AF840051

MAKING MARKET WOMEN

MAKING MARKET WOMEN

GENDER, RELIGION, AND WORK IN ECUADOR

Jill DeTemple

University of Notre Dame Press
Notre Dame, Indiana

University of Notre Dame Press
Notre Dame, Indiana 46556
undpress.nd.edu

Copyright © 2020 by the University of Notre Dame

All Rights Reserved

Published in the United States of America

Library of Congress Cataloging-in-Publication Data

Names: DeTemple, Jill Michelle, author.
Title: Making market women : gender, religion, and work in Ecuador / Jill DeTemple.
Other titles: Gender, religion, and work in Ecuador
Description: Notre Dame, Indiana : University of Notre Dame Press, [2020] | Includes bibliographical references and index.
Identifiers: LCCN 2019054896 (print) | LCCN 2019054897 (ebook) | ISBN 9780268107451 (hardback) | ISBN 9780268107482 (adobe pdf) | ISBN 9780268107475 (epub)
Subjects: LCSH: Women in cooperative societies—Ecuador. | Virgen de las Nubes Cooperative—History. | Catholic women—Ecuador—Chillanes. | Liberation theology—Ecuador—Case studies. | Economic development—Ecuador—Case studies. | Social entrepreneurship—Ecuador—Case studies. | Catholic Church—Ecuador—Chillanes—History. | Chillanes (Ecuador)—Church history.
Classification: LCC HD3424.E38 D48 2020 (print) | LCC HD3424.E38 (ebook) | DDC 334/.683730986616—dc23
LC record available at https://lccn.loc.gov/2019054896
LC ebook record available at https://lccn.loc.gov/2019054897

CONTENTS

FIGURES

All images by author.

ACKNOWLEDGMENTS

In late June 2012, I watched my kids, Molly and John, run down a long, steep hill in Chillanes's upper section, arms outstretched, alongside a few other children from town. At five and seven years old, I wrote in my field notes, they were learning to fly. Researching and writing this book has often felt a bit like that exhilarating encounter with gravity: arduous to set up, sometimes uncertain, but often joyful, especially when done in the company of friends.

For the support that made the arduous possible, I am grateful to my home institution, Southern Methodist University (SMU). The University Research Council approved two grants that allowed me to travel and work in Ecuador, and a research leave in 2013 was essential for writing early chapters. My colleagues in the Department of Religious Studies—Bill Barnard, Kate Carté, Mark Chancey, Rick Cogley, Johan Elverskog, Serge Frolov, Shira Lander, Steven Lindquist, and John Lamoreaux—have made academic life joyful, collaborative, and supportive beyond my wildest hopes. Marie Purcell and Meghan Beddingfield, brave enough to sign on with me as their PhD adviser, along with their colleagues in the Graduate Program in Religious Studies, have shown me just how good smart conversations with graduate students are for research and writing. I am also grateful to the many undergraduate students in my Religion, Gender, and Development and other classes who inspire and challenge me every day.

Outside of SMU, I am indebted to the Wabash Center for Teaching and Learning in Theology and Religion. A Pre-Tenure Fellowship funded some of the early research on this project, provided me with an amazing group of peers with whom to share ideas, and reminded me about the importance of space, care, and purpose. Thanks especially to Paul Myhre,

Tom Pearson, Joe Favazza, Amy Cottrill, and Kristi Upson-Saia for seeing the potential success in examining failure. This work has also benefited from an Individual Research Grant from the American Academy of Religion to study Catholic missions and a Sam Taylor Fellowship that supported interview transcription. Thank you to the *Journal of the American Academy of Religion*, where portions of this work first appeared (DeTemple 2013). Also at the American Academy of Religion, my colleagues in the International Development and Religion Group—Matthew Clarke, Christopher Duncanson-Hales, Nathan Loewen, Stephen Plant, and Emma Tomalin—started an enriching conversation that has sharpened my thinking and the emergent field in which it is located. Chad Seales, Heather Curtis, Lucia Hulsether, and the rest of the crew who are interested in humanitarianism broadened that dialogue at just the right time. On the anthropological side, I am grateful for enriching conversations with Laurie Occhipinti, Julie Adkins, and Tara Hefferan, who encouraged this line of inquiry, and me, from early days. In Dallas, my teammates on Limelight and biking companions with the White Rock Roadies and TXU Energy MS Bike Team make sure I don't spend my entire life inside. The Duxbury Drive Deck Sitting Society—John and Sandi Erspamer, Robin and Robert Shannon, and Beth and Scott Storm—are peerless examples of how neighbors should be. My Friday nights, and my life, are better because of them.

As some of the questions I raise here about participatory development have taken a turn for the dialogic, I am deeply grateful to my working group on the Intellectual Humility and Conviction project. Lauren Barthold, Ian and Margie DeWeeese-Boyd, Jonathan Garlick, and Betsy Hayes helped me think in new, exciting, and collegial ways about the role of cooperation and communication in learning spaces. Thanks also to our colleague and convener on that project, John Sarrouf, extraordinary friend and timely reminderer that great questions change everything. As we enter the next phase of the Listening Revolution, I can't wait to see what comes next.

Dios le pague to all those in Ecuador who made this book possible and my life rich. In Chillanes, thanks to the Municipio de Chillanes, the Registro Civil, Promoción Humana, the Parroquia de Chillanes, Padre Orlando Peña, Grupo Juan XXIII, and the Diocese of Guaranda for allowing me research access. Will Waters of the Universidad de San Francisco helped me think through issues of gender and development. Un mil gracias to the Lucio family—especially Ligia, Alfaro, and Mercedes—for hosting me, and us. It is a joy to share life with them.

Locally, I'm grateful for the unrelenting support of my family. Molly was fourteen months old when I started research on this book and turned fourteen the day I finished revisions. John proved that being two is not an impediment to helping with international research. My husband, Brian, did all the things anthropology spouses do and more: staying home to work when we traveled, feeding guinea pigs when he joined us, and finding ways to let me get the writing done. I couldn't ask for more.

Thanks to Eli Bortz for taking an interest in this manuscript and to the reviewers whose comments improved it in ways great and small. I'm also grateful to the production editors at the University of Notre Dame Press for their tireless and exacting work. This book would not be as good, and certainly not as readable, without them.

Finally, thanks to the women of the Cooperativa Feminina Virgen de las Nubes, especially Jesus Galarza, Rosa Galaraza, Julia Guamán, Lucía Alarcón, Narcisa Inca, Cecilia Miño, Josefa Arteaga, Silvia Moyano, Agustina Quinche, Magdalena Estrada, Greys Sanchez, Mercedes Huilca, and Paula Pozo. Their honesty, hard work, dedication, openness, generosity, and commitment have inspired me daily for almost twenty years. This book is for them, with hope.

INTRODUCTION

Blessed Are the Cheese Makers?

Catholic Liberation, Social Capital, Women, and Neoliberalism in Contemporary Ecuador

There have been a great many changes in Ecuador since 1960. Land reform, the discovery and utilization of Amazonian oil reserves, and seven presidents between 1996 and 2007; an economic crisis that led to dollarization in 2000; the privatization of phone service and other national agencies; significant uprisings against the proposed privatization of healthcare and water and the abuse of mineral rights; a serious earthquake in 2016; and a large influx of refugees and immigrants from Colombia and Venezuela, just to name some highlights. In 2018 an estimated 6 percent to 8 percent of the Ecuadorian population lived and worked abroad (INEC 2018). The country has been in the international news for housing WikiLeaks founder Julian Assange in its embassy in London, as well as for proposing a pro-breastfeeding resolution at the World Health Organization that was opposed by the United States under the Trump administration.[1]

Catholics may feel some sympathy. The Second Vatican Council, liberation theologies, competition from Pentecostals, calls for the ordination of women, the shift of global Catholicism to the south, the rise of charismatic movements, the abdication of a pope, and persistent revelations of clerical abuse have made for an interesting and often contentious six decades in the realm of the Holy See. In the meantime, international development has also undergone changes in its implementation and goals with the increased participation of nongovernmental organizations (NGOs), many of them religious in their heritage and mission, in the 1990s. Where economic indicators such as GDP per capita were the unquestioned measure of development success in the 1960s, social indicators such as access to education, healthcare, and gender equity now factor into a region's status as "developed."[2] The rise of neoliberal policies and benchmarks in the 1990s, along with globalization more broadly, has also colored the horizons, local and global, to which people and institutions affix their sights and measure their position.

This work focuses on the confluence of all these changes and challenges in one Ecuadorian community and specifically in one group of Catholic women. It is not that these women represent all of contemporary Catholicism, all Latin Americans, all women, all people involved in international development, or all Ecuadorians. They do not. But a careful examination of the ways in which people negotiate, use, interpret, and challenge Catholicism, development assumptions, and changing economies at the local level, in conjunction with local values and histories during this condensed period of change, can tell us a great deal about what we might call global Catholicism, shifting economic structures that include neoliberalism, gender in social and economic contexts, and international development today.

Specifically, this book is concerned with the ways in which all of the changes listed above have come to affect interpretations of Catholic "liberation" in Chillanes, the cantonal capital in Bolívar Province where I have engaged in ethnographic research since 2000. In my first book, *Cement, Earthworms and Cheese Factories: Religion and Community Development in Rural Ecuador* (2012), Chillanes is identified as "San Vicente." Since the publication of that work, and even during that earlier research, Chillanenses (residents of Chillanes) have expressed considerable frustration that the place of which they are so proud was not "correctly" named. I remedy that here, naming both the place and the Virgen de las Nubes women's group (previously called the Santa Anita Cooperative), as well as individuals when they requested that I do so. Where I do not have explicit permission, people and groups are identified by pseudonyms and other identifying factors are omitted.[3]

These complications in naming point to the complexities and relationality of fieldwork carried out over almost two decades and friendships that often span longer periods. I first came to Chillanes in 1995 when I was serving as a U.S. Peace Corps volunteer in a small community several hours away, though still in Bolívar Province. On visiting a fellow volunteer, I quickly found myself invited to the high school graduation party of Ligia Lucio, daughter of the volunteer's landlady, Mercedes Lucio. The Lucio family had rented a partially completed cement house to the volunteer in order to finance final construction. When my husband and I returned to Chillanes in 2002 for a year of fieldwork, the Lucios took us in in much the same way. We lived in two rooms in an adjacent cement building the family had purchased, contributing rent money and then labor for improvements on that structure, and on the original one the volunteer had occupied, now grown to three stories.[4] That year we attended the graduation of Ligia's younger brother from the police academy, and subsequent years allowed us the chance to attend Ligia's wedding, the birth of her second child, the fiftieth wedding anniversary of her grandparents, and many other family events. Over breakfasts and in parks as our children played together, Ligia and I discussed Ecuadorian and American politics, Catholic rituals, Protestant roles in Chillanes life, the challenges of raising children, marriage, work, pop culture, education, soccer, and what Bronislaw Malinowski (1961, 18) might call the "imponderabilia of actual life." Ligia has long been one of my best cultural and social brokers, helping me navigate everything from local politics to linguistic misunderstandings. She is a dear friend. And, to use Su'ad Khabeer's (2016) term, she is my teacher. In 2018, as she was beginning a career as a local politician (she had served as a *jefe política*, a regional cabinet member, in Chillanes since 2017), she was teaching me more than ever.

Indeed, it is Ligia's experiences as a religiously active, educated, Roman Catholic woman working full time that helped draw my attention to one of the central issues of this book: how a liberationist Catholic women's cooperative navigated Ecuador's burgeoning neoliberal economy. How did the values of liberation theology translate into a market model of development in which a cooperative was formed to make cheese for market sale? How did Ecuador's entrance into a global, increasingly neoliberal economy affect the way the cooperative was envisioned, established, and run? And what did the women who were involved in the project think about that experience, especially as it intersected with equally powerful narratives that emphasized their gender and religious identities as social capital that could be formed, saved, and spent to support their endeavors in economic spaces?

While I give a fuller history of the cooperative and its history in the chapter that follows, clarification of key terms, as well as their history in their particular Ecuadorian context, will be useful here. Neoliberalism, broadly defined, is a political, social, and economic assemblage produced in late capitalism that favors privatization and "free markets" over public or government control of goods and services, often enforced through "austerity" measures tied to international lending (Harris and Nef 2008, 15). Most scholars trace the rise of neoliberalism to the late 1980s, when the so-called Washington Consensus that favored privatization of services such as power, telecommunications, and transportation came to dominate U.S. and subsequently World Bank and International Monetary Fund (IMF) policies, especially as they were applied in international settings (Huber 2004; Harris 2008; Connell and Dados 2014).

For borrowing countries such as Ecuador, neoliberal requirements, usually referred to as structural adjustment programs (SAP), were tied to continuing access to loans for development and resulted in changes such as the privatization of water in the country's largest city, Guayaquil, in 1997; of the national phone company, Emetel, in 2005; of most major highway construction projects since 2000; and of its national airline in 2016. Despite external pressure, Ecuador has not privatized its major export, oil, and continues to run Petroecuador and Petroamazonas as public entities. Since the country converted to the dollar after the economic crisis of 2000, various politicians have moved it toward and away from neoliberal policies, with leftists such as Rafael Correa, president from 2007 to 2016, embracing a more socialistic stance even as he continued some neoliberal reforms and right-wing politicians such as Jaime Nebot, mayor of Guayaquil since 2000, advocating increased privatization of everything from infrastructure to water to the city's airport in 2003. These changes did not go unchallenged, and in 1990 and 1997 and again in 2010 there were widespread protests by indigenous peoples (*levamientos indígena*), who marched on the capital and blocked roads, objecting to the privatization of water, especially in Amazonian territories. These movements eventually resulted in a 2014 law prohibiting private ownership of water resources.

While neoliberalism is often associated with national and international policy, its free-market ethic is more expansive and has had an impact on local economic development initiatives, driving them toward market models of success measured by production and profitability. A neoliberal ethic has also resulted in the rise of NGOs as the primary institutions working in development in the Ecuadorian context beginning in the 1990s (Segarra 1994; Lind 2005). Working under the concept of efficiency, one of the guiding assumptions of neoliberalism is that private actors are always more efficient than state actors and that individuals working in their own interest are more cost-effective, and more effective, than collectives. Thus, NGOs such as World Vision International and Médecins sans Frontières are presumed to be better able to meet local needs than government-run health clinics or, in some cases, schools. At the local level, neoliberal ideals encourage individual entrepreneurship as a means of upward mobility. Individual access to and intersection with the free market is the ultimate goal for citizens in neoliberal contexts.

As Amy Lind and others document, however, the effects of neoliberalism are often unevenly shouldered, especially when gender is taken into account. In her monograph exploring development initiatives targeting women in Ecuador in the late 1990s, Lind writes:

> As the neoliberal state is privatized, women have become the primary bearers of what were previously state welfare responsibilities: they are now service providers in the realms of community development, family, health care, day care, and local produce markets. Through development policies and practices, including those of both international agencies and nation-states, these sectors of women have been brought into the visible fold of development. In conjunction with this, they have become models of the new "market citizen" and of "modern economic woman," the latter a representation of "modern economic man" in neoclassical economics that is a model institutionalized through development practices operating on the assumption that women's and men's identities, and their racialization, are defined in terms of their economic functions and their roles in the modern market. (2005, 89–90)

While Lind's subjects are urban women who find their labor repurposed (and no more economically valued) to private initiatives, the conclusion she draws is an important one that is easily transferred to Chillanes's rural location: while neoliberalism functions as a transnational mechanism, it always acts in local spaces, intersecting with local entities and people who then encounter, resist, appropriate, and reproduce it in various ways.

The primary research question for this book, then, is how religious institutions and ideologies that are traditionally collectivist, such as liberation theology, adapt to neoliberal environments in places such as Chillanes and then how this affects the people, in this case women involved in a Salesian development initiative, whose lives and livelihoods become entangled in these economic, cultural, and ethical currents. The research laid out in this book leads me to argue that Catholic liberation in Chillanes, and perhaps throughout Latin America, has taken on neoliberal features in many of its processes and cultures and, in the case of women, is suffering some of the same pains experienced by formalizing and privatizing sectors as the broader marketplace. Indeed, the experience of the women in the cheese factory is a stark example of the shift from a classic liberationist project to a neoliberal one. Though the project is founded on the archetypical liberationist principles of solidarity, communal concern, and faith engaged in the struggle to survive and thrive in the material world, the very existence of the factory and its requirement that the women enter the neoliberal marketplace as production workers and marketers changed the nature, or at least the flavor, of that liberation. Unlike my interviews in 2003, when most of the group members attributed their success at least in part to Catholic values and practices, the women I interviewed after the project failed were reticent to say that Catholicism was an important feature of the cooperative. They felt that the aspect of solidarity that they enjoyed together as Catholics and women was severely damaged when the group entered into cheese production. As they struggled to restart the cheese factory after it ceased operations in 2006, the women were markedly less sure than they were in 2003 that economic betterment, even in the hands of a group, would lead to social or religious improvement or vice versa. Solidarity is still a value they share, but the women in the cooperative are currently less likely to think that it is a value that can spur lasting and valuable economic change at the group or community level. It has become, in some very real ways, nostalgic, presumed to be unable to act in the contemporary world except as a term of comparison, an ideal to which current reality does not measure up.

A complicating factor in this narrative is Charismatic Catholicism. Defined more fully in chapter 4, the movement, perhaps most vividly in its Latin American form, emphasizes sacramental life and individual experiences of the divine. The rise of Charismatic Catholicism in Latin America, and in recent decades in Ecuador, points to a change in Catholic notions of liberation and its effects. For many Roman Catholics in Chillanes, whether or not they are part of the local charismatic group, Juan XXIII, it is striking how much the emphasis on sacraments resembles a preliberationist view of Catholic freedom: that is, one rooted in eternal concerns and marked by baptism, confirmation, communion, marriage, and burial in the church. Unlike liberation theology, which tends to describe freedom in collective and structural terms such as freedom from poverty or oppression, charismatic liberation, often evoked as a state of grace in which one's sins are forgiven, harkens to an older and more individualized notion of liberation as a profoundly personal rather than structural project. Individual conversion and encounter with God are the key to liberation, not fundamental changes in living conditions or social systems, which are signs of liberation but not the necessary conditions of it.

In many ways, then, this book is about how ideas of liberation—social, economic, gendered, religious—work in a specific place during a specific time in history. Here some caution is warranted. Though Chillanes is identifiable on a map, in government documents of various kinds, and even in its virtual existence on everything from Facebook sites to group chats arranged for expats and family members, it is not static. The town of Chillanes, where about 5,000 residents of the canton live, accounts for less than a third of the canton's total population of 17,406 (INEC 2018). The rest of the population is spread between one larger town located in the coastal mountains, San José del Tambo, with the remainder of the population in 241 rural areas with small population centers (*recintos*). People from the recintos often travel to Chillanes and to Tambo on market days in order to purchase essentials, receive medical care at the hospitals, attend religious services, or visit family members, many of whom are high school and college students who have been forced to emigrate to the population centers in order to complete secondary education or, in the case of Chillanes, which has had a branch of the Universidad de Bolívar, a technical or bachelor's degree. Such educational pursuits are not cheap, and many rural families cannot afford to board students away from home, a factor that continues to contribute to Bolívar's 13.9 percent illiteracy rate, though this number has continued to fall in recent years as more children are educated through the primary years and more indigenous communities gain access to education.[5]

Still, Chillanes remains the second poorest canton in Ecuador (INEC 2018), mostly due to substandard educational achievement and very little industry outside of small-scale agriculture. Many of the recintos in the canton of Chillanes are losing population as young people emigrate to larger population centers within and outside Ecuador seeking social and financial opportunity and as the birthrate falls.[6] Such realities made national headlines in September 2018 when a 6.3-magnitude earthquake centered in the Chimbo River Valley in neighboring Chimborazo Province severely damaged more than 240 houses in the canton, the majority in the outlying recintos. A provincial official, Minister of Risk Leonardo Espinosa, appeared on national television explaining that "people constructed their own houses without following the codes," seeming to blame a largely rural, poor population for whom the building materials to construct such houses are a significant investment and for whom hiring building crews and contractors is outside of financial and logistical reach for the effects of the quake ("Sismo afecto 240 viviendas en Chillanes Provincia de Bolívar" 2018).

The lived experience of poverty in Chillanes, which is location-specific but also mirrors other places in Latin America and beyond, is one reason I have chosen to engage in ethnographic research there and one reason the canton and its people remain a target of economic development efforts: national, private, or international, or various combinations of the three. Though 90 percent of men and 94 percent of women are "economically active" (INEC 2018) and though there is a growing middle class, a topic I treat in chapter 4, most people still consider themselves "poor," cut off socially and physically from resources, opportunities, and services.[7]

Being poor, and engaging in "la lucha," or the daily struggles of everyday life, is an embodied experience. Being a poor woman in Chillanes is often markedly different from men's experiences of poverty, and development interventions are often targeted to specific genders, as was the case with the Virgen de las Nubes cheese project. For these reasons, I treat gender as a significant variable in this study, not because I believe it is a fixed or innate trait, or because the women I spoke with do (though they construct gender as innate to greater and lesser degrees), but because the social construction of femaleness—by Chillanenses, the Ecuadorian government, development organizations, the Roman Catholic Church, and other entities—has significant bearing on how the women of the Virgen de las Nubes group conceived of their work and of themselves as religious and economic actors. Gender matters, and one of the concerns of this book is to delineate how, especially where narratives from different social, intellectual, religious, and economic spheres collide.

One way that gender matters has been in the use of gender-targeted development initiatives that rely on ideas of gendered social capital. I give an in-depth account of social capital as a development intervention strategy in chapter 2, but a brief treatment here is helpful to orient readers to my aims and research objectives. Broadly defined, social capital is a concept, originated by Pierre Bourdieu (1977) but more fully developed by Robert Putnam (2000), that explores social relationships as capital that can be invested, built, and leveraged for social, economic, political, or other gains. Some social capital comes with relative power and privilege, but other forms of it, usually the kind that is built through shared social experience from positions of relative weakness such as gender inequality, may be utilized for social inclusion or social change. In international development contexts, social capital is often perceived and utilized as a resource on which marginalized groups can draw to aid in cooperative economic efforts (Lomnitz 1988; Molyneaux 2002; Roy 2010). Microlending interventions, for example, often depend on ideas about women's social capital—expressed as "cooperativeness," "trust," and "reliability" when in a group—as an explanation for their structure and self-defined success.

A major concern of this book is the question of social capital as an asset that is wagered when offered as a basis for development work. Like financial capital that is marketized, social capital may be lost when the project in which it is invested fails. One reason the women in the Virgen de las Nubes Cooperative were less likely to speak about solidarity as an asset after the collapse of the cheese factory, I argue, is that the loss of the project also meant the loss of such socially cohesive ideas. Especially where tied directly to core aspects of identity, as in the case of the group's roots in Catholicism and gender identity, the wagering of social capital in development endeavors is a profound wager of those core identities. For the women of the Virgen de las Nubes Cooperative, the failure of the cheese project has resulted in deep changes in the ways they think about their identities as Catholics and as women, and about the Catholic Church as a sponsoring partner in the development project. The failure of the project has also reoriented them to their community. To paraphrase Amy Lind (2005, 58), who comments that "neoliberalism has multiple definitions and meanings" and thus is produced and experienced locally, all social capital is also local, as are the repercussions of its loss, even if invested internationally. One goal of this work is to explore the effects of such loss and then to reexamine the role of social capital in development interventions, where its use is becoming increasingly widespread.

Getting at these themes—poverty, development, social capital, gender, failure, religion—is a complicated business, and the methods I have used to gather the data I present here are varied. Much of my research is ethnographic and includes well over one hundred structured and unstructured interviews with cooperative members and their families, members of the greater Chillanes community, and representatives of Promoción Humana (PH) and Fondo Ecuatoriano Popularum Progressio (FEPP), parent organizations of the project. I began fieldwork in Chillanes with short trips in 2000 and 2001 and then returned for extended field stays: nine months from September 2002 to May 2003, six weeks in 2006, twelve weeks in 2009, six weeks in 2012, and one week in 2015. During these field stays I conducted interviews and participated in meetings and other activities hosted by the cooperative and other development organizations in the province. I also attended activities sponsored by various groups associated with the Catholic Church, including Juan XXIII and the Diocese of Guaranda as it trained mission recruits and lay parishioners running a Holy Week service in a recinto. In addition, I conducted walking surveys of the Chillanes center designed to assess gendered access to public spaces. Those surveys were conducted at random times on different days of the week in order to craft a comprehensive picture of the use of space. For interviews about Santa Rita as a local religious figure, I began with one local, well-known devotee and then asked her for recommendations of others who might be willing to share their experiences. In a similar manner, I was able to interview various municipal employees about their experiences in development work in the canton and was granted access to the local records office (Registro Civil), where I was able to glean data on births, deaths, and marriages in the canton, as well as information about businesses registered in town. The local priest, Orlando Peña, granted me access to church records dating to the founding of the parish that record baptisms, confirmations, marriages, and deaths. He also sat down for several interviews from 2009 to 2015 in which he described the current state of Roman Catholicism in the parish and in Ecuador, as well as his investment in a growing mission movement, outlined in chapter 3. Since I began to focus on this project in 2006, cell phones have become ubiquitous in the Ecuadorian Sierra, even in places like the recintos where landlines were never present. As a result, I have been able to chase down dangling questions and to check my research results by calling cooperative members, Ligia, Padre Orlando, and others and simply asking. Because Chillanes received broadband service in 2012, some of this work has been via internet applications such as Facebook and Skype.

Finally, since my daughter made her first trip to Ecuador at the age of fourteen months, she and my son have been an entrance into valuable conversations about gender, parenting, work, and other topics this book addresses. Taking them to Chillanes's parks during our extended field stays in 2009 and 2012 often opened up conversations with mothers and other caretakers similarly engaged about child rearing, play, the difficulties of work, cooking, nutrition, and marriage. While Padre Orlando let me know he was worried that I was a woman traveling on my own (my husband had to remain in Texas for work), the presence of my children made me less susceptible to suspicion and allowed him to invite me to parish events from which I might otherwise have been prohibited. Indeed, conversations about what I was doing, how I brought my children into it, and why led to some of the connections between gender, work, economic realities, religion, movement, and change that this book addresses, not only because of the questions people asked of me, but also because of what I could see, hear, and learn through my children's experiences. While not precisely an ethnographic strategy, Molly and John were certainly an asset.

These themes are addressed in this work in the following manner. The first chapter, "Why Catholic Women Make Cheese," explores the genesis of the women's group in the context of 1970s liberation theology movements in Ecuador, local Catholic histories that emphasized male confraternities, and the group's parent organization, FEPP. Chapter 2, "Reproducing Women: Gendered Social Capital in Local Contexts," highlights the ways in which the group reproduced and valorized traditionally female roles in group spaces such as the cheese factory, where food and clothing production were transferred into direct economic activities in a neoliberal environment. The third chapter, "Marketing the Domestic Church," explores various constructions of gendered religiosity in Chillanes, from a local saint famous for her protection of victims of domestic violence to the Vatican's recent emphasis on the "domestic church" as a venue for genuine piety. Chapter 4, "Las Juanes: Charismatic Catholicism, Women, and the Market in Chillanes," continues this theme as it explores changing modes of Catholicism in Chillanes, some of which seem to reflect neoliberal approaches to poverty, poverty reduction, and gender. The fifth chapter, "'We Are Also Outside': Religious and Gender Identities When Development Fails," draws on the voices of cooperative members, community members, and development promoters as it focuses on the reasons for the failure, as well as the impact of that failure, on cooperative members' religious and gender identities.

All of these chapters take basic questions about the relationship of religion and development as their core. As in my earlier work, I "read development religiously," attentive to development's teleological and ontological expressions that often cause it to address questions of meaning and being in ways almost indistinguishable from assemblages such as Christianity (DeTemple 2012, 16). In addition, I work in this book to read religion economically, looking for the ways in which actors use religious institutions, understandings, connections, and habits as sites of exchange and resources that can be saved, bartered, or exhausted in ways that reflect, bolster, and challenge identities. Here, I draw on recent work, especially studies that consider secularity, that focuses on capitalism as an expression of American Protestantism (Long 1986; Chidester 2005; Lofton 2011; Seales 2013). Just as Lofton argues for the dissolution of clear boundaries between Oprah as icon and Oprah as marketer, I ask questions here that presume meaning is made not only in the epistemological shadow of a sacred canopy (Berger 1967) but also that of a late capitalist one. Such a stance allows me to ask how religious change might affect economic development goals, understandings, and processes and how development failure might affect religious identity and affiliation. It allows me to explore how "liberation," a term claimed by actors in religious, development, and certain economic circles, is being asserted, rejected, mixed, matched, and negotiated by those whom these discourses touch. To paraphrase the Gospel of Matthew and Monty Python, will the cheese makers be blessed? These words from Padre Orlando are telling on this point:

> Social, political, economic, cultural—there are many kinds of slavery, and Christ comes to us to give us complete and full liberation, right? So, in this sense, sure, there have been various exponents of liberation at the Latin American level: Gutiérrez, Leornardo Boff . . . but lately, as they themselves say, we are in the resistance. . . . [With the missions to the countryside around Chillanes] I think I have continued what my colleagues before me have done.

ONE

Why Catholic Women Make Cheese

The acme for the Virgen de las Nubes Cooperative may have been October 26, 2002. Thirteen years after the group formed, the women were throwing a party to dedicate and bless a new two-story building that housed their cheese-making operations and group meetings. The completion of the *quesera* was a major accomplishment for the cooperative, which had been making cheese in borrowed spaces that included a group member's house and the house of a local man active in Catholic causes since 1998. Though the Italian organization Mani Tese donated money for the building materials, cooperative members either performed or paid for all of the construction labor, doing everything from mixing cement to providing meals for bricklayers and other artisans. The structure, protected from thieves and roving animals by a newly completed chain-link fence, was the tangible fruit of many years of planning, negotiation, and hard work by the roughly thirty-five cooperative associates (*socias*) and a smattering of friends and relatives who counted themselves as supporters of the group.

Most of those same group members and supporters were there on the Saturday of the dedication when, after a frenzied morning of cooking and preparation, a battered Land Rover made its way down the dirt track to the quesera. Pulling past the loading dock where milk deliveries were processed and into the small courtyard on the west side of the building, the vehicle stopped and disgorged its passengers: two Italian Salesian priests, two Ecuadorian women, and an Ecuadorian man employed by Promoción

FIGURE 1. Virgen de las Nubes Quesera

Humana, a human development organization working under the auspices of the Catholic Diocese of Guaranda.

The dedication unfolded with a celebratory mass, lunch, dancing, toasting, the unveiling of an image of the Virgen de las Nubes, a ribbon-cutting ceremony, and fireworks. Speakers emphasized hard work, dedication, community, and cooperation. Mateo Panteghini, the younger of the two Salesians, conducted the eucharistic rite in vestments thrown over a green reporter's vest and jeans. Fr. Antonio Polo read from Mark, using the passage in his homily to communicate the message that success comes from the combination of faith and community, solidarity, and hard work. Any effort without all of these elements, he concluded, is bound to fail.

These comments echoed opening remarks given by a group member at the beginning of the service, in which she invoked Paul's writing about the importance of solidarity for successful Christians. And, indeed, on that happy day as the priests threw holy water on the tiled floor of the cheese plant and the Promoción Humana community promoter responsible for the group took pictures, solidarity, community, faith, and economic success were palpable realities. Cheese—mozzarella, andino, parmesan, and *queso fresco*, the soft, fresh cheese favored by campesinos throughout rural Ecuador—was the culminating expression of the promises made by Catholic liberation theology, international economic development, women's movements, and Ecuador's participation in the global economy. With the completion of the quesera, the women of the Virgen de las Nubes Cooperative seemed poised to take advantage of the confluence of all these philosophical, theological, and economic transformations as they came together in stainless steel vats, reaching maturity one milky round at time.

This chapter explores the genesis of these events, and of the quesera itself, as it seeks to answer the question, why do Catholic women in Chillanes make cheese? Answering this question will do considerable work in addressing the larger issues of changing notions of Catholic liberation, development, gender, identity, and market economies to which this book attends. It also raises an important question of network: when events, structures, organizations, and enterprises form as the result of the confluence of multiple philosophical, ideological, institutional, and material discourses, what happens when one, or many, of those discursive structures changes or fails? If the Virgen de las Nubes Cooperative produced cheese because liberation theology, international economic development, women's movements, and changes in the Ecuadorian economy made cheese production possible and economically and socially profitable, then it is also possible that failure in one area may have wrought consequences that are equally entangled, widespread, and powerful. Understanding how the entanglement happened—how it is that Catholic women came to make cheese—enables a much fuller understanding of the consequences when that cheese production ceased, when some of the many threads that formed a tapestry of possibility unraveled and fell away.

WHY CATHOLICS?

Despite more than thirty years of an increasingly varied and dynamic Protestant presence in Bolívar, and in Chillanes more specifically, the fact remains that most people in the region are Catholic. While government census data do not account for religious affiliation and therefore no comprehensive figures are available, in 2008 the civil registry office for the canton of Chillanes recorded 394 births. The Catholic church in Chillanes, which includes slightly more than half the canton in its geographic reach

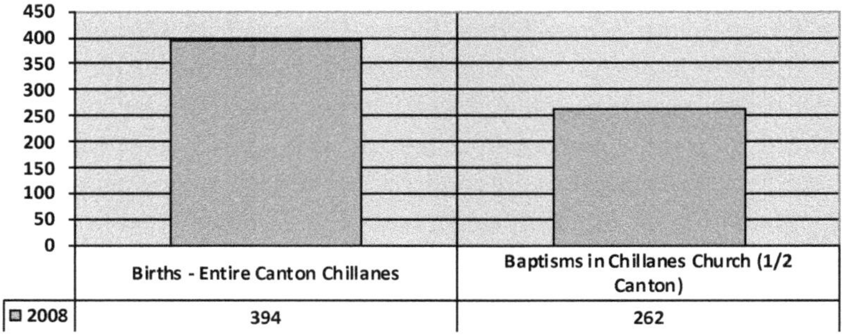

FIGURE 2. Baptism and Births, Chillanes, 2008

after a parochial split dividing Chillanes from Tambo in 2003, recorded 262 baptisms.

Even taking into account that baptism often occurs well into childhood, these numbers suggest that the majority of the population of Chillanes identifies as Roman Catholic and has some official, sacramental relationship with the church. In this sense, Catholics are making cheese because almost everyone engaged in dairy production in the region is Catholic.

That the priests who performed the mass and dedication of the quesera were Italian, Salesian, and not from the local parish, however, indicates that the Catholic nature of the women's group is not simply a matter of demographic happenstance or cultural osmosis. Indeed, the history of the women's group, and of the cheese-making enterprise in which it is engaged, is directly dependent on recent Catholic history as it has played out in Latin America and in Bolívar Province. Chillanes Catholics, in other words, make cheese for a reason.

The roots of this reason lie in liberation theology, *teología de la liberación*, the 1960s and 1970s movement in the Latin American Catholic Church that posited that spiritual salvation can only be achieved in concert with efforts to improve the material conditions of those living in need. In 1968 a group of Catholic bishops from Latin America issued a declaration from their meeting in Medellín, Colombia, declaring that a "preferential option for the poor" was the moral responsibility of the church, especially in Latin America where the vast majority of Catholics lived in crushing, seemingly inescapable poverty. Not long after that meeting, Gustavo Gutiérrez, a Peruvian priest working in the poorest sections of

Lima, published *A Theology of Liberation: History, Politics, Salvation* (1971). The book introduced an extended exegetical argument for the eradication of poverty as a necessary if not the primary aim of the church. It also gave the movement a name, even as it drew the attention of the Vatican, which advised Gutiérrez to revise some key writings so as to make them less dependent on Marxist analyses and their emphasis on class struggles as the primary explanatory lens for history.

Indeed, the liberationist movement was not immediately, or ever fully, accepted by the Vatican, which was leery of the Marxism and revolutionary tendencies some fear liberation theology represents. Leonardo Boff, a Brazilian liberation theologian, was silenced for a year in 1985 by the Vatican Congregation for the Doctrine of the Faith led by then-Cardinal Josef Ratzinger for his book *Church: Charism and Power* (1985), which critiqued the strict hierarchy of the Roman Catholic Church and called for greater involvement of the church in the political sector. In a six-page letter, Ratzinger (1985) accused Boff of "endanger[ing] the sound doctrine of the faith," beginning with the Brazilian's views on church hierarchy and ending with the role of the church in the world. Boff later resigned from the Franciscan priesthood. Jon Sobrino, a liberationist Jesuit priest from Spain working in El Salvador, was similarly accused and censured in 2007 for, among other things, deemphasizing the divine nature of Jesus. Gutiérrez, Boff, and Sobrino survive today, however, unlike many of their compatriots. Six of Sobrino's Jesuit colleagues, as well as Archbishop Óscar Romero, were killed by forces sympathetic to government causes after they publicly condemned government abuses of human rights during an ongoing civil war in El Salvador.

The actions of the priests point to a defining feature of liberation theology: praxis. By forming small ecclesiastical base communities (CEBs) within larger churches, liberationist believers are encouraged to reflect on scripture in the context of social problems and then act on that reflection in tangible and sometimes overtly political ways. Orthopraxis, as liberation theologians refer to actions motivated by faithful reading of the scripture combined with Freirian attention to local circumstances, is the way in which the church, through its members, can enact the necessary change to enable all people to live with the dignity the faithful believe is granted them by God.

Such orthopraxis was interpreted by many, both supporters and rejecters of liberation theology, as a call for revolution, an invitation into the political sphere where the church was either required to go or did not rightly belong. Gutiérrez, writing in an essay meant to give an overview of liberationist thought, highlighted praxis: "All this means that the life of faith is not only a starting point, it is also the goal of theological reflection. To believe (life) and to understand (reflection) are always part of a circular relationship. . . . [O]rthopraxis and orthodoxy need one another, and each is adversely affected when sight is lost of the other (Gutiérrez, quoted in Rowland 1999, 29). To this end, Gutiérrez maintained that no theological reasoning could be complete without a considered and contextual accounting for local circumstances, an accounting best done by and for lay believers in the CEBs, a consideration that is almost by definition political as it takes into account structures that invite and perpetuate poverty and oppression.

Where Gutiérrez sees praxis as a necessary part of a dialectic, however, his critics have seen and do see it as misleading and the source of a dangerous relativity and illicit interference of faith in politics. In a document Ratzinger's office for the Defense of the Faith released on liberation theology, Ratzinger (Ratzinger and Messori 1985, 184–185) pointed to this emphasis on praxis as a fundamental error in liberationist thought: "Absolutely fundamental [to liberation theology], finally, is the stress on *praxis*: truth must not be understood metaphysically, for that would be 'idealism.' Truth is realized in history and its praxis. *Action is Truth*. Hence even the ideas which are employed in such action are ultimately interchangeable. . . . Ultimately what is normative for interpretation is not historical research but the hermeneutic of history experienced in the community or political group." Such a hermeneutic, the man who would become pontiff continued, is too local, and too political, to be of divine origin. The revolutionary potential of the movement, he concluded, is a theology misplaced.

These controversies continue today, even as the influence of the liberationist movement appears to be waning.[1] The Polish pope John Paul II was careful to winnow "care for the poor" from the more overtly Marxist theories some theologians employed, and many in the church applauded the censure of Sobrino's work under John Paul II's leadership in 2007. Clodovis Boff, once one of the most outspoken liberationist priests in Brazil and brother of Leonardo Boff, critiqued the movement in an article in the *Revista Eclesiástica Brasileira* published shortly after Sobrino's censuring. In its emphasis on the poor, Clodovis Boff argues that liberation theology wrongly overshadowed a foundational emphasis on God or Jesus, something he characterizes as a "fatal error."

"Nothing but dismal effects," he writes, "can follow from this error of principle. . . . When the poor acquire the status of an epistemological 'primum,' what happens to the faith and its doctrine on the theological and pastoral level? . . . The inevitable result is the reduction of faith, its politicization; the transformation of faith into *ideology*" (Boff 2007, 1005; original emphasis). Indeed, he continues, liberation theology reduced the church to something like an international aid organization.

> The "pastoral action of liberation" becomes one of the many branches of the "popular movement." The church becomes like an NGO [*A Igreja se "onguiza"*], and so also loses substance physically: it loses workers, militants, and faithful. Those "on the outside" feel little attraction for a "church of liberation," because the militants already have NGOs, while for religious experience they need much more than simple social liberation. Moreover, because of the failure to perceive the social extent and relevance of the current spiritual malaise, liberation theology shows itself to be culturally myopic and historically anachronistic, or "alienated" from its time. (1007)

Whether it is because of this "error" or because, as Andrew Chesnut (1997, 2003a) and others have contended, the church failed to compete effectively in the "religious marketplace" of Latin America, overtly liberationist churches are losing ground to more charismatic modes of Catholicism at the beginning of the twenty-first century.[2]

Indeed, the concept of liberation theology does not have much obvious currency in Bolívar, where liberationist practices and organizations abound but without the title given them by Gutiérrez. Small groups that gather for prayer, "reflection," and social action are common in Chillanes, but very few people refer to these using the liberationist language "ecclesiastical base communities." Rather, they are "groups" or, especially in the case of male organizations, "confraternities." Though I have lived and worked in Bolívar for significant periods since 1994, outside of conversations with clergy I have never heard anyone volunteer the term "liberation theology" as a descriptor for Catholic thought or practice, though liberationist terms such as "consciousness raising" and "solidarity" frequently arise. When I have asked about the impact of liberation theology in the area—in settings as diverse as prayer groups, the women's cooperative, interviews, celebratory masses, and casual conversations over meals in private homes—I have been consistently greeted with confused looks and shrugged shoulders. This 2009 conversation with Elena Sanchez, a forty-six-year-old Charistmatic Catholic active in mission work in Chillanes, is typical.

ES: Because before [we started the recent mission work] they didn't share, there wasn't—only the priests were missionaries and we Catholics were rooted in our chairs, comfortable.
JD: So when [the people in the communities receiving missionaries] saw you, they noticed that you were different.
ES: Yes. Yes, because before it wasn't like it is now, open. Everyone has the opportunity to read the Word of God and also of being a testament of life [*siendo testimonio de vida*]. That is, trying to come, to share. I believe that has come to pass.
JD: So, for you, is this another type of liberation, of liberation theology in another form? Something different?
ES: What? What?
JD: If you understand me, that what you are doing is another form of liberation theology? Or is it something different?
ES: This . . . part of the religion, you say?
JD: It was a movement here in the 1970s, liberation theology.
ES: Yes—
JD: Is what you are doing now something similar, or is it something different?
ES: I didn't know about the other mode, I wasn't familiar with it. No, no, I wasn't familiar with it, and I can't say if this is the same or if it's better or worse. No, no.

Elena did go on to use the term "CEB" in her interview to describe a small group active in the charismatic Juan XXIII movement, but she clearly does not associate it with liberation theology and has no real sense of the 1970s liberationist movement.

Elena's response and those of the other Chillanenses with whom I talked do not mean that liberation theology missed Ecuador. Far from it. Just over the mountains from Chilllanes in the province of Chimborazo, Msgr. Leonidas Proaño spent the better part of his tenure as bishop of Riobamba working to improve the material and spiritual lives of the majority indigenous peoples in the area, often in the face of overt criticism from urban whites and mestizos, as well as from more conservative members of the Catholic hierarchy. Proaño was an active member of CELAM, the bishop's conference calling for a "preferential option for the poor," and also founded Juan XXIII, a group of Ecuadorian priests dedicated to liberationist causes (Gavilanes 1992, 100).[3] In Riobamba and its surrounding communities, Proaño helped to establish several ecclesiastical base communities and, in 1963, Tepeyec, a warehouse and school that aimed to promote indigenous rights and teach artisanal and agricultural skills.

More than twenty years after his death in 1988, Bishop Proaño remains the best-known liberationist priest in Ecuador, not least because of his participation in the 1964 land reform. He was not the only member of the Catholic episcopate interested in applying the lessons of liberationist teachings, however, and Chimborazo was not the only region in which liberationist clergy were, and are, active. In 1970, the Diocese of Guaranda, the capital of Bolívar Province, which includes the Chillanes parish, established Promoción Humana, an organization dedicated to sponsoring small credit and technical training programs in the region. The organization often worked in conjunction with the Lauritas, a Colombian religious order with the specific mission of educating women. In 1973 Bishop Cándido Rada of Guaranda founded the Fondo Ecuatoriano Popularum Progressio, in concert with Salesian priests and laypeople working in the indigenous community of Salinas. FEPP's mission, and its name, came from Pope Paul VI's 1967 encyclical letter, *Populorum Progressio*, in which he called for a "common fund" for the "assistance of the most disinherited," all of this in the spirit of "solidarity human development." For development to be authentic, wrote the pope, "it cannot be restricted to economic growth alone. To be authentic, it must be well rounded; it must foster the development of each man and of the whole man" (Paul VI 1967).

In this vein, FEPP sponsors sustainable economic ventures and microcredit programs in Bolívar and several other provinces, providing training, technical assistance, and oversight to the communities that undertake them. Cheese making, which FEPP coordinates with Promoción Humana and a Salinas-based marketing consortium, Fundación de Consorcios de Queseras Rurales Comunitarias (FUNCONQUERUCOM), is one of the most successful of these programs.

The genesis of the Virgen de las Nubes group in 1989, then, was sparked at least in part by a nascent liberationist infrastructure dedicated to development within the church. FEPP and PH promoters were working to form artisanal groups and microcredit organizations throughout the region as a part of a larger effort to bring "disinherited" peasants and poor urban dwellers into the marketplace, and also into the Kingdom of God.

That this movement toward "integrated" development was successful is indicated by the existence of the women's group, and to a certain degree by the fact that the women do not identify themselves as particularly liberationist, a theme to which I return in later chapters. Rather, groups like the Virgen de las Nubes Cooperative participate in economic activities and Catholic practices such as the mass and "reflections" on biblical passages at the beginning of meetings, engaging in liberationist praxis even though they do not use the term. As Josefa Arteaga, president of the Virgen de las Nubes Cooperative in 2003 and a PH technical adviser for microcredit and knitting, put it:

> When we start a group, we are with the Word of God in every meeting. We are reflecting on what the Word of God says, and how to put it into practice. . . . That is, that we put into practice what is the actual Word of God, what God teaches us. . . . It's the same in the community banks. When we promote a bank, we identify ourselves as from Promoción Humana. . . . I identify where I'm from, what it is we're looking to be, where we want to go. That is, we want them to know that the Word of God comes first, more than anything. So we always start meetings with the Word of God. This is the way of communicating to the people. We identify where we're from, what we want to do with them, that the project is by the poor for those who are poorer.

Virgen de las Nubes Cooperative members also pointed to reflection and the Word of God when I asked about the Catholic nature of the group. Narcisa Inca, who joined the cooperative in 1994, described it this way.

> JD: Is it important that the group is Catholic?
>
> NI: I don't know, that's something for each person. For me it is important that one accepts Catholic [teachings]—that only God is our Father because others come from far away and contradict the Word of God.
>
> JD: What do you do that is Catholic in the group?
>
> NI: When we met we read the Bible, we reflected that way, among all the *compañeras*. We haven't met that way in a while. We aren't together right now. Not like before.

Paula Pozo, who joined the group in 2004, had something similar to say, though she also mentioned the importance of hierarchy and institutional affiliation.

JD: Is it important that the group is Catholic?
PP: Yes.
JD: Why?
PP: Because we take our problems with leadership to Padre Mateo [Panteghini]. He always evaluates us; he has given us advice when we were starting to fall, starting to become disorganized. We have always had Catholic support at our backs.
JD: Have you done anything particularly Catholic in the group, or is it more of an identity?
PP: Yes, we always start with the Word of God. It's the first thing in the Order of the Day.
JD: And are there other things?
PP: Readings and reflection.
JD: And are these important, or just words?
PP: It's important because they are things that happen to us and it's like, a reflection for us. So we think, "This isn't good, what we are doing." We have to change, we have to have to stop in order to feel better among ourselves, and then later with others.

Narcisa's and Paula's comments, especially in conjunction with Josefa's emphasis on cooperatives as "the poor helping those who are poorer" and the emphasis on solidarity and community during the dedication of the quesera, point to the predominance of liberationist ideals and practices in the cheese-making operation. Catholics make cheese in Chillanes because it is what Catholics interested in solidarity and the "Word of God" *should* do. To promote such progress is the presumed job, and goal, of the institutional church.

WHY CHEESE?

Cheese is not a native food in the Andes, having been introduced only with the Spanish and their livestock during the Conquest. Since that time, however, queso fresco, a soft, white cheese that does not need to mature, has become popular in the Ecuadorian diet and is served in soups, with fresh corn and hominy, in the potato *llapingachos* popular in the Riobamba region, and inside the stuffed corn tortillas particular to Bolívar. Queso fresco is available for purchase in local markets, and many women make it at home with the aid of rennet tablets. Hard or mature cheeses—parmesan, andino, mozzarella, cheddar—are gaining popularity in urban centers and are now readily available in supermarkets, which sell an ever-expanding selection from producers around the country, including those in Bolívar. In addition to cheese, yogurt is popular as a drink and is available in kiosks and the small dry goods stores that serve rural and urban shoppers.

The particular story of cheese production in Chillanes, and indeed in the province, however, has less to do with urban tastes and supermarkets than it does with the legacy of liberation theology. At least in Bolívar, hard cheese has always been Catholic.

Cheese: The Fruit of Juan Bosco in the Andes

Antonio Polo and Mateo Panteghini, the Italian Salesian priests who came to dedicate the Chillanes quesera, have been in Bolívar since the 1970s, when they arrived as part of Operation Mato Grosso, a liberationist endeavor that placed Salesian priests in isolated communities to engage in community organizing, social work, and technical training.[4] Polo, then a young priest who led the first-ever student strike at an ecclesiastical university when he protested the suspension of radical priests at the Salesian University in Turin, arrived in Salinas, a remote community high in the mountains outside of Guaranda, in 1971, at the invitation of Guaranda's bishop, Cándido Rada. A self-described "radical priest," Polo decided to join Operation Mato Grosso at the suggestion of a professor. "Little by little the decision is made," wrote Polo in his autobiography, "and longings and thoughts concentrated themselves on the new frontier. What if in place of so much talk about change, I could have the opportunity to live it?" (Polo 2002, 18).

The situation that Polo found in Salinas was one that certainly needed some practical, and practiced, change. At 3,550 meters above sea level, Salinas does not possess the mild climate that characterizes the rich agricultural lands in the lower valleys of the province. Rather, Salinas's majority indigenous population was forced into the area during the Spanish conquest and occupation and made a living as laborers in a salt mine and agricultural interests owned by the Cordovex family. The work was notoriously brutal, and Polo is not alone in describing the relationship of the indigenous population in Salinas to the salt mine owners as one that was "harshly exploitative," characterized by "servitude," "desperation" and "stagnation" (Polo 2002, 25–26). Recalling his arrival in Salinas in his autobiography, Polo writes that he did find unity among the population, but it was a "solidarity of emergency" rather than the concerted and constructive solidarity he hoped to foster as a community organizer and religious leader (30). Indeed, when Polo arrived, Salineritos had tried to take community control of the salt mines and industrialize their production in 1962, an attempt that ended in failure (201).

Padre Antonio, as he is known throughout the region, worked with Jose Tonello, director of FEPP, to start savings and credit programs in Salinas and its surrounding communities from almost the day he arrived. Though he eventually wanted to help people move out of salt production and into artisanal goods and other businesses that would lead to self-sufficiency and the kind of "solidarity development" outlined by the papal encyclical, Polo felt that basic savings and credit programs were a good beginning as they would help bring people together and encourage them to strategize about the future (Polo 2002, 31). He was particularly concerned with teaching accounting procedures that were "simple and effective," especially as he found a "resistance to regulation" such as accounting rules that could be an obstacle to sustainable development initatives (Polo 2002, 32). Polo, in cooperation with Tonello, was successful in creating an initial saving and credit cooperative, Cooperativa de Ahorro y Crédito (CAC), in Salinas in 1972. Community banks (bancos comunitarios), as Promoción Humana has come to call them, are still flourishing in the province, and PH promoters help organize several every year.

In Salinas, the success of the CAC led to community development efforts, including the improvement of the road to Guaranda, tree planting for conservation and harvest, and, in 1974, the initiation of the Centro Artesenal TEXAL (commonly referred to as "Tejidos Salinas"), which organized women who produced knitted goods for sale. Youth groups dried mushrooms, community men organized a carpentry shop, and by 1982 UNORSAL, the Union of Salinas Organizations, was formed to represent these "base organizations" in the parish. UNORSAL was reconfigured and officially recognized as a foundation, FUNORSAL, in 1988, and is the entity responsible for collecting the goods created by affiliate cooperatives, finding markets, and negotiating prices. By the late 1990s, Salinas was recognized internationally as a success story in sustainable development, primarily because of two products: wool yarn produced in a factory and then knit into sweaters by women in cooperatives associated with FUNORSAL and cheese marketed with the FUNCONQUERUCOM consortium throughout the country.[5]

Cheese production began in Salinas in 1976, when one of the cooperatives began a relatively small queso fresco operation that processed 400 liters of milk a day. The plant was not an immediate success and closed for a brief time, largely because of problems with transportation, marketing, and pricing. The real ascendancy of cheese in Salinas began in 1978, when the Swiss technician José Dubach suggested that Salinas had the perfect climate and, with ready and willing cooperatives, the labor resources required to produce mature cheeses, which are better suited for transport to cities such as Quito and Guayaquil. Working with FEPP director Tonello, Dubach and Polo arranged for an accord between the Ecuadorian government and Switzerland. COTESU, the Swiss bilateral aid agency, funded the construction of the quesera along with credit provided by FEPP and support from Promoción Humana. Dubach provided training and technical assistance. Cooperative members, as in the Chillanes example, provided labor and also sent members to Switzerland to be trained in mature cheese production. To facilitate marketing, the consortium opened a store, Queseras de Bolívar (Cheese Producers of Bolívar), in Quito in 1978 and one in Guayaquil in 1989. Business was so good that a separate consortium, FUNCONQUERUCOM, formed in 1991 with the sole mission of overseeing cheese-producing cooperatives around the province.

By 2002 there were more than twenty-two queseras operating in Bolívar and about eighty nationally, under the auspices of FUNCONQUERUCOM, including that of the Virgen de las Nubes Cooperative. An agreement signed with the grocery chain Supermaxi in 1990 gave the consortium access to the largest supermarkets in the country. Meanwhile, oil money from the Amazonian discoveries in the late 1970s led to the formation of the Ministerio de Obras Públicas (MOP), the government agency with the primary mission of road construction. With the completion of a major highway between Guaranada and Ambato in 1986 and the improvement and paving of the road from Salinas to Guaranda in 2001 following a presidential visit by Gustavo Noboa, transportation of hard cheese and even milk to major markets became ever more possible and profitable. Catholics were in the cheese business, and doing very well.

When the Promoción Humana promoter Eugenia Montero approached the Virgen de las Nubes group in 1997 and asked if it would be interested in starting a rural cheese-making operation, then, she was offering the women a chance to become even more involved with what is arguably the most successful sustainable development project in the province if not in Ecuador. Though the women were already knitting sweaters and other goods for sale with FUNORSAL, cheese production offered the possibility of full-time employment and marketable production on a much larger scale. With cheese production, the community praxis of a small-scale base community could go national as the women entered the larger marketplace as owners, architects, and entrepreneurs.

Non-Catholic Interests: Cheese and the Market beyond Liberation

The success of the Salesians and their base communities around the province in dairy production did not go unnoticed by businesses and non-Catholic development agencies, nor did it exist in a vacuum. Nestlé, the Swiss company specializing in dairy-based products, first came to Ecuador in 1965 and took advantage of relatively cheap wholesale milk prices and rebounding cacao stocks to produce everything from chocolate bars to baby formula and especially powered milk, popular where refrigeration is unavailable. Though the prime milk-producing region in Ecuador is just south of Quito in the wide valleys around Latacunga, Nestlé also established a presence in the provinces of Chimborazo, Tungarahua, and Bolívar once the company had built a processing plant outside of Guayaquil, taking advantage of the rich milk of the highlands and the newly improved, and improving, highways to the coast. In Chillanes, the company built a milk collection plant on the southeast side of town in 1995 and hired truck owners to drive rural routes, gathering the milk for the plant, where it was chilled until it shipped to the production plant on the coast. Though the collection station was certainly never one of Nestlé's biggest interests in Ecuador, the plant did provide work for several Chillanenses. It also raised community members' awareness of the potential for the province in dairy markets.

Guillermo Mesías was a collection driver for the plant before it closed in 1998, after the Ecuadorian government eased restrictions on the importation of powdered milk as part of neoliberal restructuring. He described a small boom in cheese production and dairy interests in the region as the

FIGURE 3. Nestlé Milk Chilling Station, Chillanes, 2009

result of Nestlé in combination with the Salinas success story. When Nestlé shut down its collection plant in Chillanes, Mesías used the skills he had acquired in the Nestlé operation to start his own production on some unused family land.

GM: So, I began to make the cheese there, and I was working more or less with an average of 800 liters of milk a day. And it was that way for a while. For a good while it was a good business. But later there was strong competition, because as industrial dairy plants and also milk collection plants closed in other provinces, it was the same in Riobamba, in Santo Domingo, in Latacunga. There was no one to supply the milk to, no one to sell to, so they opted to build queseras, to make cheese. And there was a cheese competition, an overproduction of cheese.

JD: What year was that?

GM: More or less twelve years ago.

JD: So in 1998, around then.

GM: Yes.

Mesías would eventually shut down his quesera when his hired drivers began to take cheese orders on commission for delivery and fail to return with the money from his clients. This, along with the competition, he said, forced his cheese plant into bankruptcy despite demand for the product.

No longer in the role of producer, Mesías once again became a driver and ended up working for the recently started Virgen de las Nubes effort, as well as for other burgeoning production centers in the region, transporting milk from rural producers to the plants. At one time, Mesías recalled, he was driving for the Universidad de Bolívar in Guaranda, which had a technical program in dairy production, the Virgen de las Nubes group, and also for Plan Esperanza, a plant sponsored by the Catholic Diocese of Guaranda. The Esperanza plant initially specialized in pasteurized, bagged milk but was taken over by the Salinas consortium for cheese production in 2005 when it could not find a large enough market for its fresh products. For Mesías, who is now out of the dairy business and works as a driver for the *municipio* (municipality) of Chillanes, that cheese production in the province is almost the exclusive domain of the Salesian project makes sense. "Just look at Promoción Humana . . . excellent!," he concluded. "They have a market, they have exports, everything! Promoción Humana is doing very well." Mesías could think of only one remaining non-Salesian cheese producer in Bolívar, though it still had Christian ties. The evangelical development organization World Vision entered the cheese business in 2008 by opening a quesera in the community of San Simón.

When Eugenia Montero proposed that the Virgen de las Nubes group start cheese production in 1997, then, she was proposing that associates engage in a project with a strong and successful liberationist history, and also one with real market potential. By producing both soft and hard cheeses, the women would not only be participating in liberation theology, but in an increasingly neoliberal marketplace. They would work in solidarity, for the good of the cooperative, even as they entered the competitive environment of 1990s cheese production in Ecuador. They got involved in cheese production, in other words, because cheese was the hot commodity of the day, especially and notably most successfully, in Catholic circles.

WHY WOMEN?

Having traced the liberationist and economic roots of the Virgen de las Nubes cheese plant, one question remains: why a women's group? Here the story once again goes back at least in part to liberation theology, which has a history, if an uneven one, of targeted gender inclusion. The formation of women's cooperatives for microcredit and enterprise, however, is not limited to Catholics but also has deep roots in international development and the women's movements of the 1960s and 1970s. Women's social circles and women's work especially are one place where the networks and discourses of liberation, development, human rights, and market ideologies come together.

Though women are widely considered "more religious" and "more cooperative" than men throughout Latin America, women's place in the larger struggle for liberation within the Catholic Church has been, and continues to be, contested (Burdick 1993, 2004; Molyneaux 2002). When base communities began to form in response to liberationist ideals, many women found the groups an extra burden, not relevant to their particular struggles in household spaces or an uncomfortable space in which to handle issues of marital tensions or domestic abuse. John Burdick's research in Brazil in the early 1990s documented that groups focused on systemic change did not always take into account more local, and pressing, issues for female participants. As one of his informants phrased it, "They say 'struggle, struggle, struggle!' But they mean unions, and neighborhood associations, and political parties, things like that. But I struggle here in my own home every day. They don't speak about that" (Burdick 1993, 96). Struggling in the context of a community committed to societal change was not necessarily what she felt to be in her best interest.

Indeed, scholars studying the liberation movement in Latin America often point to the tensions inherent in balancing consciousness of women's rights in the context of a patriarchal and communitarian organization (Molyneaux 2002, 174). Sonia Alvarez (1998, 311), writing about the globalization of feminist movements in Latin America, also highlighted the discordance many women felt between wanting to be better represented in and by institutional systems and the need to see those systems fundamentally re-imagined and reformed.

The fact remains, however, that as liberation theology became actualized in Latin America through the formation of base communities, many of those communities were, and are, composed mostly or solely of women. In many cases, liberationist women's groups emerged from already active lay organizations of women organized for purposes of charity, prayer, or education. In the barrio of San Juan Pamba, home of the Virgen de las

Nubes Cooperative, a group of women met regularly for devotions to the Virgen de Rosario before the women's cooperative formed. Similarly, there has been a long history of religiously sponsored women's education in Chillanes. The Lauritas ran a high school in town from about 1950 to 1979. When they left, some of their programs were continued by a group of Dominican sisters. When the liberationist Promoción Humana first offered to train women in piece knitting for export in the 1980s, they did so in the convent, taking over where the nuns had left off.

While gender has not always been a clear category of oppression against which liberation theology and its practitioners have struggled, then, women have been historically targeted as willing and effective agents of change. Certainly this is true in the case of cheese making in Bolívar. When Antonio Polo first arrived in Salinas, women's groups were the first successful microcredit and artisanal enterprises he encouraged. When TEXAL was formed in 1974, it was overseen by an entirely female committee from the Salinas cooperative. The consortium employed sixty-five women engaged in production knitting in their homes. In a 1993 interview, Polo (1993, 26) mentioned gender as an important factor in the success of the Salinas enterprise: "In the countryside women have been very expert in all their work, but this is not to say that this automatically translates into power." In starting projects geared to women, Polo and the participants in the Salinas projects endeavored not only to include women but also to enable them to foment and use some of the power historically denied to them.

The cheese factories have certainly emerged as one place where women have made a claim to, and a mark on, liberationist practices and ideologies. At a 2003 International Day of the Woman gathering in Guayco, a shrine marking an apparition of the Virgin Mary in the province, women's groups from all over Bolívar gathered to worship and reflect on their identities as religiously committed Catholics engaged in an enterprise meant to improve their material and communal well-being. At the gathering, the priests reminded the women of their special place in the liberationist enterprise as the gender gifted with "compassion" and "communal sense," qualities especially suited for the enterprise of taking action to help the poor. Though the Virgen de las Nubes quesera was the only one in Bolívar operated solely by women, most of them have women as stakeholders, often as the majority stakeholders.

One reason for the relatively high number of women participating in cheese production is the lack of employment available to women outside of industry they create themselves. Bolívar is overwhelmingly agricultural, forcing almost everyone interested in work outside of farm labor, shop keeping, or government jobs to look elsewhere (INEC 2018). This lack of employment is felt more intensely by women, who are just beginning to enter the formal labor sector. This is certainly true in Chillanes. Indeed, one reason the women of the Virgen de las Nubes Cooperative were willing to try the cheese factory was its potential to create job opportunities. As Jesus Galarza, a founder and recent president of the group put it:

> Here we haven't studied, and we can't work in any factory, in anything important like that, you can't earn money. Here, what we do is work in the fields. . . . And I do what I can in the house. And on top of this I can't leave. . . . I can't go somewhere else [to work]. And so . . . we formed the group, [and] my husband joined the group Jesús de Gran Poder. And so the wives of the men, they came to train us, here, FEPP came here to offer us training in knitting, all of this we did that way. . . . And so we started, we started meeting that way, and it used to be very nice, the group was very organized.

Julia Guamán, also a founding member and recent president, echoed these sentiments.

> JG: The first thing I do [in a day] is the household chores. Then, if I have outside work, I go to work. I, for example, I work here in the church office. I spend the day working here. Most women spend their days like this. Most women here are dedicated to household chores, taking care of the home. Children, their husband, and everything, they do most of everything. There are very few that go out and work at something else.
>
> JD: And for those that want to work go out and work, is there work here?
>
> JG: No, there isn't. There isn't. This is why when someone has a job they have to take good care of it, because here there isn't any work. It's the same in the countryside, working as a laborer.
>
> JD: So do many young women leave here to look for work?
>
> JG: Yes. The majority emigrate to other places in order to look for work.

An important facet of the cheese plant as a liberationist project was the creation of local jobs, freeing women to stay in the community.

Such a pragmatic approach to liberationist projects is not unique in Latin America, or among women. In her research on women's liberationist groups in early 1990s Brazil, Carol Ann Drogus concluded that what she called "religious personality" colored women's perception of and participation in base communities and subsequent political action more than specific teachings of the church. More women in Brazil were "traditional" and "Samaritan" in her study, preferring liturgy, historical church structure, and charity over anticapitalist or overly political ("liberationist") views of the ideal role of the church. But this did not mean that women disregarded the specifically female aspects of the base communities in which they participated. Rather, "women's ability to discuss the movement in terms that touched their common cultural notion of womanhood and a related continuum of religious values (charity-love-social justice) unified them where liberation theology could not" (Drogus 1997, 113). Women's experience of liberation theology, then, was more closely related to their experiences as women than to their particular mode of melding politics and faith. Liberationist settings allowed a solidarity of gender but not one that led to an automatic political revolution or unified religious views.

The experience of liberationist Catholicism in Bolívar, and in much of rural Ecuador, has been similar. Women make cheese as part of a push toward empowerment and expanding opportunities but not necessarily as part of a concerted effort to radically change the political or economic systems in Catholic circles or in the greater area. This appears to be indicative of the timbre of liberation theology as it has played out in local environments. This is not the politically forward or radical revolutionary ethic often associated with the movement, especially in places like El Salvador. Rather, this manifestation of liberation theology is more akin to a basic-needs approach to development; one that works to change existing conditions at the local level, seeking to increase opportunity by making the system work for traditionally marginalized groups, including indigenous peoples (in the case of Salinas) and women.

There is a politics here, and it is, in many ways, revolutionary, but it is a quiet and productive revolution, one waged and counted in sweaters, rounds of cheese, access to markets, and improved income rather than street protests and raised weapons. Inverting Clodovis Boff's critique, the church is indeed the NGO, and one that the revolutionaries possess. Those revolutionaries, however, are not stereotypical political dissidents marching in the streets or overthrowing a government through violent means but women looking to expand on their roles as those responsible for households, as community citizens reluctant to emigrate in order to find economic opportunity, as visionaries and entrepreneurs looking to make the best of a difficult economic situation.

WOMEN IN INTERNATIONAL DEVELOPMENT

While there is a clear connection between liberation theology and the targeting of women in Chillanes, liberation theology and its attendant economic development programs did not arise in a vacuum. Women's groups have played an important role not only in Catholic cooperatives, but across a broad range of development initiatives. Women and women's groups have come to play a key role in international development, especially in the past thirty years.

Like liberation theology, international development was late to focus on women as a marginalized social group and key constituency. Until the 1970s women were often seen as antithetical to the "progress" economic development offered as they were the bearers of "tradition" (Bergeron 2000). The rise of women's movements, however, helped raise gender as an issue to which international development must attend. In 1970 the United Nations Committee on the Status of Women passed a resolution encouraging the "full integration of women into the total development effort" (Tinker 1990, 29). In 1973 the United States joined the concerted attempt to involve women in international development programs when Congress passed the Percy Amendment to the Foreign Assistance Act, an effort that established Women in Development (WID) programs as a part of USAID in order to "give particular attention to those programs, projects and activities which tend to integrate women into the national economies of foreign countries, thus improving their status and assisting the total development effort" (Tinker 1990, 31). These programs took gender into overt consideration in development projects.

The emphasis on women, and specifically women's roles in development, continued as 1975 marked the start of the UN "Decade for Women." The focus on women was paired with, and in many ways made possible by, a concomitant shift in strategies and theories about international economic development and its implementation. Robert McNamara, who headed the World Bank from 1968 to 1981, adopted a "human needs" approach to development, which essentially switched the bank's core mission from one of macroeconomics to one targeting food, medical, and other insecurities. In many cases, these were insecurities felt mostly by women, who were largely excluded from formal economic activities recognized by the bank.[6] This shift led to the popularly held notion in the early 1980s that women were the "missing link" in development and that their inclusion would make development programs more successful as their relative lack of progress in eradicating poverty was becoming clear in the "lost decades" of the late 1970s and early 1980s, when world poverty was on the rise.

WID was not without its critics, however. Carolyn Moser (1993, 27), especially, is credited for her work calling into question WID's failure to account for women's "triple burden": reproductive household, productive extrahousehold, and community managing work. Moser called for a deeper accounting of gender roles and the replacement of WID programs, which she said inadequately represented the role of gender in society, and thus in development, with Gender and Development (GAD) programs, which would allow for more flexible, local, and realistic assessments of the role of gender in development programs. Moser did not disagree that women had a role to play in development, and that women were necessary partners for successful development, but she did a great deal to trouble notions that women's only useful role was as part of the formal economic sector.

When Martha Nussbaum proposed a "capabilities approach" to development in 2000, one modeled on the economist Amartya Sen's theory that good development will maximize available resources and human capabilities, she attempted to take these critiques into account. Development, according to both Sen and Nussbaum, allows people to live up to their capabilities as economic and human actors. "We ask not only about a person's satisfaction with what she does," wrote Nussbaum, "and not just what she is in a position to do (what her opportunities and liberties are). We ask not just about the resources that are sitting around, but how those resources do or do not go to work, enabling [women] to function in a fully human way" (2000, 71). Effective development, according to Nussbaum, considers the needs and capabilities of women, attempting to maximize human potential in areas such as life, bodily and emotional health, imagination, play, and control over one's environment. Nussbaum's approach, one often cited favorably by development critics such as Arturo Escobar, has also been adopted to a certain extent by international development programs that utilize "participatory" or "integrated" models for programs and projects. The Participatory Analysis for Community Action (PACA) model used by the U.S. Peace Corps, for example, encourages development workers to survey communities in which they work for gendered uses of time, communal spaces, and other resources (United States Peace Corps 1996).

By the time the Virgen de las Nubes Cooperative was founded in the late 1980s, then, it was not unusual for many development programs to target women as partners and recipients of development projects. By the time "gender mainstreaming" became a formal development practice in 1997, the United Nations Millennium Development Goals specifically targeted gender inequality in 2000, and the World Bank released its seminal *Engendering Development* report in 2001, the women's group was already part of a growing, global movement. This movement not only included women in international economic development; it also targeted women with specific programs, usually in areas of reproduction, microcredit, and community organizations such as cooperatives. Whereas development programs in the 1960s and 1970s viewed women primarily as reproducers—as people in need of birth control to stem rising population growth—in the 1990s the view shifted. With the introduction of the "basic needs" approach to development and the concomitant rise of "alternative development" programs that stressed local solutions to meet those needs, women were not just reproducers of populations and households; they became potential, necessary, and even uniquely endowed participants in economic and community spheres.

SOCIAL CAPITAL: WHY THE WOMEN ARE SMARTER

This shift in the way development programs have approached women and their roles has been supported by and has in turn supported the rise of the notion of social capital. A concept whose intellectual roots are found in the work of Pierre Bourdieu, social capital refers to social networks, alliances, and relationships that are not formalized in political or economic realms, though, as in all networks, some overlap and interconnection may occur. These informal networks are often where women and other marginalized groups find ways to change or improve situations when formal or macrosystems are not working. Social capital thrives in what Larissa Adler Lomnitz (1988, 43) calls "informal exchange networks," which involve activities that are "socially embedded transactions that obey a symbolic-cultural logic that differs from (and often clashes with) economic rationality or the formal ideology of the state. The rules of sociability that govern informal exchange vary from culture to culture." Social capital, then, is the ability of an individual or group to tap into and utilize these activities.

Broad acceptance of social capital has driven much of the "participatory" development programs in Latin America since the 1990s, though, as Maxine Molyneaux (2002) points out, participation and community-mindedness as strategies for local change have been on the continent since the invention of liberation theology. "Long before social capital and its policy derivative, 'participation,' became an integral part of development policies," she writes, "the Catholic church and the left were engaged in forms of development and activism through Christian Base Communities" (170). And, like many of these base communities, many participatory programs target women.

Indeed, despite the absence of the term "social capital" in *Engendering Development*, the notion that women are especially rich in networking skills and community-mindedness has driven many microcredit and other communitarian programs. The assumption of these programs, and one at least originally shared by many Virgen de las Nubes Cooperative members and promoters, is that women are (naturally) more community-minded, generous, understanding, ecologically oriented, trustworthy, and even more religious than men. Josefa Arteaga, one of the founders of the group who now works as a community bank organizer for Promoción Humana, discussed this in a 2003 interview.

JD: Which is more important, that the group is female or that it is Catholic?

JA: For me the two things!

JD: You can't decide?

JA: The two go together, you can't separate them. Because women, we are always a little more thankful to God. We are always giving thanks to God. The men—pff!

JD: Why is that?

JA: Because they are more concerned with what they are going to do, what they want to have. They don't think about other people.

> Also, as women we feel the necessity to come to, to other women, to the poorest people. We're more unified. If [the men] get together it's to talk, to, I don't know, do their things. . . . We pay more attention, we know what we want to do. Men, on the other hand, get into arguments and everything ends, it stops. They are left with nothing. There is discord, and sometimes they just drink at meetings.
>
> It's because of this that the project came especially for women. Because they say that women are more inclined to save, more responsible, we see what's missing in the household, we're responsible for our children, our husbands, for everything. So this project is especially for women. . . .
>
> What we want to do when we meet, whether it's in the community banks or in the groups, is to obtain a space where a woman can develop herself as a human being, where she can have ideas, where she, too, can play an important role in the community, not just in the weekly market. We can do many things.

In Josefa's view, the cooperative targets women not just because they need to claim a larger role in society, but because they are especially well suited to do so. What the groups provide in this model is a space where women are afforded the chance to develop their especially feminine skills of cooperation, savings, foresight, and willingness to work in and for community.

How much this notion of women's social capital penetrated the Virgen de las Nubes Cooperative and what the failure did to change these ideas among cooperative members are the subject of the chapters to come. For now, it should be clear that the members of the cooperative, and of many cooperatives like this one, made cheese *as women*. Cheese making was meant to be an action of liberation, not only from the confines of poverty, but from disempowerment and constraints to public life placed on women as a class with many responsibilities but few opportunities.

The women of the Virgen de las Nubes Cooperative, then, began making cheese as Catholics, as women, and as women taking part in international economic development projects. Josefa's reluctance to break any of these discourses apart when I asked her to rank them in terms of importance, and also their larger histories, indicates that once entwined, these discourses become very difficult to disentangle. Together, they create what the anthropologist Dorothy Holland calls a "space of authoring," a live and connective assemblage where women work out identity and purpose in alliance and opposition to ideas, material objects, and other people (Holland et al. 1998; see also De Landa 2006). How this "space of authoring" was composed and the consequences of its unraveling with the failure of the cheese factory continue to shape identities and possibilities for cooperative members, Chillanenses, and development specialists in Bolívar and beyond. The next chapter examines the particular places in which women in Chillanes author their lives and then moves to the use of gendered social capital in order to understand how that social production is invested, and risked, when used as a resource for development work.

TWO

Reproducing Women

Gendered Social Capital in Local Contexts

When the Virgen de las Nubes Cooperative was founded, there was no middle class to speak of in Chillanes, or in much of Ecuador (Central Intelligence Agency 2012).[1] For this reason, the opening sentence of the cooperative's Libro de Actas, written in 1997 to describe the founding of the group eight years earlier, was self-evident.[2] It reads, "With the proposition to provide support and motivate the advancement of peasant women out of marginalization by their own effort, this group began on the 28th of August 1989" (Libro de Actas, 1). Because the group was composed of peasant women, there was no need to describe the marginalization of which the book makes mention. As peasants, the women forming the group did not have access to the upper tiers of a capitalist economy where they could profit from manufacturing. As women, they faced double marginalization in that their labor was largely constrained to the sphere of domestic production and reproduction. Their vulnerability as social and economic actors was twice that of peasant men, who, though also limited in their ability to access financial capital, did have greater access to economic and social opportunities outside the home.

This lack of access to financial capital and lack of social opportunity are two of the reasons Promoción Humana focused development strategies on women soon after its founding. Every board of directors for PH's community banks — local groups established for microlending — must include women and are often exclusively female. When cheese making began in Bolívar Province in the 1980s, PH implemented a policy of "supporting" women, though the Chillanes cooperative was the only one that did not have men either working in production or on the board of directors. When Promoción Humana began its microcredit program in 2000, it was exclusively for women, a policy that remained in place until 2002, when Mateo Patenghini authorized the formation of cooperatives with as much as 30 percent male membership, though men remain barred from serving on boards. Aside from official policies that encourage women's participation at the programmatic level, PH boasts a provincial staff on which women are well represented and hosts, in conjunction with the Diocese of Guaranda, a celebration of International Women's Day every March 8 that is well attended by groups from throughout the province.

As discussed in the previous chapter, Gender and Development initiatives and theories of social capital played key roles in making women's groups attractive as development options. The often tacit belief that women are better at saving, more interpersonally cooperative, highly responsible, and more attentive to household needs—and thus better suited for microcredit projects and cooperative development programs—drove many development projects beginning in the late 1980s and remain at the fore of development strategies in the early twenty-first century. The 2006 Nobel laureate Grameen Bank, for example, incorporated in Bangladesh in 1983, gives 98 percent of its Grameen credit loans to women. No collateral is required for the loans, which rely on "trust" in systems of community to ensure that the loans are repaid (Grameen Bank 2012).

Feminist critiques of social capital theories such as those employed by Grameen, and to a certain extent, Promoción Humana, assert that by imagining women as "more responsible" in their fulfillment of household needs—and more susceptible to community pressures to conform to gender norms of charity, honesty, communitarianism, and hard work—gendered social capital programs reify gender stereotypes in ways that may reinforce subordinate roles for women. In a 2002 article, "Gender and the Silences of Social Capital: Lessons from Latin America," the sociologist Maxine Molyneaux expresses concern that social capital programs may be used as a substitute for political action aimed at changing the status of women in economic and public spaces. She also worries about the ways social capital programs may uphold "tradition" to the detriment of women's rights and entitlements (Molyneaux 2002, 174). The economist Ben

Fine joins Molyneaux in these concerns and, while not focused specifically on gender, worries that development that relies on social capital is not necessarily more successful but is simply less quantifiable than previous, failed, development policies. "From a moment's reflection," he asserts, "it is apparent that such endeavors have nothing new to contribute through appeal to social capital which merely serves as a convenient peg on which to hang collections of dull and mechanistic empiricism" (Fine 1999, 6). Worse, for Fine, a continued (mis)focus on social capital continues to deemphasize the role of the state in social welfare. Like other neoliberal policies, he argues, development based on social capital diminishes the role of the state and places the burden of economic well-being on individual, and often relatively powerless, actors.

Experiences in the Virgen de las Nubes Cooperative reflect these tensions and also point to embedded assumptions about the regenerative abilities of gendered social capital, which is often perceived as a "natural" quality, not unlike gender itself. Like financial capital, which is vulnerable to economic failures of various kinds, social capital may also be lost when relationships break down. There is risk and vulnerability when capital is put on the market, even if that capital is perceived as a natural, renewable resource, as in the case of gender.

This chapter examines these risks in context, beginning with an overview of cooperative members and their lives as women and economic actors in rural Ecuador. It then moves to an exploration of gendered social capital as it was deployed in the cooperative in order to understand how it both replicated and challenged gender and economic roles in wider society. The chapter is also designed to give readers a sense of cooperative history (a time line of that history is available in the appendix), beginning with its early days when women engaged in knitting, moving through cheese production, then into the period of early economic failure. Throughout, the chapter attends to the ways in which social capital models of gender paradoxically replicated the gendered vulnerabilities it was intended to overcome.

CAPITALIZING THE HOUSEHOLD: VULNERABILITY, PRODUCTION, AND CONSUMPTION IN DOMESTIC MODES

"Jill! Jill!" Climbing up the set of cement stairs to the suite of rooms that made up the living quarters of the Lucio house, I heard my name as I returned from an interview in the late afternoon one July day. Ligia, her hand barely extending beyond her belly at thirty-eight weeks' gestation, was motioning me over to the room that she and her husband, Alfaro, shared next to the one they had lent to me and my two children, in town for a research stay. "Mi mami!," she proclaimed in a slightly panicked stage whisper, "It's her birthday! Can you make a cake?" Ligia was well versed in a ragged Peace Corps–Ecuador cookbook that is standard issue to volunteers serving in the country and that I still bring with me whenever I visit for extended periods. She knew her mother was fond of a chocolate pastry included in the dessert section and hoped I could put one together before Mercedes returned from a workday in her blackberry (*mora*) fields. In the midst of Ligia's pending delivery, some intense work at her internet café on the bottom floor of the house that had kept her up until early morning for almost two weeks, and other family concerns, everyone had forgotten about Mercedes's birthday until that moment.

Rallying my kids and Ligia's daughter from a game they were playing with neighborhood children, I set to work in the kitchen, measuring ingredients while my helpers mixed them up, and then supervised some spirited decoration after we had baked our mixture in an industrial gas oven the family owns from a time when they made bread for sale. Later that evening, when Mercedes had sent her *peones* (day laborers) home after feeding them supper, we gathered in the upstairs living room and sang the Happy Birthday song as Mercedes smiled, her eyes half closed with exhaustion after a long and physically arduous day.

Quehaceres Domésticos: Work, Class, and Community in Rural and Semirural Settings

The hustle and bustle of the Lucio household, in which I have participated as a friend and researcher since the mid-1990s, is typical of many households in the rural and semirural sector in Ecuador. Mercedes, raised as one of ten children on a farm in a small community 10 kilometers from Chillanes proper, never married and is the matriarch of the two-story cinderblock house built on land given to her by her father. The house is a hub for her extended family. Mercedes, Ligia, Alfaro, Ligia's young daughter, and their infant son were the current permanent human residents on any given night during my fieldwork (Mercedes includes the family's chickens, pigs, dog, and guinea pigs whenever she speaks about the "household" (*hogar*), but most weeks at least one of Mercedes's brothers or sisters and their families, one of her two sons and their families, her mother, or close family friends traveling from out of town sleep at the house. In the summer months, the family played host to a teenage niece and nephew from Guaranda who helped with household tasks and the downstairs store and acted as baby-sitters for the younger set, which was especially helpful when my children, aged fourteen months to seven years over the course of my fieldwork, were part of this extended family.

Even when the extra beds go unoccupied, the kitchen table is often busy as family or friends passing through to the farm stop for a bite to eat, or Mercedes rises at four o'clock in the morning to begin cooking for the two or three peones she needs to hire to sow, weed, or harvest the crops she keeps on several plots of land she owns and rents on the circumference of town. Though the family bought an electric clothes washer in 2006, freeing them from a day of labor each week, there is still much to do to keep things running.

The Lucio household is not unlike those of the women in the cooperative, and Ligia was a member for several years in the 1990s at the same time that she was finishing a college degree at the local branch of the Universidad de Bolívar. The internet café on the first floor places them on the cutting edge of business innovation in Chillanes, however, and Alfaro's work as a heavy-machinery operator gives them a steady income that is the envy of many who rely on less predictable agricultural or commercial revenue. Like many of the households occupied by women in the cooperative, the Lucios depend on agriculture in combination with other sources of income, and like many women in the cooperative, Ligia has well beyond an average education for Ecuadorians in general, especially in Bolívar Province.

According to the 2010 Ecuadorian national census, 91 percent of all Ecuadorians have completed the prescribed "basic course," roughly six years of standard schooling, though this number is weighted heavily by those under twenty-five years of age, who are much more likely to have an education than older Ecuadorian citizens. Average Ecuadorians had 9.04 years of education in 2010, up from 6.61 years in 2001. Also in 2010, 6.3 percent of Ecuadorians had attained a higher degree, mostly in two-year technical programs. In Bolívar, these figures are lower. Bolivarenses average only 7.8 years of schooling, placing it second to the bottom in education levels in Ecuador. Bolívar's citizens also have the highest rate of illiteracy, at 13.9 percent (INEC 2018).

Of fourteen associates remaining in the cooperative in 2009, five (36 percent) had either completed or were in the process of obtaining a college degree, three (21 percent) had some secondary schooling, and six (43 percent) had at least some basic schooling, ranging from two to six years. This degree of education translated for several of the women into occupations outside the household. Four women, three of them with college degrees, held professional positions with organizations in Chillanes, primarily NGOs. In addition, one woman runs her own cottage industry selling fried pork, one does laundry for families around town, and another works as a domestic servant with a local family, a position she has held since she was thirteen. Almost all of the women do some sort of agricultural work on family holdings or rented lands, two were married to salaried professional men, and two were married to nonsalaried wage earners, working in occupations like truck driving. Both of these men were also engaged in agricultural work. Six of the women owned their houses, and the remaining eight either rented or lived in parents' or in-laws' residences.[3] Domestic partnerships also varied among group members: nine members lived with husbands, often in multigenerational households, three members were married but separated from their husbands, and two members had never married.[4]

As a group, Virgen de la Nubes Cooperative members represent various modes of households in twenty-first-century rural Ecuador and span several social classes in a rural society that generally values education and outward signs of professionalism, as well as embedded social status gained through success in business and/or politics. The permanent administrative position for the cheese plant as well as the coordinator position through PH were granted to women with college degrees. Positions on the board of directors, however, rotated at the minimum on an annual basis, did not favor those with higher educational status. The most frequent presidents of the group were those who had completed only some primary schooling but were older than other members and thus regarded with a certain respect and as having leadership capacity.

Despite higher than average educational attainment, none of the cooperative members came from Chillanes's handful of elite families—primarily doctors, lawyers, politicians, and owners of large businesses located in the center of town—though the group tried to recruit female members of these families in its heyday in the early 2000s, extending special invitations to knitting sessions when the Promoción Humana promoter, based in Guaranda, was also attending. Rather, most members of the group came from households with modest landholdings and diverse small economic enterprises, though a lack of these things was not a bar to entrance, as exemplified by the women working in washing and domestic services.

While the women varied in educational attainment, and to a certain degree in access to economic resources outside of agricultural income, the group was substantially more homogeneous when it came to race and perceptions of access to societal wealth. Every woman in the group considered herself *mestiza* (of mixed indigenous and Spanish descent), and none came from the many indigenous communities that surround Chillanes. And to a woman, each considered herself poor (*pobre*) in comparison to elite families in Chillanes, and especially in comparison to women in Ecuador's urban centers.

Indeed, a shared sense of rural poverty was an important source of communal identity for group members, one that also frames the ways in which the women saw themselves as women, especially in household settings. In group meetings, when women would speak formally, group members often began with "Somos pobres," "We are poor," before asking for greater cooperation among associates, requesting that the group aid people in greater need, or inducting a new member, a process that required that the new member pledge to work for the "benefit of the group."

Cooperative members also mentioned class and the need for household income when they spoke about why they joined the group, something they then linked to rural women's experiences more broadly. Mercedes Huilca, a past president of the group who spent several years living in a small building at the cheese plant in her capacity as caretaker, answered my question about why she became a member of the group by citing the economic benefits of the group's knitting project in the context of women's domestic life.

> MH: Because I was knitting sweaters, and because they paid us. And with that I was buying things [*cualquier cosa*]. That's why I joined the group.
> JD: So you were knitting in order to sell?
> MH: Yes. And that helped out here in the house. I bought whatever [*cualquier cosa*] with that.

Mercedes contrasted the ability to buy "whatever" with the money she made from knitting to standard women's activities, which she described as "a little difficult."

> You have to work, help your husband, just to get to a place where you can have anything. [My husband] works in agriculture, so I help with the animals, and here in the house, and there, I help him in the fields. I wash, I cook, everything.

Lucía Alarcón, who worked in the cheese plant as a full-time employee, shares much of the same sense of rural struggle. When I asked her to talk about women's lives in Chillanes, she replied, "We're very sacrificial."

> JD: Very sacrificial?
> LA: Surely! We get up early to cook, to clean the house. If there are plants to take care of, we take care of them. We ourselves do laundry. It's not like, poverty doesn't let us—that is, our economy, the salaries here are very low, we don't earn much. We don't have anything to pay to anyone to cook, we don't have domestic help. We don't hire someone to wash clothes. We do it ourselves.

One area of commonality for the Virgen de las Nubes women was "doing it [them]selves" when it came to domestic tasks, unlike many of their urban counterparts, whom they presumed hired help for the daily grind of cooking, cleaning, washing clothes, childcare, and other household chores. Cecilia Miño, a group member for ten years at the time of a 2009 interview, commented on this as she discussed the possibility of men entering the cooperative.

> CM: If there were men, it would be better.
> JD: Do you think men will join the group?
> CM: I don't know, they haven't talked about that. They really haven't talked about that.
> JD: Are the lives of women here more difficult than the lives of men?
> CM: Yes.
> JD: How?
> CM: Because women work the same as men. Or better, maybe more. For example, in the fields, I work as hard as men. Imagine if I couldn't! You go out into the fields, you use the same tools, and work the same as men. And you can work, in all the work we are equal. It's not that if you're a woman you can't do it. In the fields more than anything, it's like that. But in the city, it's different.

There girls are prepared, and they have better work, better possibilities. But in the country—

JD: So for them, life isn't as hard as it is in the country?

CM: Clearly, because they're prepared. Imagine what it's like for those that have only a basic education. I can't perform any function in an institution because of this. I can't work because of this. All I can do is swing a hoe, here in the fields.

It is not uncommon for young women from the Chillanes region who do have an education to emigrate to Ecuador's urban centers, usually Quito and Guayaquil, though many end up with jobs that do not require the education of which Cecilia speaks. Julia Guamán, a recent president of the group, foregrounded this phenomenon during a discussion about women's lives.

JD: In order to understand more about women's lives here, how do you spend your days? What do you do from the time you get up until you go to bed at night?

JG: The women here?

JD: You, yourself.

JG: Just speaking for myself, we do chores [*labores domésticos*] first. From the time we get up, we do various tasks. Then, if we have outside work, we go to work. For example, I work here in this office. I spend my days working. Most women do the same. The majority of women here are dedicated to housework [*quehaceres domésticos*], tending to the household. The children, the husband, and all that, the majority are. Very few go out and have other jobs.

JD: And are there jobs for those who want to go out and work?

JG: No there aren't, there aren't. This is why when one has a job, one has to protect it, because there are so few jobs here. And for those in the countryside, it's the same, for those who work the land.

JD: And are there many young women who leave here looking for work?

JG: Yes. The majority emigrate to other places looking for work. . . . With luck, they go out a little prepared and seek good jobs. If not, it's just the same, they're going to work in housework, and just do it there [in the cities].

Julia's assessment of "quehaceres domésticos"—the household work of cooking, childcare, laundry, agricultural work, and support of spouses as the major occupation for women in Chillanes—was shared by every cooperative member I interviewed, and also by women in the community who had never been involved in cooperative efforts. On average, women reported rising between five and six o'clock in the morning, cooking breakfast, attending to children's and spouses' needs, washing clothes, tending animals, assisting in agricultural labors, and, where applicable, working in outside jobs, until they went to bed at about nine o'clock at night. Most reported watching television as a leisure activity, something they usually did in the evening, and most spoke about women's lives in terms similar to Lucía's, describing women as "very sacrificial" with "difficult lives," especially when domestic production included agricultural duties.

The shared experiences of this domestic production, as well as those drawn from geographic proximity, were an important source of social capital for Virgen de las Nubes members. Most of the women came from San Juan Pamba, a small, dispersed agricultural community approximately one kilometer from Chillanes's church and park, with no center to speak of apart from its small church and accompanying dirt plaza. Much of the casual conversation at group meetings and knitting sessions revolved around the community and local events or discussions about the relative merits and problems of living "in town" (*por el centro*) instead of in San Juan Pamba's more rural environs. Group members living in Chillanes's center often referred to agricultural activities and family members from smaller communities, something that aided in maintaining social harmony.

When Promoción Humana sought to employ strategies to grow what organization employees perceived as significant preexisting social capital within the group, then, the organization was often relying on a replication and reproduction of activities commonly associated with normatively female household roles defined by a predominantly agricultural environment. Group members frequently cooked together, and shortly after they purchased the land on which the cheese plant would be built, they planted corn and rented out pasture for cattle grazing, endeavors that clearly replicate rural household activities.

For several years, this strategy worked. When group activities were limited to replicating household tasks, members reported high levels of the social qualities of care and cooperation often afforded them in gendered social capital literature. When the project became marketized with cheese production, however, they pointed to a lack of these qualities as being among the culprits for the collapse. Gendered social capital was effective, but vulnerable, when it replicated the conditions that, ironically, it sought to overcome, particularly those typically associated with household labor in agricultural settings.

THREADS AND SMOKE: KNITTING AND COOKING IN GROUP SPACES

Two activities in particular highlight the ways in which the women reproduced typically gendered household activities in the space of group. The first of these, knitting, was introduced by Promoción Humana as a way of supplementing household incomes and as a productive activity that added resources to the group and to the homes of individual cooperative members. The second, communal cooking and food production, was supported both overtly and tacitly by PH, as well as by the federal government, but was more localized in its implementation as it was perceived by PH as a support activity and never a primary means of generating income or social benefits. The ways group members negotiated and now remember these activities suggest that gendered social capital that reproduces typically gendered household activities may be more effective when deployed in modes of production rather than consumption, for example, activities that involve knitting for outside sale rather than eating together using external resources. This is especially true when that production creates flexible, voluntary spaces where gender identity is valorized.

"Unburdening One's Mind": Knitting as Household Reproduction and Escape

Of the fourteen cooperative members who remained active in the group in 2009, all but one stated that knitting was what initially drew them to join the group, even if they joined after cheese production began. At the time of the group's formation, cooperative members met on Sunday afternoons, when a promoter from Promoción Humana came from Guaranda to Chillanes, bringing wool from the mill in Salinas along with consortium orders for knit pieces and the technical skills necessary to fulfill them. At the meetings, the promoter taught group members knitting skills, assigned consortium orders to group members to fulfill, oversaw the distribution of wool, and collected finished pieces to take back to the consortium. Eventually, PH trained a local woman, Josefa Arteaga, to become technical adviser to the group for knitting, meetings moved to twice a week on Monday and Thursday afternoons, and the group branched out into crochet and lacework, also sold through the PH consortium. Group members paid for the wool they used in the pieces and earned a fee for every piece they completed, with sweaters and detailed lacework fetching the highest prices and hats, scarves, gloves, and socks netting less for their makers. Promoción Humana marketed the finished work in its Salinas stores and also to local and tourist markets in Quito and Riobamba. Knitting was the primary activity for the group from its inception in 1989 until the introduction of cheese making in 1997, though the group engaged in both activities until the cessation of knitting in 2004, when the volume of orders became too low to sustain continued activity, and at the same time the knitting coordinator was hired by PH to facilitate community banks through its nascent microlending programs.

When speaking about the group in the era when it focused on knitting, cooperative members display palpable nostalgia. Magdalena Estrada, forty-eight years old at the time of a 2009 interview, joined the group in 1994 and has served as secretary and president. She described her decision to join as one motivated by economic concerns. "Because I was poor!," she answered in response to my query about her reasons for becoming a group member.

> I had my children, and I didn't have a way to support them like my husband did. And I knew how to knit a little, I knew a little. And so I said, "I'll go!" They paid us for the work that we did, and so I decided to go and at least have a little for my house. So that's why I went. We were always there. After, we kept making the organization stronger. We got ahead, and we started making the cheese, and from that the plant, all the things that are there now.

While she misses the economic opportunities that knitting provided, it is the social space that group knitting allowed that she emphasized when I asked if it was important that the group was female. "It's important," she responded. "It's very important."

JD: Why?

ME: There are women's groups like ours because it's like therapy. Because when we go out from it all, from this amount that we have in the house with the children, husbands, with what needs to be washed, ironed, and all that. It's not simply because we go to gossip, to tell stories. But it's a change of environment, and it's a kind of therapy for a person. One de-stresses, forgets. At the least, if one has a big problem, one feels a little lighter. You go out, you forget a little, and that's good, right? It's good. . . .

The knitting was very important because everyone participated in that. Everyone could participate in one thing or another. So it was very important. I got a little money from my work, from what I did, from what I can do, from what I can learn. This is why it's so important. It's what one does to make one feel better, to make one grow as a person. To feel like a person in one's own house.

Narcisa Inca, forty-nine at the time of a 2009 interview and a cooperative associate since 1993, echoed Magdalen's sentiments when I asked about the benefits of group membership: "We would all get together and sometimes, just not to be alone here thinking about household things. To unburden our minds a little." When I asked about the worst attributes of group membership, she said, "What we've lost, what was good. Before there were loans [through the microcredit branch of PH], and when one knitted, one earned. It was help for a person when we sold the sweaters like that." This was not the only benefit of group activities, however. Narcisa also valued the exclusively female aspect of the group. "It's always between women," she told me, "and we completely understand each other because, for me, sometimes there wasn't that same kind of understanding in my home."

While knitting replicated household labor in the realm of economic production, it clearly also had a high social value for the women. They cited feelings of cooperation, a sense of self-worth, and a safe space to talk about domestic issues as the tangible benefits of the knitting project. It was a way of "helping" the household that provided an escape from the grind of household labors and domestic disputes, though one that did not disrupt gendered work patterns as knitting is generally conceived of as a women's hobby that contributes to but is not a primary source of economic production. Though the knitting had economic benefits, these are subordinated in cooperative members' minds to the social benefits of a gendered space outside of their immediate households.

Indeed, public spaces for women to gather are not common in Chillanes's social structure, and while private gatherings among friends happen in domestic settings, there are few places for women to simply come together. In walking surveys conducted at random hours during the periods of my field research, I found women more likely to be outside the house in the morning, usually doing marketing or other tasks that required them to come into the commercial areas close to the church. Before noon, when many elementary schools dismissed classes for the day, it was common to see women in Chillanes's central plaza, especially on a set of four benches that surround a statue of Homer Villagomez, who is credited with founding the canton of Chillanes in 1967. Women would often sit for a while, letting children run on the cement paths of the park or play on the statue, which featured cut stone sides ideal for sliding. In the mornings, as many as twenty women would gather. Few men joined them on the benches or on the steps nearby, though it was not an exclusively female space, especially for men caring for young children.

By two o'clock in the afternoon, however, men would begin to play ecuavoley, a popular Ecuadorian pastime in which two teams pass a soccer ball over a high net using their hands. A set of large steps leading from the ecuavoley court to the upper part of the park provides an arena for the games, which are played on two level courts (*canchas*) slightly higher than street level, across from where interprovincial buses arrive and trucks for hire wait for business. The street is also home to a municipal cock fighting ring, a popular bakery, a pharmacy, and the town's first video arcade. On weeknights, it is typical to find fifty men playing and watching ecuavoley, with only a handful of women in the upper part of the park, away from the courts. On weekends, especially on Sunday afternoons and evenings after market days, it is common for up to ninety men to be at the park, drinking, watching, and playing the game. Most women are uncomfortable in those spaces, and in Chillanes's handful of bars, and actively avoid passing by them when they are likely to be crowded.

In interviews and casual conversation, men and women often commented on the ecuavoley games as a sign that machista culture, while perhaps diminished from its past prominence, is not entirely dead in local settings. Silvia Gaibor, a fifty-year-old woman who makes a living as the janitor and cook for Chillanes's high school, a job that demands at least twelve hours per day while school is in session, commented that while she thought that women in Chillanes might be better off than their more rural compatriots because men were less likely to physically abuse them, gender parity had not arrived, especially in the space of the household.[5] "Here in Chillanes," she commented rather unexpectedly in the middle of an interview on local religious expressions, "we can still crudely categorize our husbands as 'machista.' In the fiestas, who do you see? Which gender is there?" Our interview continued.

JD: There are some women.
SG: Men are at the fiestas.
JD: Sure, but it depends on where; women are at the mass.
SG: Yes, women are at the mass, women are at the mass, but if you're talking about a soccer match, an eucavoley game—
JD: Men.
SG: Who are they? We women aren't there.
JD: No.
SG: Why? Because we have obligations. And it would be nice if men would come home and say, "Because I work, and you work, let's both work in the house. What can I help you with?" That is, if he did one thing and I did another thing, it would lessen the burden of all the things there are to do. Because if one was cooking, the other could be cleaning the room, tending to babies, and if there are animals, to see to their needs. Because here almost everyone has a dog or a chicken.

This is why I don't want to see, that it isn't, "I'm tired. I have the right to come home, sit down and take a rest." Women don't have [rights], they aren't human? Women don't have the right to rest? Mothers are the first to wake up and the last to go to sleep. . . . We need someone to come and educate [men] so that they understand that not only women have obligations.

Silvia's comments highlight not only traditional gender roles in household settings and what has been well documented as a machista culture that makes "the street" men's space but also the tensions these roles cause as more women take on routinized economic activities outside of the home with the increasing formalization of the Ecuadorian economy. The 2009 tax rosters for the city of Chillanes indicate that of 155 businesses registered in town, 63 (41 percent) are owned and operated by women. Many of these are businesses, such as small dry goods stores and food stalls, that were previously part of an informal economic sector that operated largely outside of state regulation. In an effort to shore up a recovering national economy in 2006, however, Ecuador's national government started enforcing a sales tax law that had been on the books, but largely unenforced, since 1963. Every business was required to register with the government and receive an individualized Registro Único de Contribuyentes (RUC) number, which business owners use to report and pay taxes to the Servicio de Rentas Internas (SRI), in addition to taxes paid to local authorities. With the implementation of the law, women selling *fritada* (fried pork) by the side of road, paper to children on their way to school, or phone cards to passing motorists became official entrepreneurs, with responsibilities to national agencies in ways that were unprecedented in Ecuadorian history. Whereas such activities had previously been treated as cottage industries, to supplement home incomes and thus outside the purview of the formal economy and state control, the RUC law formalized women's industry and women's economic spaces.

This is not to say, however, that the law revolutionized the work itself. Chillanes tax records reveal that work in the canton remains gendered in predictable ways. Businesses registered by men often require travel, such as bus companies and truck rental consortiums, or advanced education. The largest commercial enterprises, including a large electronics store, grocery, and hotel owned by a single family, are registered under men's names and require the owners to travel for buying and supply trips. The broken-down brothel at the edge of town and all but two of eight local bars are also registered to men, though all of the town's four internet cafés list females as their owners and operators (Gobierno del Cantón de Chillanes 2009). For service work that does not require a tax listing there is mixed gender representation. Teachers and municipal workers are almost evenly divided between male and female. All but one of Chillanes's lawyers are male, however, as are all its doctors in private practice, though the town does support a female dentist. The Chillanes police force is exclusively male.

When the Virgen de las Nubes Cooperative was knitting, then, it was reproducing an economic and social model of work centered on flexible household production as part of an informal economy, even as it contributed to a formalizing women's sector through the marketing of the goods the women produced. With the cessation of organized knitting in 2004, many associates reported losing the camaraderie and social space that the knitting allowed, along with frustration that they were no longer able to earn money from piecework that would directly benefit their households. Agustina Quinche, fifty-three years old at the time of an interview in 2009, described joining the cooperative twenty years earlier as an extra activity to supplement her work as a live-in domestic servant. The best part about being a group member, she said, was "mutual support [*aportar entre nosotras*]," in conjunction with the opportunity to learn new skills and to supplement household income. In her opinion, the introduction of cheese production put an end to both benefits. "We took a turn when we put in the cheese plant," she explained. "It was different then. It was different then. For five years, we really haven't had anything. In contrast, when we would knit a hat, knit a scarf, knit sweaters, there were benefits. Even though it was only a sucre,[6] there were benefits and they paid us. But it was temporary."

Communal knitting provided a place for the women to reaffirm their identities as women concerned with domestic well-being, at the same time that they acknowledged the "stresses" that this identity imposed. The knitting sessions were an important, rare space where women both upheld and critiqued social positioning. Knitting was a way of easing social and financial burdens, and it provided a space in which they could assert identities as learners, as women capable of mastering and deploying new skills valued in the marketplace, but commensurate with the household activities they could not leave behind.

When Promoción Humana approached the cooperative about cheese production, many women embraced the project as an extension of what they saw as a successful endeavor. It would require extensive technical training, which would then be shared among members as they rotated as workers in the cheese plant, and bring in significantly more revenue for the group and for those members who would draw salaries as administrators and laborers. The Promoción Humana facilitators in charge of the Chillanes project promoted these benefits to group members, and as early as 1999 they envisioned expanding them through a store in Chillanes's central plaza where group products, "cheeses, ice cream, and the like," would be sold, with profits to be reinvested in group activities and infrastructure and, eventually, among group members as store employees and shareholders (Libro de Actas, No. 12, 12).

While records show that most associates present for a vote to embark on the cheese factory were wholly in favor of the project, they also reveal tensions about the project's scale and potential to disrupt social harmony. Jesus Galarza (no relation to Rosa), a founder of the cooperative who served as president several times, objected to opening the cheese plant because she worried the group wasn't organized enough to support it and was leery of the risk involved, preferring to stay with the tried and true knitting model. These tensions were still on display in 2009 at a meeting with a PH administrator to discuss reopening the cheese plant after it had been shuttered. Several women pulled knitting out of bags and began work as they sat on the grass outside the plant (the group had given the key to PH in a 2007 agreement in which Mateo Pateghini settled most of the group's outstanding corporate debt, mostly to water and electric utility providers), only to be told by the cooperative president to put it away as the meeting "wasn't about that." No longer a way of banking and reproducing gendered social capital, knitting had become divisive, distinctly set apart from the cheese plant as the focus of group activity and identity. Though women still brought money to buy wool from the remaining group stores on the rare occasion a PH administrator was in town and allowed them access to the cheese plant where it was warehoused, knitting was no longer a professional activity of the group, no longer considered a productive activity but rather a detriment to much needed group capital to continue in the cheese factory. Knitting had reverted to the households from whence it had come.

Culinary Capital: Cooperation, Cooking, and Conflict in Group Spaces

Knitting was not the only mechanism through which gendered social capital was employed in the cooperative. Communal food preparation and consumption also played a major role in group activities from the group's inception until the onset of serious financial difficulties in 2006. It was so important that the cheese plant included a kitchen space that the women used to replicate a traditional hearth and so meaningful that it could lead to a major rift between the plant administrator, charged with the care of group resources, and the group president, who disagreed vehemently about how the food should be used. Culinary capital, the communal production and consumption of food, was vastly important to group identity and cohesion.

I employ the term "culinary capital" to describe the use of food in the cooperative before its failure for a number of reasons. First, the food that the group used for communal meals at the cheese plant on meeting, group work, and knitting days was a collective economic and social resource. The Ecuadorian Ministry of Social Well-Being (Ministerio de Bienestar Social) provided registered social groups such as the women's cooperative with tuna, rice, and cooking oil, products that it also provides to public schools to feed students. Groups that received the supplies were to use them in an "equitable" way to support group activities and the stated mission of the organization. Receiving the food supplies gave the group recognition as an official entity in the eyes of the state and also bolstered its reputation as an "official" organization locally. When the Ministerio sent a small sign that marked the cheese plant as part of the national "nutrition program," the women promptly placed it on the outside of the building. The economic resource of the food supplies was social even before it was put to any use for group activities.

Within the group, the donated food became an important focal point for weekly meetings as the women would cook for everyone present, as well as for husbands and children left at home, whom group members assumed would not cook for themselves. Indeed, as the weekly meals began to be a regular occurrence in late 2002 and early 2003, school-aged children learned to stop by to grab a bite to eat on their way home from classes or afternoon chores.

Along with the knitting sessions, the meals became a place where cooperative members engaged in many of the therapeutic behaviors that Magdalena recalled as the best part of group work. Reproducing a traditional kitchen space, complete with fire and large pots in the middle of the room, the women ignored the gas cooktops in the back of the room as they boiled huge pots of rice, creating copious amounts of smoke that could not escape through the modern zinc roof of the cheese plant. "Why are you crying?," they joked as smoke-induced tears streamed down their faces. Once the food was prepared, women who had been knitting or working at agricultural projects on group land joined the cooks, and typical conversations ranged from concern over family issues to plans for the future to gossip about the new priest and his stricter rules for receiving sacraments in the church. Instated in the summer of 2002, the weekly meals became an important ritual for the cooperative and marked peak attendance for weekly group meetings, with more than a dozen of the forty registered cooperative members there at any given time.

The value of the goods was economic, certainly, but it was thus also social. The culinary capital of weekly meals drew in new members, gave the women a gendered space in which to gather, and eased some of the burden of their work as they could take the food home to hungry, and often suspicious, husbands and children. In this regard, like knitting, the food was in many ways flexible, and like knitting, it represented the reproduction of household activities in which women engaged when not occupied with group work. Though not an economically productive activity, communal meals tapped into and replicated gendered social capital as they required and fostered cooperation based on common women's skills around the hearth.

As activities focused on consumption and requiring outside, communal resources, however, cooking and eating were vulnerable to group harmony in ways that knitting was not. In spring 2003, the plant administrator, Silvia Moyano, began using some of the Ministerio supplies to feed the rotating workers at the plant, which some group members perceived as threatening an important social resource. Jesus Galarza was deeply displeased with the idea that only women currently working at the plant would benefit from the food, which she saw as a group resource not meant for those benefiting in other ways. During a regular group meeting to discuss microcredit loans to individual women and plant finances, she very publicly castigated the plant administrator for "selfishness" (*egoismo*) and made the case that the food was meant to benefit *all* the members of the cooperative, not just those working in the plant, who in any case were drawing a salary. Silvia, also endowed with a forceful personality, fired back that the women working in the plant were also group members and therefore eligible for and deserving of the resource. These exchanges are recorded in the Libro de Actas as "discussion of plant operations" and are paired with an entry in which Silvia, speaking as the president during a visit with their Promoción Humana promoter, "asked that we don't hurt each other as it is certain that we all make mistakes." The log goes on to record Silvia's assertion that cooperative members needed to work together to resolve their problems so that "work can continue in the cheese plant" (Libro de Actas 33, 34). Eventually, the group came to consensus on the issue, and plant employees retained rights to a limited amount of food for their lunch breaks, so long as ample supplies remained for group activities, which cooperative members deemed crucial for good relationships between women.

What is striking about the "food fight" is that Jesus and Silvia, and by extension the membership of the cooperative, were not only arguing about some fish and grains of rice. They were arguing about what the cooperative was doing, where its values were, and how it should produce, reproduce, and consume gendered social capital. Those who sided with Jesus in the dispute faulted Silvia for seeing the food as simply another resource at her disposal as an administrator. She had not, in their opinion, understood the real value of the food, which lay in its potential to be invested in the kinds of social relationships the women had enjoyed when they were knitting. Used in domestic reproduction, the food was not simply a marketized or marketizable consumer good, but an extension of social relationships that the group valued, perhaps more than any economic activity with which it was concerned. Used to feed factory workers, however, it lost this socially productive quality. It was just another consumer item, another reminder of class divisions that keep rural Ecuadorian women from "having things" even as they are occupied constantly with the needs of a household.

SE FUE A LA QUIEBRA: INVESTMENT, RISK, AND VULNERABILITY IN GENDERED SOCIAL CAPITAL

One phrase that kept appearing in interviews and casual conversations after the closing of the cheese plant is that the cooperative "se fue a la quiebra," "went bankrupt." The description was certainly correct in terms of group finances. The documents putting the cheese plant into receivership with Promoción Humana list more than $5,000 in outstanding debts, mostly to milk providers but also to utility providers and individuals who had provided services when building the plant. It also seems an accurate assessment of the conditions the remaining group members faced as they attempted to reinstate the kind of social environment that had existed when the women met regularly for knitting and cooking. Having once had substantial social capital in those areas, they were now bankrupt, hoping to find some way to restructure the loss.

These experiences highlight the strengths of gendered social capital but also expose major vulnerabilities. In the case of the Virgen de las Nubes Cooperative, programs that invested in women by reproducing rural women's roles of flexible household production, specifically the knitting program, were effective in creating an atmosphere of camaraderie, mutual support, and empowerment. Women recall the group as a place that both replicated and improved their households, allowing them to speak freely about domestic roles and stressors, a place where they felt welcome and where they were able to acquire skills that allowed them to contribute to their households in an environment in which outside employment is hard to find. The cooking component, in some ways more organic in its genesis and implementation, was also effective in these ways, though its dependence on outside resources made it substantially more vulnerable to disagreements and personal clashes that exposed, or even created, rifts in the social fabric that it was meant to support. Though the women sought to use their gendered social capital to patch those rifts, the need to explicitly do so called attention to the limits of social capital when physical resources were at stake. The need to "cooperate" so that "work at the cheese plant could continue" demonstrates a keen awareness among the women that the success of this business endeavor was directly tied to their ability to leverage the cooperation and camaraderie they identified as being the most beneficial part of group membership. When they were unable to do this, they failed not just as businesswomen and cooperative members, but as rural women working to have "something" for their homes.

This sense of failure resonated in group meetings and personal reflections after the plant went into receivership and was no longer operational. When I asked the remaining cooperative members what had caused the failure of the cheese plant, Agustina's answer was typical.

> At times it was bad administration, and at times it was because of the selfishness of the members themselves. It all went downhill [with] the selfishness of the group members themselves. Some would say things are one way, others would say no. Sometimes there is a lot of selfishness among the group members. They didn't understand each other. Some are good, but some are not sincere. We have to speak sincerely from the beginning, but there wasn't always that.

While Agustina blames "bad administration" on the part of the woman managing plant finances, she also blames "selfishness" and a lack of "mutual understanding" among group members for the downfall. Because women involved with the cooperative were not "sincere" enough with each other, because they did not exhibit the qualities the women sought in the safe environment of the knitting circle where honesty and openness were valued commodities, the group failed.

Mercedes Huilca, also commenting on the cause of the failure, cast it in remarkably similar terms. After commenting that "bad administration" is what caused the group to "go bankrupt," which she found especially disturbing as the salary she had been earning at the quesera disappeared, she concluded, "It was nice [*bonito*] but only when we understood each other. When we didn't understand each other, it wasn't. Now no one feels obliged to one another." The loss of the cooperative was not only, or even primarily, seen as a loss of financial capital, but was experienced much more keenly as a loss of the very things that women used to bring the group together in the first place: common experiences as rural women with few outlets for socializing or for economic or social advancements.

When development based on gendered social capital replicates the conditions it seeks to overcome, it is risky business. In the case of the Virgen de las Nubes Cooperative, gendered social capital was the most effective when it reified many of the social conditions, particularly related to rural household work and social relations, that the group was founded to "advance" beyond. It was also effective when it replicated those conditions in a productive mode as opposed to consuming outside resources. For this reason, the act of cooking and knitting together strengthened the social qualities of mutual support the women valued and created a space where they could share the stresses of rural life. When outside capital was introduced in food commodities, however, it opened space for public conflict over its use.

Indeed, it is this conflation of social and material capital that most clearly exposes the risks inherent in social capital in development efforts, as well as the difficulty of moving that capital into sustainable positions in public sectors. One way GAD programs in general and FEPP specifically work is to identify women as vulnerable in society but then to overcome vulnerability by using strengths related to it. So when vulnerability is identified in formal banking sectors where interest rates are high and loans almost impossible to obtain, microfinance programs enroll participants who have a sense of commonality because of exclusion from the larger banking systems. Where the vulnerability is identified as a lack of power roles in the public sector, or attributed to bad decisions made by men, women's groups are invented, again using common experiences to hold them together.

At least some of the social capital employed by these programs, then, is that forged in the crucible of vulnerability, creating an intricate connection between vulnerability and social capital programs that seek to turn such vulnerability into strength.

It is precisely this logic of strength through a shared sense of vulnerability that many critics of microfinance and other social capital programs point to. When weighing the value of microfinance programs, critics have been especially concerned that while they seem to be effective on the small scale, they appear to do little to increase the relative economic standing or financial resources in communities and/or nations where they are employed. Where social capital appears to be a locally useful resource, it does not appear to translate easily to global or even regional capital and therefore effectively re-creates the very vulnerabilities it seeks to overcome (Wong 2007; Fine 1999, 2010).

While it is too strong to argue that the history of the Virgen de las Nubes Cooperative supports this critique, the experiences of cooperative associates do point to related weaknesses in gendered social capital, especially as it is marketized and where, as in all development efforts, there is a risk of failure. Indeed, the risk of this kind of failure was apparent to the women from the beginning, as recorded in the Libro de Actas. "In this group of people," a section of the book's first entry confesses, "there doesn't exist that collaboration, that equity, as a group. There are many who don't participate in the Word of God, or whatever aspect. If we aren't conscientious, this group will simply disappear" (Libro de Actas, No. 1).

Reproduced as women in the space of the group, as people required to make the most of their vulnerabilities through strengths generally assigned to their gender, associates failed *as women* and subsequently lost what was most important to them, both in terms of economic production for their households and in terms of the social outlet group meetings provided. How this gendered loss intersected with religious identities, especially as these have been constructed with increasing frequency in the realm of the "domestic church," is the focus of the next chapter.

THREE

Marketing the Domestic Church

Every month on the Thursday that falls closest to the twenty-second, Catholics in Chillanes remember their patron saint, Santa Rita of Cascia, who was born and died seventy-six years later on that same day in May. In September, Santa Rita's mass is augmented with celebrations for the Virgin of Merced, patroness of the city of Quito and of the Ecuadorian armed forces. A favorite among people in Bolívar, Merced is the namesake for the largest market plaza in Chillanes, and her festival is marked with novenas, dancing, and parades, as well as with masses and liturgical commemorations.

On September 21, 2009, in the middle of the novena and celebrations that would culminate with her feast day on September 24, Merced performed a miracle. Encamped in her place in the market that bears her name, a market that had only recently been updated to include indoor covered stalls and the shrine in which she spends part of the year, Merced was the focus of devotions that included a sea of candles placed about her feet, close to the ceremonial robes she wore to mark the festival. Witnesses do not remember exactly how the flames escaped the confines of wick and wax, but in short order a wall of fire was headed toward the image, made even more vulnerable by its velvet adornments. Just as the conflagration reached Merced's feet and just as suddenly as it started, the fire ceased, leaving a path of charred cement and evaporated candle wax but sparing the patroness any damage.

The next evening I walked to a mass dedicated to both Merced and Santa Rita with Agustina Quinche and Noemi Jaramillo, who share a house across from the market. Fighting to be heard over the cacophony of trumpets, drums, and assorted brass instruments that accompanied Merced as she traveled in procession from her shrine to the church, the women expressed admiration for her power and also gratitude for the new building that allows her presence in the lower part of town. Their sentiments were repeated by the local priest, Padre Orlando, in his homily in which he mentioned the "miracle in the market" as evidence that the saint, and by extension God, had not forgotten the people of Chillanes. At the same time, he warned, the miracle is a reminder not to confuse temples made of blocks and bricks or icons made of wood with the true house (*templo*) of God. This, he concluded, is found in the home and the family, the "domestic church" (*iglesia doméstica*), which is primarily in the care of women exemplified by the saints the gathered devotees had come to honor.

Miracles and markets, homes and families, are spaces where people in Chillanes author their identities in religious contexts. Women of the Virgen de las Nubes Cooperative understood religion as an essential factor in their early success, and they have reevaluated religious institutions, actions, and beliefs in light of the cooperative's failure. Merced, after all, is not the only religious woman in the marketplace, not the only religious woman at risk when market structures are threatened by flames of various kinds.

There are many ways to evaluate the role of Catholicism in the Virgen de las Nubes Cooperative. For development scholars interested in social capital, religion is sometimes listed alongside gender as a potential source of social cohesion and preexisting networks (Drogus 1997; Bergeron 2003; Radcliffe, Laurie, and Andolina 2003). In the burgeoning scholarship on faith-based organizations (FBOs) and their roles in international development programs, religion is a complex, often international, institutional means of delivering relief and development assistance that may have significant advantages due to mutual understanding between those receiving aid and those giving it, long-standing networks developed through missionizing, and longtime commitments to missions and aid that are sometimes lacking in the governmental or secular development arenas. Elizabeth Ferris (2005), for example, points to religious networks as important mechanisms for disseminating both relief and information about humanitarian crises, and Jonathan Benthall (2008) explores issues of religion in the context of humanitarian aid more widely.

Other scholars are less interested in religion as a broad (and notoriously ill-defined) category and focus instead on the ways particular FBOs involved in international development handle specific issues, often related to sex and sexuality, HIV/AIDS, or views of charity and commitment. Laurie Occhipinti (2005) and Tara Hefferan (2007) have explored the role of Catholic ideas of charity and partnership with overseas development projects. Erica Bornstein (2005) and James Howard Smith (2008) have examined the ways in which World Vision combines evangelical Christianity and Western capitalism in African experience. Jonathan Benthall (2015) has explored the role of Islamic Relief since the rise of Islamic terrorism, and Emma Tomalin (2009), Stacy Leigh Pigg (2002), and others have explored the role of Buddhism and Hinduism in local development in the South Asian context.

This chapter focuses on local expressions of and interactions with Roman Catholicism. Cooperative members often cited Catholic values, especially in their liberationist articulations and especially as they overlap and define households and gender identities, as an important part of group cohesion and success, as well as the yardstick by which they measured group goals. Renewed emphasis on families and sacraments by the institutional church, often accompanied by mission programs, shaped the way cooperative members saw themselves as mothers, wives, and religious actors in professional, domestic, and community settings. Even as the Roman Catholic Church in Chillanes was emphasizing a more sacramental, accountable, and personal form of Catholicism, one supported largely by women as catechists and home specialists in the "domestic church," it was working to increase its public relevance, sending missionaries into communities in order to reassert an Ecuadorian Catholic identity in places where other forms of Christianity were growing or where institutional forms of the religion had lapsed or never taken hold. Negotiating these changes at the same time the group entered marketized production required many of the women in the cooperative to reevaluate the Catholic Church and their place in it. Negotiating these changes, along with the shifting financial terrain the cheese factory brought, required cooperative members to engage with several forms of social capital—domestic, spiritual, and interpersonal—all of which were wrapped up in fluctuating iterations of Catholic piety and practice.

GOD ON THE PLAZA: CATHOLICISM IN CHILLANENSE LIFE

As in many Latin American communities, the Catholic church in Chillanes is the geographic and social center of town. Built in 1981 after the previous building burned in a fire, the church is constructed of cement-covered cinderblocks and is located on the upper plaza with the *municipio*, the seat of the cantonal government. While the civic building is blocky and nondescript, the church boasts a steep, swooping roofline and a modernist bell tower that make it a distinctive landmark often used in images of the town produced for tourist literature and expatriate web pages. The plaza in front of the church is home to the Sunday market, benches, and a statue where children often play, as well as the ecuavoley court where men gather in the evenings and weekends. The church also dominates much of Chillanes's soundscape as bells announce regular masses in the mornings and evenings, and the mass itself is often broadcast over loudspeakers affixed to the bell tower.

Chillanes's Catholic church is also the center of much of the town's social life and many of its social networks. Announcements after masses alert parents to school closings and parishioners to deadlines for municipal events such as tax payments and planning sessions for everything from parades to protests against changes in state or provincial policies. Chillanes's annual fiestas, held in May to commemorate the birth and death of Santa Rita, bring locals and expatriated Chillanenses back into town for masses, parades, feasting, and fireworks. The liturgical calendar is thus intimately bound up with civil calendars, creating a Catholic environment even for those not actively involved in (or even actively opposed to) the church.

In this way, Chillanes is, and has been since the establishment of the parish in 1809, an overtly Catholic place in its public spaces. Such overt Catholicity is expressed in the names of local businesses, many of which adopt the name of either Rita or Merced. In 2015 Chillanes was home to a pharmacy, bakery, dry goods store, funeral supply store, and gas station named after Santa Rita and an internet café, restaurant, and taxi service named after the national patroness (Municipio de Chillanes 2009). Merced, as previously discussed, is also the namesake for the lower, covered market, where she has a permanent shrine.

Catholic images and practices are also common in Chillanes's private spaces, in what might be best described as *quotidian Catholicism*: the acts

FIGURE 4. Chillanes Church with Image of Santa Rita, 2015

and materials that comprise everyday activities. Catholic families often have images of saints or souvenirs from pilgrimages adorning their houses, and crosses fashioned from the palms used in Palm Sunday processions are ubiquitous on doorways for several months after the event. Neighborhood associations and other small groups also care for church icons by rotating them through homes. Families play host to the Divino Niño, Merced, and other images for a night or two at a time when the icons are placed on tables next to lit candles inside the house or on special tables outside as the object of prayer and devotion.

In recent years, small weekly prayer groups have gained in popularity in various barrios in town. In these groups, men and women come together to share concerns and offer prayers and various forms of support from emotional to financial when crises arise. When a fire destroyed the upper floor of the Lucio residence in 2011, for example, including the visiting icon of the Virgin of Guayco, the La Merced Neighborhood Prayer Group moved quickly to raise funds to replace the burned statue, valued at more than $950.

Much like the medieval maps that show Jerusalem at the center of the world, then, much of Chillanes's physical, temporal, and social structures

FIGURE 5. Homework with Saints and a Visiting Virgin

are centered on church buildings, calendars, and social institutions. When men and women in Chillanes craft their identities, they do so in a Catholic environment formed from the global church and local interpretations and iterations of that church. Catholic teachings, Catholic practices, and Catholic worldviews are intimately entwined with gendered and economic identities in this context.

NI MOJAS NI SANTAS (NEITHER NUNS NOR SAINTS): WOMEN AND SANTA RITA

Nowhere is this entanglement more apparent than in the way women relate to Chillanes's patroness, Santa Rita de Cascia. Santa Rita was brought to Chillanes by a Spanish priest, Ramón Pizarro, when the parish was established in 1809, late in the colonial era. Most Chillanenses believe the icon of Santa Rita originated in Europe and credit Pizarro with bringing her to the parish church via an arduous journey over the mountain range and plunging Chimbo River Valley that separates Bolívar from its neighboring, and politically more powerful, Chimborazo Province. A 2009 radio program dedicated to the saint recounted the journey, as well as her rescue from the 1981 fire.

> Following the arrival of Padre Ramón Pizarro, we continue to honor our patroness after more than 201 years [*sic*]. Our faith in her persists even after three fires in the church built to honor our patroness, and it continues to grow as she arrived in Chillanes on the shoulders and backs of the faithful and devout, coming a long distance over inhospitable mountain roads from San Juan de Trigoloma and then to Tacaló Ensillado all the way to Chillanes. Just think how much faith and hope there were to bring the image that still exists today, even after the last fire in our architecturally unique church, built by the able hands of our artisans. Fire is terrible, and on August 2, 1981, at 2:00 in the afternoon, all was lost within minutes, but we still retain our powerful church.
>
> We gave thanks [on yesterday's program] for the bravery of so many Chillanenses for rescuing the image from the flames. Indeed, the fire was produced by an act of faith for the patroness because in an eagerness to receive grace, a candle was placed on her altar, perhaps at her feet, in order to ask for a miracle. (Radio Amiga Chillanes 2009)

Currently, the saint resides in a permanent alcove in the church, where she receives regular attention from parishioners who come to pray and light candles, now kept at a safe distance from the icon. She also enjoys regular time at the main altar of the church when her feast day draws near, a season when she is also the center of several processions throughout various Chillanense neighborhoods.

As Chillanes's patroness, Santa Rita enjoys the respect of local Catholics, who often pray to her for assistance with healing, difficult business relationships, or more general financial difficulties. Rita's history as a godly woman who overcame domestic violence, however, has also made her a particular intercessor for problems that arise within households, especially regarding issues of gender roles, household responsibilities, and violence. For many women in Chillanes, Santa Rita, often described as a "saint of the impossible," understands not only suffering in general, but their suffering as women in a presumably machista society that can sometimes render the "domestic church" a place of contention, inequality, or danger.

One place this is especially evident is in Rita's hagiography, to which Chillanenses have added details that do not appear in official accounts. Born in Roccaporena, Italy, in 1381, Rita is said to have exhibited religious tendencies from an early age, when she is reported to have taken great joy in prayer and was unusually obedient to her parents (Barbé 2001, 5–6). Despite her wish to enter religious life, Rita was married at fifteen to Pablo, a man described in official hagiographies as "presumptuous, violent, with tendencies to get drunk and swear" (Barbé 2001, 7). Committing herself to "Christian marriage," including obedience to her wayfaring husband, Rita endured years of neglect and abuse as Pablo is said to have continued to drink excessively, beat her, and squander household resources on nefarious activities. Despite his frequent "blasphemy" and abuse, Rita continually prayed for Pablo's conversion, petitions official accounts say God favored as, little by little, Pablo repented of his violent lifestyle, eventually reforming such that he forewent the worst of his drinking, ceased beating his wife, and became a responsible, loving husband and father to the couple's two sons.

Although Pablo repented, his previous entanglements with the underworld of Renaissance Italy remained, and he was murdered by acquaintances who were unhappy with his disaffection. Rita, now head of a household with no means of income, is said to have prayed not that God would send means of support but rather that her two teenage sons would not seek revenge for their father's death. Her petition was granted when both sons succumbed to the plague. Alone, Rita presented herself at the local Augustinian convent as a novitiate, where she was twice denied entrance as the order did not accept women who had been married. The third time she appeared at the convent, Rita miraculously gained entrance through a locked door in the early morning and was kneeling in the chapel when the nuns arrived for morning prayer. The abbess recognized Rita, allowed her to pray, and then successfully lobbied the bishop for Rita's inclusion in the order, where she exhibited stigmatic marks on her forehead beginning in 1441, a condition often accompanied by grave illness. The marks did not disappear until Rita's death in 1457, when her body is said to have emitted an odor of flowers. Her incorruptible body was exhumed in 1625, and Rita was beatified in 1626 and then canonized in 1900 by Pope Leo XIII.

Chillanense accounts of Rita's life generally follow this narrative, though people often tell the story without specific dates or details about Cascia or its location in Europe, and stories about the death of her sons, Pablo's conversion, and her entrance into the convent have significant variations. In one rendition, Pablo is converted to Christianity as the result of Rita's prayerful interdiction after one of the couple's sons is murdered and she asks God to stop Pablo from taking revenge. The woman who explained Rita's history this way also recounted that Rita was accepted into the Augustinian convent after she miraculously appeared there, having been mysteriously conveyed into the locked building directly from her bed.

The most striking variation in local stories from Rita's official hagiography, however, comes when Chillanenses describe Rita's life with Pablo, which all accounts agree was one of misery and abuse. Iván Burbano, a doctor in Chillanes and head of a confraternity (*cofradía*) dedicated to San Vicente, began his brief narration of her life this way.

> So she, she wasn't a normal religious, right? She was a housewife, a lady of the house, but her husband was bad. . . . He abused her, he attacked her, he insulted her. I think he was drunk as well, and he didn't give Rita anything [to buy] food. And then one day he demanded that she give him something to eat, probably in the evening, so he would have been demanding meat, and she didn't have any. So she cut off a piece of her buttock to give him, to satisfy her husband.

Lola Chauquinga, a woman who credits Santa Rita with a miracle that saved her child, also mentioned Rita's supreme sacrifice when I asked about her relationship with Pablo.

> This is all I know about the patroness in regard to that, that he [Pablo] was very bad to her, and she came to suffer. And, how do I tell you? She didn't have anything, not even anything to eat, even though the rosary that priest has given us tells us so! . . . And they say that, he, her

> husband, was bad. She was never going to steal, but she never had anything to give to him to eat. So she cut off some pieces of her body and gave them to him to eat.

Though not part of the official account, it is this extreme act that gives Rita much of her identity and power as a saint in local settings and that raises questions for many Catholic women about the domestic church and their roles in it.

Indeed, Lola, Iván, and most of the Chillanenses I interviewed admired Rita as an example of idealized Catholic womanhood. Iván, who is a bit unusual for a middle-aged man in Chillanes as he regularly washes dishes after meals and was cooking lentils when I arrived to interview him and his wife, asserted that while Rita is known for the miracles she has performed locally and abroad her most impressive feature is her "love for her spouse, her loyalty, her sacrifices. How much she loved [Pablo] and didn't care how much he offended her. So much so that she took pieces from her own body even though it left her in a bad way, just to satisfy her spouse." Lola also admired such domestic fealty, agreeing, though not elaborating, when I asked if she was an example for women in the home.

> JD: Is Rita an example of how to be when one has a spouse like this?
> LC: [quietly] Um hmm.
> JD: Ah . . .
> LC: [quietly] Um hmm.

Aurora Ballesteros, a sixty-two-year-old woman to whom several people pointed me when I began to ask about Santa Rita, shared much of Lola's ambivalence about Rita's actions. Aurora and her family run a radio station in Chillanes that frequently features Catholic themes, and they have organized several masses in honor of Rita in Quito and other places for Chillanenses who have left the province but want to pay homage to the saint. Aurora has been devoted to Rita "from the age of reason" and regularly prays to an image of the saint she keeps in her house. In her general description of the saint, she emphasized her importance to women.

> We know Santa Rita here as the saint of the impossible, of desperate causes, as the intercessor of mothers, of widows, so we keep her in our minds and in our presence. She is a saint that comes in the role of all

> the stages of women. . . . Here, the majority of husbands are like Pablo: they're drunks, they drink, they fight with their women. Now the young people are changing, but before, the husbands, uy! The poor women didn't stand a chance.

While Aurora greatly admired Rita, she was also, after a more extended discussion of changing gender roles in Ecuadorian society, moderately critical. "She was mute," Aurora concluded after describing what she saw as the continuing prevalence of domestic violence, especially in rural homes, and also the continuing machista culture that requires women to do more work in the domestic sphere than their male counterparts. "She was mute."

Aurora's comments that women's lives are changing, that there is a difference between urban and rural households, and also her willingness to be critical of a saint for not denouncing gender-based abuses encapsulate themes of change and negotiation in domestic and religious spheres. These changes and spaces of negotiation were prevalent themes for many women in Chillanes, who often commented in interviews that domestic spaces were simultaneously marked by intense religious devotion and ongoing gender inequality, both of which formed their experiences as Catholic women. The domestic church was, for them, still evolving, deeply embedded in local contexts that were variable, unequal, and deeply problematic but always Catholic, the site of most Catholic actions they undertook on a daily basis.

Noemi Jaramillo, a longtime devotee of Santa Rita and the woman with whom I walked to mass in September 2009, joined Aurora both in her devotion to the saint and in her assessment that Catholic values are often acted out in homes. "Catholic women," she asserted in a 2009 interview, "what they do here is, they are in the home, they are in the home, they observe the fiestas, they speak with the priests. When we suffer we go to the church to vent [*desfogar*] because that's the only place that's honest [*sincera*]." Noemi lamented what she considered a lack of sincerity and religiosity on the part of machista men, whom she described as having a "complex."

> NJ: It's difficult to describe Catholic men here in Chillanes.
> JD: Why is that?
> NJ: Most of them don't go to church. My husband, for example, he almost never goes to church. But he does pray a little, I don't know . . .
> JD: And why is it different for men?

NJ: I, I really don't know. It's very hard to change them. They have these characteristics, and in general those characteristics are very strong. They're very machista.

JD: How?

NJ: It's that they say that [women] have to obey, and when they don't, there are fights.

JD: Ah—

NJ: There are arguments.

JD: So, to say that men are machista, it's to say that they aren't going to church? That they aren't doing those things?

NJ: No. It's that men have a complex [*complejo*].

JD: A complex?

NJ: It's a complex, that they're everything [*de que ellos son todo*], and that they say it's their way, their way of venerating God. They believe in God, in the Virgin, also in the saints, but they don't have to be going every moment to the church. . . . It's that way in meetings, too. They have this character, here, in the province. It's not like in Quito, in Guayaquil, in Ambato, where the men are truly, truly, truly Catholics.

Noemi's comment that men in Bolívar are not "truly" Catholic in the way that men in Ecuadorian cities are conflates religiosity, class, geography, and a sense of varying gender inequality in a manner that is common for Chillanense women. Carmen Pérez, who works as a clerk in the municipio offices, summed up the differences between women in rural areas and those in centers even as small as Chillanes in stark terms.

CP: In general, for the women that live in the *campo* [countryside] it's hard, because they work on the farms, they have to cook for many people, and then they have to go out and work in the sun, so it's very hard for them. . . . Here in the center, life is easier.

JD: And how is life for men here?

CP: The same. Here in the center it's easier, at least for those who have work.

JD: And what's it like to be married here?

CP: The men are machista here.

JD: How?

CP: I mean, women do everything. . . . But it was worse before. They say men, before, they were bad, they mistreated women. But now, there's almost none of that. More than anything here there's none of that, but still, in the campo, I believe that there are men that hit their wives.

The domestic church, then, is a complicated and changing space formed in the crucible of geography, class, and social perception. It is also a space that has changed in its basic structure as family relationships continue to evolve socially and legally in the Ecuadorian context. Birth records at Chillanes's Registro Civil reveal a strong trend away from the kind of nuclear family centered on marriage emphasized by Catholic preaching and teaching. In 1975, for example, the Registro recorded 644 births in the canton, 168 of them to unmarried mothers, an out-of-wedlock birthrate of 26 percent. In 1995, 34 percent of children were born to single mothers, and by 2011, 72 percent of all children born in the canton listed a single mother as the parent. In addition, Registro data reveals that many in Chillanes are taking advantage of Ecuador's 2008 domestic partnership (union civil) law that allows couples to declare such a partnership without the legal or religious responsibilities of marriage.[1] These changes have caught the attention of the institutional Catholic Church, which has focused on family issues in recent years through a renewed emphasis on sacraments within the church and on a revitalized mission movement to local communities.

PARTICIPATORY DEVELOPMENT: PROCLAIMING AND RECLAIMING THE FAMILY THROUGH SACRAMENTS AND MISSIONS IN THE TWENTY-FIRST CENTURY

Arriving to speak to a crowd of an estimated 250,000 people in Guayaquil's Parque de los Samanes on July 6, 2015, Pope Francis could have addressed any number of issues. Two weeks before, a political rally convened by Guayaquil's longtime mayor, Jaime Nebot, loudly protested President Rafael Correa's policies, an act repeated in the capital, where marches and protests were ongoing. The pontiff could have spoken about his recent encyclical on environmental protection, a topic relevant to a country that has benefited financially from oil reserves and shrimp fisheries, even as those activities have caused tremendous environmental damage to delicate ecological areas. Instead, the pope delivered a homily focused on more intimate subjects. "The family," he explained,

> is the closest hospital—when one is sick they take care of him as best they can. The family is the first school for children, it is the fundamental reference for youth, it is the best haven for the elderly. The family constitutes *society's best social capital*, for which other institutions cannot substitute, which should be enhanced so as never to lose the correct sense of the services that society gives to its citizens. In effect, those services that society gives to its citizens aren't a form of charity, but a real social debt in regard to the institution of the family, which is the foundation that strongly supports the common good of all. The family also forms a small church, the so-called domestic church that, along with life, channels tenderness and divine mercy.

In giving the domestic church credit for being the society's "best social capital," however, Pope Francis was not completely celebratory. "The family today needs a miracle," he concluded, asking that God would "make us recover pride in being family, the pride in living in family. Let it be so" ("Homalía del Papa sobre la familia en el Parque Samanes en Guayaquil 2015"; emphasis added).

Francis's concern with family, which he would continue as he traveled to Quito and Quinche, site of Ecuador's most popular apparition of the Virgin Mary, underscored an institutional concern with the domestic church that has deep roots and also more recent branches. The term "domestic church" was first used in *Lumen Gentium*, a document drafted by members of the Second Vatican Council and then promulgated by Pope Paul VI in 1964. In the document, which traces church structure and hierarchies, "all people" are identified as that which constitutes the church. Article 11 of *Lumen Gentium* describes the role of the sacraments, asserting that it is through the sacraments and the exercise of the virtues that "the sacred nature and the organic structure of the priestly community is brought into operation." Marriage is the last sacrament mentioned in *Lumen Gentium* and receives almost as much attention as the previous six combined.

> Christian spouses, in virtue of the sacrament of Matrimony, whereby they signify and partake of the mystery of that unity and fruitful love which exists between Christ and His Church, help each other to attain his holiness in their married life and in the rearing and education of their children. By reason of their state and rank in life they have their own special gift among the people of God. From the wedlock of Christians there comes the family, in which new citizens of human society are born, who by the grace of the Holy Spirit received in baptism are made Children of God, thus perpetuating the people of God through the centuries. The family is, so to speak, the domestic church. (Paul VI 1964, 11: para. 2)

Articulated in the context of the Second Vatican Council, the domestic church as vital to Catholic sacramental life was an idea that seemed tacit in church teachings but rarely specifically mentioned in papal documents or, according to those I asked in Chillanes, by priests. This began to change when Pope Benedict XVI paired concerns about changing social mores, which he saw as directly contradictory to nuclear families, with evangelization, which he saw as a Catholic imperative that had been neglected in the modern world. Indeed, Benedict XVI tied church teaching about families to a renewed emphasis on sacraments for Catholics and to revitalized efforts at evangelization. Addressing participants at the Plenary Assembly of the Pontifical Council for the Family in December 2011, Benedict proclaimed:

> The new evangelization depends largely on the Domestic Church. In our times, as in times past, the eclipse of God, the spread of ideologies contrary to the family, and the degradation of sexual ethics are connected. And just as the eclipse of God and the crisis of the family are linked, so the new evangelization is inseparable from the Christian family. The family is indeed the *way* of the Church because it is the "human space" of our encounter with Christ. ("New Evangelization Inseparable from Family"; original emphasis)

For Benedict, the domestic church was the place in which Catholics were created, the church grown, and social order maintained.

Pope Francis has continued this concern, most notably by convoking a bishops' synod examining the family in the context of the church. Meeting at the Vatican beginning in 2014 and continuing to 2015, the synod surveyed Catholics from around the world about their experience with church teachings on family, marriage, sexuality, and children, following Benedict's lead by framing the synod in terms of evangelization. The first document released by the synod, *The Pastoral Challenges of the Family in the Context of Evangelization* (2014), reasserts this linkage between evangelization, the future of Catholicism, and families as a fundamental part of society.

This concern with the family and with evangelization more broadly has certainly been felt in Chillanes. Sermons such as the one excerpted at the beginning of this chapter often focused on families, especially on issues of spousal harmony and "understanding." The priests in Chillanes, both Padre Orlando and his predecessor, also began to emphasize and enforce sacramental compliance in a way that was unfamiliar to most Chillanenses, who had become accustomed to flexible schedules and requirements for baptisms, communion, confirmation rites, and marriages in the church. With the new emphasis on sacramental correctness, parish priests began vetting potential godparents for baptisms, confirmations, and weddings, being sure that they themselves had undergone the rituals. Orlando refused communion to those he knew were divorced and marriage rites to couples who had not thoroughly repented and separated if they lived together before an ecclesiastical ceremony. In 2002 women in the Virgen de las Nubes Cooperative often discussed the new "strictness" of the priest when it came to sacramental issues, and signs listing the requirements for sacraments now hang prominently in the *convento* (church office), ready for consultation when parishioners come to inquire about the rites.

The renewed emphasis on sacraments as imperative to Catholic identity and practice did not arise in a vacuum. Long-standing critiques of Roman Catholicism in Latin America, both internal and external, often decried a general lack of formal participation on the part of Roman Catholics in the regular rites of the church. Because of poor catechesis during the imperial era, lingering indigenous religious sentiments, and not a small dose of racism that persistently insists that non-Europeans are never "really" Catholic, many secular and religious scholars point to a "cultural" or "fiesta" Catholicism that is large on feast days but lacking in regular attendance at mass and a catechized knowledge of church practices (Burdick 1993; Cleary 2011; Scheper Hughes 2009).

Conservative Catholics join this critique, especially in the wake of Vatican II, which they perceive as dismantling the centrality of sacraments in favor of a secularized and worldly church that elevates social issues over more sacred concerns. This critique only grew with the invention of liberation theology, as we saw in the first chapter. Contemporary Catholics in Ecuador, both lay and ordained, make similar comments, describing "true Catholics" as those who regularly attend mass and, increasingly, as those who participate in sacramental life. Indeed, it is through sacramental compliance that the institutional church is beginning to measure, and encourage, renewed participation of its members. Missions to rural communities, youth programs, and the training of lay catechists to serve rural areas, as well as tolerance and encouragement of charismatic movements within the church, are all designed to increase parishioners' participation in sacramental life and characterize an increasingly lay-led, liturgical church that simultaneously focuses on family issues.

This inward-facing movement, which shifts the liberation theology emphasis on the public back to private spaces, reflects larger neoliberal trends. Individuals and private spaces are highlighted over public or structural causes. The domestic church is the private church, shaped by individuals through private actions, even as those actions are learned and reified in institutional spaces. This shift is also observable in the renewed mission movement, where lay Catholics replace the institutional church, and often the state, as they teach, preach, and in the summer months take part in development projects.

THE EMPIRE STRIKES BACK: CATHOLIC MISSIONS IN THE TWENTY-FIRST CENTURY

In Bolívar, missions to rural areas began in the 1980s, when priests and others in the Catholic hierarchy became concerned about Protestant competition and communities where there was no active participation in church programming, to the point that some churches had disappeared in communities where they had been extant since early imperial times. Missions occur annually at the beginning of August, during Christmas, and during Holy Week, lasting between seven days and two weeks. The structure and emphasis of the missions vary, as does the missionary corps, but sacramental Catholicism, often in conjunction with specific teachings about families, is always at the center of mission efforts.

Working in Ecuador as a Peace Corps volunteer in the mid-1990s, I never encountered Catholic missionaries, though even the small community where I lived and worked had its fair share of Protestant visitors hoping to make converts on the mountain slopes. When I returned to Bolívar in the early 2000s for fieldwork, the mission movement, though extant, was still small, and no one in Chillanes mentioned it in interviews or in casual conversation when I asked about Catholic practice. In 2009, however, several people spoke often and with admiration about Catholic missions, prompting me to seek out missionaries and others who had participated in one of the programs to describe their experiences. In 2012 I attended a mission training camp with the Diocese of Guaranda, and in 2015 I was able to participate in the Holy Week missions in one of Chillanes's peripheral communities. I attended both events at the invitation of Padre Orlando, Chillanes's resident priest since 2005.

Padre Orlando has long been an advocate of missions, and he estimated that 120 Chillanenses participate in them annually as missionaries. During Christmas and Holy Week, the missions take place in the center and in recintos in the canton. The longer, two-week missions that take place in August are targeted at these smaller communities on a provincial level and combine Bible lessons and services in the evening with community development projects during the day. Where possible, missionaries live with the people they go to serve, though some with paid work in town commute to the communities for the evening services after they finish their regular jobs. Missionaries train for this task in a weeklong, annual mission course sponsored by the Diocese of Guaranda. The event is attended by potential missionaries from all over Ecuador who then operate missions in their home parishes and is normally held at the diocesan retreat center outside of Guaranda during the last week of July.

Missionaries from Chillanes often describe the missions as fulfilling a need for sacramental and social knowledge in small communities that share a priest with many others, rendering it difficult to benefit from regular religious instruction. Padre Orlando ministers to fifty-six communities and several barrios, or discrete areas in larger towns that may have chapels, making him responsible to more than sixty individual congregations. He credited the missions with an increase in sacramental participation throughout the province and with the continued Catholic affinity of people in communities where Protestant evangelizing has been especially noticeable. "There has been a notable increase in Christian believers coming to the Eucharist," he commented when I asked about religious change in a 2009 interview,

> I notice a greater valuation of the Eucharist by the people, and that's the fruit of evangelization. They have a hunger, an appetite, for the Word of God, to receive Christ in the Eucharist. I notice valuation of the Eucharist and the other sacraments has improved. . . . And we also have in Gualcalgoto [a recinto roughly 10 km from the center] communities where other religious groups were beginning to come in, but with evangelization people have made a discernment and opted to continue in the Catholic Church.

In 2012, his enthusiasm had not waned. When I asked in an interview how he saw the state of the church in Chillanes, he commented that things were "improving," something he marked by an "increased participation" in church activities.

> JD: So more people are coming to church? Something else?
> PO: Yes, they keep coming. There is a valuing of sacred things.
> JD: Ah, and how is this? How do you know?
> PO: Yes, you see people confessing more. They confess more, and with greater frequency. Their behavior in fiestas, for example, when they have them, is better. They have gotten rid of the excesses when they eat and drink; the drinking has decreased. . . . One indication is Holy Week. So take for example Good Friday. Two years ago we had a procession that was about two and a half blocks long. Now it's full of people—four blocks long! Between four and five blocks long. There is participation. And the people who come bring their video recorders and make videos of it, that they've done it.
> JD: So they're participating more actively.
> PO: More actively here in the center. And that has spurred similar activities, like with the missionaries, in the recintos. There it's the same, improved participation with more people, a more active participation, more conscious, and also with fruit.
> JD: What kind of fruit?

PO: The fruits—you note them in life, no? Their behavior is better, they have a better appreciation for Godly things. Some of them have married.

JD: Those who weren't married—

PO: Of those who weren't married, some have married. And some youths who weren't confirmed are now confirmed, are in the process of receiving confirmation, doing their first communions. It's good, but at that level, there are about sixty of them.

JD: Sixty—

PO: People who haven't done, normally, the—in the years they have prepared—and with that, with the evangelization, it isn't necessary that they [come to Chillanes to do] confirmation or communion, and now many of them are getting ready to marry.

JD: So they're doing more sacraments.

PO: Yes, yes.

In Padre Orlando's view, the missions have led directly to greater sacramental participation on the part of his parishioners, which in turn has led to what he considers more Godly, and thus better, life choices.

His concern about sacramental participation was reinforced, and occasionally challenged, in the mission training session I attended in 2012. In an opening afternoon session on the day the sixty-one mission trainees arrived at the Diocese of Guaranda Retreat Center, a sprawling cement building in Balta Pamba, a tiny recinto tucked into the mountains to the west of the provincial capital, the Salesian priest Padre Luis welcomed his charges by reminding them of their purpose. "We're in a very difficult moment [with the missions]," he told the crowd as we gathered after lunch, elaborating that previously people accepted Catholic authority with something like unquestioned faith. "Now," he continued, "they want analyses. They question things and they aren't content to just hear answers." In the campo, he continued, people only know the few things they learn in church on Sundays. The missionaries will be taking a more complete version of Catholicism, and the purpose of missionary training is to make this possible. Luis's message was immediately, and perhaps more succinctly, followed by that of Carlos, a young priest from one of Bolívar's subtropical regions near the coast. After leading trainees in a game of telephone, he used the resulting confusion over the garbled message to convey his sense of missional purpose. "What we're trying to do is bring a clear message to our communities," he stated. "Better clear than big."

When the bishop of Guaranda, Msgr. Ángel Polivio Sánchez Loaiza, spoke later in the afternoon, he emphasized the clarity of the message the missionaries were to give. Quoting then-Pope Benedict XVI, he stated that the biggest problem in the world is that people have a relationship with God that does not include the church. If people don't need the church, he continued, still paraphrasing Benedict, they don't need the sacraments. They don't need others. "It's just Dioisto y yo" (God—in the colloquial language favored by rural Ecuadorians—and me). "We're entering into a Christianity that's just me and God." One reason for this, he continued, is that modern children "don't know how to pray." "Why don't kids today know how to pray?," he asked. "Because their mothers don't teach them, and fathers even less." For these reasons, he said, the Ecuadorian Bishop's Council voted at the 2008 meeting to focus on the family. "If we don't evangelize the family, we are not going to gain much," he remarked to the attentive crowd. Citing documents from the Aparecida gathering of Latin American Bishops (CELAM), specifically article 403, Bishop Sánchez emphasized that missionaries and the church more broadly are called to work with whole families, including young people and single mothers. This will require a change in culture, he continued, asking, "Who do we find in church? Women." Referring to the confirmation services he had attended the day before in Chillanes, where more than one hundred youths had received the sacrament, he complimented Padre Orlando for his work but expressed concern that such shows of piety were impermanent. "How many will come back?," he wondered.

The job of the missionaries, he concluded, was to continue the "new evangelization" called for in Vatican II and undertaken seriously by Pope John Paul II. Referencing the latter, the bishop made it clear that it is not the gospel that changes in the new evangelization but the means of spreading it. The missionaries gathered in the room were that new means.

As mission training continued for an additional four days, priests and seminary students who were in charge of the sessions continued to weave together the themes of mission, sacrament, and family in various ways. Discussions touched on questions of youth participation—or a perceived lack of it—in sacramental life, and several missionaries wondered if lack of preparation to receive sacraments may be the reason that people do not take them seriously. In another discussion that followed a presentation on theological understandings of the sacraments as reenactments of Jesus's actions on earth, a priest turned the conversation to families by pointing out that marriage is a way of giving one's life to God outside of the priesthood, a position he was sure to say was not "yet" open to women. Because marriage stands in for ordination, he continued, the Catholic prohibition of divorce remains in place and is considered a mortal sin. The priest then told a story about a young woman who had been married unhappily but had now found another, more suitable partner and wanted to be married in the church. The priest related that he had told the woman that he was sorry, but the best he could do was hear her confession.

This caused one mission trainee, a college student who had traveled to Balta Pamba from her home in the south of the country, to ask the priest about instances when a woman is married to an abusive husband, "living like a slave," and enduring physical abuse. If she finds another, better man, she wanted to know, what does the church have to say about that? The priest rubbed his neck a bit as he worked into an answer, then explained, "Christ came to save, not to condemn." Some people, he said, can "normalize" the situation within church laws, though he sounded none too convinced as he said this. The young woman persisted, wanting to know about priests who renounce their vows and have families. Here, the priest was empathetic. "Marriage ends with the death of a spouse," he explained. "Priestly orders never end." He was not entirely done with questions from the missionaries, though, as another woman suggested that the church had to be careful. If priests refused communion and other sacraments to those who remarried or the like, they should also refuse them to people who had committed theft and other sins.

After a longer discussion of hypothetical situations, including a case where the priest advocated helping unmarried couples living together to receive marriage sacraments if their desire to do so is genuine, he turned the tables a bit and asked the mission trainees, the majority of whom were under the age of twenty-five, why marriage rates in Ecuador were declining so sharply. The same young woman who challenged the morality of staying in an abusive marriage offered an abrupt answer. Her grandparents, she explained, had married too fast, at too young an age. "Now we're afraid of marriage," she said. "We're not going to live well or be able to study." For her, as apparently for the many trainees in the room who nodded as she spoke, the domestic church was not an easy or obviously beneficial social or ecclesiastical structure, especially for women. The domestic church did not necessarily offer adequate social capital for flourishing or for a satisfactory life. The sacramental emphasis on the part of church elders came across as constraining, even dangerous in the case of abusive relationships.

Still, most missionaries used a sacramental yardstick to measure the success of the missions, even as the missions themselves opened up spaces for women's participation in ways far broader than standard ecclesiastical practice. Carlota Inca, a thirty-four-year-old widow who lives in the recinto of San Juan Pamba, participates in three missions per year, an activity for which she makes time in addition to continuing university studies, work as a seamstress, and heading a start-up day care that keeps her occupied from eight until eleven o'clock weekday mornings. "Yes, thanks to God, with the help of God, the missions have been a success—not only in the community where I was, but in the rest of them," she commented.

> The missions changed them. The August missions from a year ago changed them. The missionary that was there, he was full of the Holy Spirit, and the people unified and changed. And now, many of them go to mass, they go to mass and help the priest. They didn't before. The priest said that before, they came and told him, "Get out of here!" But now they don't. Even in school and in their houses they are celebrating the mass, saying their rosaries. There still isn't a church [in that town]. Many of them were separated [brothers],[2] and now, now they have changed.

Walter Ayala, a fifty-four-year-old man who has been participating in missions since 2001, echoed Carlota's emphasis on Catholic ritual and sacramental training, though he linked this directly to improved family and community relations.

> Yes, we've had this [success in the missions]. There has been a lot of change, a lot of change in the communities where people have participated. There have been homes that were on the point of destroying themselves, and they have come to realize, "Why are we doing this?" They're getting along better among neighbors because we were talking about this: "Why fight among yourselves about a road, about water,

> about land when it's all going to stay here when we die, right? So please realize this, and get along among sons and daughters, between brothers and sisters."
>
> So there has been a good response from the people. . . . We go to give religious formation to kids from the time they're little, right? But, to older people, it's possible they have never received, that they never had catechism, because in the campo there are families sometimes that never go to mass. So it's really important that we go on the missions because we go where the parents, we prepare the parents so they can teach the children from a young age, because from a young age they see that we pray, that we make the sign of the cross.

Mission success in this context is measured through the lens of continuing quotidian Catholic practice that instantiates Catholic values such that social relations are improved.

Mission success is thus rendered legible in improved community and familiar relationships and increased participation in the sacraments, further cementing the link between evangelization, sacramental participation, and the domestic church. As the young woman's challenge to the priest in the mission training demonstrates, however, the missions are also sites where the nature of the domestic church is exposed, tested, and in many ways redefined.

Recinto Nubillado, April 2015

Holy Week 2015 began with mud and raging rivers as torrential rains from the week before left parts of Bolívar Province and several locations on Ecuador's Pacific coast digging out from devastating floods and landslides. Blocked roads created hazards for travelers, and a presidential order forbidding the collection of *palmas* for use in Palm Sunday processions created confusion and dismay among many Roman Catholics, who looked forward to the annual processions reenacting Jesus's entrance into Jerusalem before his crucifixion. The order, designed to protect an indigenous species of parrot that President Correa believed nested in bushes sometimes harvested to make elaborate garlands used in the processions, effectively halted the celebrations in urban areas as police were under orders to seize the newly illegal flora. In Chillanes, the combination of rain, closed roads, and lack of palms made the processions the smallest in recent history.

Outside of town, however, in the small recinto of Nubillado,[3] people gathered with their garlands and with the guidance of two local catechists marched in a circular path ending at the small chapel that, along with a water system, a school, and a one-room community center, gives the scattered collection of houses a focal point. In Nubillado, Holy Week and what have become regular Holy Week missions had begun.

Though Nubillado has sometimes enjoyed visiting missionaries, primarily during the August mission season, the Holy Week missions are usually handled by the local catechists with occasional help from the parish church in Chillanes. The year 2015 was no different, and every night between Palm Sunday and Good Friday the lay missionaries Danilo and Maria and one of their sons pulled up to the chapel in a four-wheel-drive SUV, opening the church and ringing the bell to call residents to the evening services. Soon an average of thirty-five men, women, and children were seated on chairs that formed a semicircle in front of the altar and pulpit, arranged so that every participant could see the others.

Danilo and Maria led the mission services using a guidebook produced by the archbishop of Cuenca titled, *Celebration of the Easter Mystery Directed by Authorized Laypeople: Sunday, Day of the Lord and Holy Week* (Cisneros 2002). Following the suggestion of the pamphlet, they welcomed people by asking them to pray "with our hearts, not just with our lips." Danilo then asked God to bless families, the community, and their time together during the missions. One night, he reminded the gathered parishioners that "we are all catechists here," emphasizing that as members of the church, everyone had a voice.

And indeed, a notable feature of the missions was the amount of participation on the part of people who attended. After reading a passage from the Bible, usually from scenes leading up to Jesus's crucifixion, Danilo and Maria told people, "You have the word" (Uds. tienen la palabra), and waited to hear what the gathered community members had to say. After reading about Jesus's flagellation, for example, a man dressed in the polyester slacks, sweater, and rubber boots typical of campo men commented that he always focused on the part of the reading where Jesus is identified as "King of the Jews." Danilo nodded and explained that this was an insult, and a way to get Pilate off the hook for what he was about to do. He then went on to explain that this kind of shirking of responsibility is "something we all do" and "something we should all reflect on." Maria then read from the pamphlet, "Let us be like Jesus, accepting insult" without retribution. This started a conversation about accepting bodily pains and being patient, especially in the course of raising children. There was widespread participation by those in attendance, all of whom agreed that patience is a difficult virtue.

The participatory nature of the conversation that opening night and the direct ties the catechists pointed out between biblical texts and family relationships continued throughout the week of the mission, which included a foot washing ceremony and communal dinner on Thursday and ended with a *via crucis* procession and subsequent Seven Words service on Good Friday. Both the procession and the service emphasized ties between biblical events and contemporary realities in Latin America, and the Seven Words service, especially, focused on the importance of family relationships as part of that reality.

The service takes place immediately after the via crucis procession during which those who have attended the missions carry large crosses through the streets of the recinto and out onto the highway, stopping at each station of the cross to read scripture, pray, sing, and connect the events that led up to the crucifixion to events in modern-day Latin America. At the fourth station, for example, when Jesus sees his mother as he is walking with the cross through the streets of Jerusalem, the reading from the guidebook reminds processioners that Mary "is the most loving of mothers." But Mary is not the only focus as the guide elaborates, after detailing the pain she must have at seeing her only son on the way to his death:

> How many mothers in Latin America see their young sons leaving home! The laborers that go in search of work in rich countries, to be oppressed or dead, those that have to go and fight in absurd wars, or those youths from the countryside that disappear, victims of repression and barbarity all over America. (Cisneros 2002, 147)

At the seventh station, which recalls Jesus falling for a second time under the weight of the cross, the reading reminds listeners:

> All over Latin America laborers are fallen. Peasants, indigenous peoples, the poorest of the poor, those who extract gold from mines, those that cultivate corn and coffee, those who work iron and refine petroleum, those who produce the riches of the continent and those

> that fall in sickness, old age and that are abandoned. No one helps them in their daily lives.
>
> Lord, don't make me deaf or blind to the misery of my brothers, but abandoning my security and comfort, that I go and help. (Cisneros 2002, 150)

As they walk, participants are encouraged to connect the events of Good Friday to their own cultural and political climate in the particular context of Latin America, reflecting not only on Jesus's pain (and Mary's) but also on broader issues of social dislocation, inequality, and solidarity.

The Seven Words service that follows immediately after the via crucis also encourages participants to connect biblical content, in this case Jesus's reported sayings as he was nailed to the cross, to issues in the contemporary social world. Unlike the more formal procession, however, the Seven Words service encourages flexibility in its presentation and content that opens a space that both reinforces and challenges the reality of that social world.

In Nubillado, the service started with Danilo welcoming the approximately fifty people who had gathered and then introducing the Seven Words as "a synthesis" of Jesus's teaching "to love one another." He then asked for seven volunteers, each of whom would come to the pulpit, read a scriptural passage and commentary from the same book the catechist had used throughout the mission services, and offer a reflection, a free-form commentary, of his or her own.

The first reader, a woman in her thirties who had come to the service from a neighboring community, read from the guide, which indicated that the "first word" was "Forgive them, for they know not what they do" (Luke 25, 34). She then read the brief commentary that emphasized God as a father, capable of love, and the need for forgiveness in all circumstances. Looking up from the book, she then continued, still at the pulpit, to render her own interpretation of the passage, commenting, "Jesus was like a child. And where do children go when they need something? Their mother. Mother! Father! It was the same with Jesus, who was crying out to the father he knew he had. He was crying out because he was hurt by the sin we inflict on him every day." Continuing to reflect extemporaneously, the woman quoted Don Bosco, who once commented that demons are more likely to be found in monasteries than parks as they are enemies of

God and work to defeat him. Of course, she said, demons are also in bars and places "where temptation is," but they are most insidiously "in homes." "We have to use the power of God to accept our spouses," she concluded, "to accept the shortcomings of our children."

The second reader, assigned "You will be with me in paradise" (Luke 33), also touched on family and domestic issues, commenting, "If you're fighting with your spouse, and then go and sleep with a neighbor, that doesn't do—you're not being brothers in Christ." Maria, who read the third word, "Woman, behold your son. Son, behold your mother" (John 26), commented that Mary was a "true spouse," an example of obedience in the home. The last reader, a sixteen-year-old boy, commented in regard to his portion, "I commend my soul to God" (Luke 46), "We have to treat our spouses differently, because when we become a pair, we aren't two people, we're one person."

The missions, then, reinforced ideal notions of the domestic church while at the same time recognizing that those ideals are not always met. Calls to become better families embedded in the mission guide connected the domestic church to larger stories of Catholicism even as they allowed laypeople, most notably laywomen, to comment on familial imperfections from the space of the pulpit. In a similar manner, mission training opened up room for the young woman and others to challenge church teachings about divorce and sacramental constructions of family as she raised the issue of abuse and remarriage. Throughout the missions, the domestic church was presumed to be a good specifically supported in liturgical and sacramental contexts, even as that good was recognized to be imperfect or even harmful in the case of abusive relationships.

As "society's best social capital," then, the domestic church is a social and spiritual ideal that women embody as they use it to form notions of ideal homes supported by an increasing emphasis on the sacraments in missions and in daily life on the part of the church. At the same time, it is capital that Ecuadorians, especially Ecuadorian women, are using to question the value of those sacraments when used to support the maintenance of harmful relationships and to a certain extent a religious hierarchy that would normally restrict women's voices in liturgical settings. When women reflected on Jesus's words during the Holy Week missions they were for all intents and purposes preaching. They were claiming spaces not via protest but via channels afforded to them through liturgy. They were garnering social capital through the mechanisms of spiritual capital.

BEING WOMEN, BEING CATHOLIC: THE DOMESTIC CHURCH AND CATHOLIC VALUES IN COOPERATIVE LIFE

As discussed in the previous chapter, many Virgen de las Nubes Cooperative activities reproduced domestic acts such as cooking and knitting, effectively re-creating a household setting in the space of the cooperative. Beyond these economic and social activities, the cooperative was also a space where women practiced, discussed, and sometimes questioned Roman Catholic teachings that related to the domestic church, often under the rubric "improvement" or "change." The cooperative was another space in which members authored their identities as Catholic women.

All of the cooperative members who were still active in 2009 considered themselves Catholic, though their participation in church activities varied, as did their descriptions of the cooperative as a Catholic enterprise, especially given the recent emphasis on sacramental Catholicism as vital to Catholic identity. In interview questions designed to gauge the extent of Catholic activities among cooperative members, most women described going to mass as their primary Catholic practice, though many commented that this was difficult given the distance between their rural homes and the church, either in San Juan Pamba or in Chillanes proper. When I asked about the Catholic identity of the group, and specifically if it was important, the women were in unanimous agreement that it was very important but then faltered a bit when trying to describe why or how. Magdalena Estrada, for example, described her Catholic practice outside of the group as going to mass once a week when her work schedule and that of her husband allowed it. She also emphasized her duties as a parent. "I'm a Catholic," she responded when I asked what she did as a Catholic on a daily, weekly, and monthly basis.

> I'm a Catholic, and what I try to do is to live my life as a Catholic. Once in a while, when I can, I go to mass. The one thing I do also when it comes to religion is, when it comes to parents, we have to baptize our children and complete the sacraments. That's what we have to do. These are our responsibilities as parents. We always have to guide them, our children, on a good road. And that's what we've done.

"Within the group," she explained,

> it's that, it's different from the mass, it can't be like that. I mean, it's important that we always had the practice of reading scripture. We did all of that, and that was good. But sometimes we weren't aware enough of what a religion is. If we had really understood the true message of the Word of God, we would have tried to improve and change. But sometimes, we didn't do that.

For Magdalena, the lived Catholicism in the group, while rooted in the some of the same liturgical and scriptural values of the home, had failed in its impact. While she felt she had succeeded in the domestic church of her home, the group had failed in replicating that church as it regularly considered scripture but apparently failed to embody its message.

Magdalena's assessment was shared by most of the cooperative members, who often commented on scripture reading as the primary Catholic practice, even as they faulted the cooperative for not living up to its Catholic ideals of solidarity and cooperation. Narcisa Inca, an original member of the women's group and one who had to struggle to attend meetings as she lives several miles from the Chillanes center on the far side of San Juan Pamba, conflated Catholic practice with "being together" when she recalled what was specifically Catholic about the group. "When we met we read the Bible and reflected on it. We all did that together. We haven't met that way in a long time. We aren't so together these days. It isn't the way it used to be." Julia Guamán, a former president of the group and one of its founders, also located Catholic practice in shared practice and community. "We're very Catholic," she commented when I asked about the religious aspects of the cooperative, "and it's beautiful when we organize, when we come together we pray the rosary. We used to invite each other over to our houses to pray. When we were in the group, when it functioned, we used to invite the father to celebrate the mass, the whole thing, so we could share with each other." For Julia, the failure of the group was a failure to fully embrace church teachings about cooperation within families such as the one the cooperative created: "What happened was, as you are starting to understand, it was something economic. It didn't have anything to do with religion. Nothing to do with it. We're each human beings, and we make mistakes. . . . In the group, we're all believers, and we're all active in the faith. Yes, all of us. It's beautiful to serve in a group, to serve with people who serve God. You feel fulfilled. Now I'm going to go on a mission. In three weeks I'm going there [to mission training]."

While the group re-created aspects of the domestic church, then, especially assumptions about the power of spiritual capital to create social cohesion, cooperative members joined the institutional church in emphasizing sacramental participation as the hallmark or, as Padre Orlando put it, the "fruit" of Catholic identity. The failure of the cooperative could thus be written off by members as their own failure to successfully re-create idealized aspects of the domestic church, most notably cooperation and kindness that they feel were reinforced by shared sacramental participation. It is not the domestic church that failed them but themselves, in not implementing that church.

Women in Chillanes shape and are shaped by a dominant Catholic culture that in its institutional iterations is increasingly emphasizing sacramental elements as foundational for genuine Catholic life. At the same time, increasing lay participation in the liturgy and the sacraments is opening space for public reflection on the realities those sacraments are meant to describe and define. As women retold the story of Santa Rita in ways that questioned her muteness in the face of domestic violence and as they reflected on the difficulties of domestic life from the space of mission pulpits, they were crafting new and notably public expressions of the domestic church in local contexts. While Pope Francis's comments idealize families as refuges from illness, ignorance, and other problems, men and women in Chillanes are broader in their thinking, expanding the matrices of the social capital network even as they include the possibilities of misconnection or failure, especially where there is not an overt space for women's participation.

Once again, social capital, and more specifically in this example, gendered spiritual capital, emerges as a contested value that may strengthen women and their position in society or leave them vulnerable. Francis's description of the family as society's "best social capital" highlighted women's roles as reliable caregivers, educators, and community members, even as fewer and fewer women are entering motherhood as partners in nuclear families. The renewed missions in the Ecuadorian countryside also targeted families as the loci of a revitalized Catholic faith, along with improved personal and community relations, tying sacramental participation to domestic and communal well-being.

Certainly, families have always been central to Latin American Catholicism. The renewed emphasis on the domestic church, however, does change the spiritual and social capital matrices in which the Virgen de las Nubes Cooperative members operated. At the same time that women were to use their talents to be sure their children were cared for and present for the sacraments, they were to use their gifts as women "more prone to cooperation" to work together to produce cheese for market sale, an activity that required them to be away from the home for hours every day. They were asked to reproduce the domestic church in the space of cooperative even as they used that space to challenge the more difficult parts of domestic life. They did all of this in a neoliberal context that emphasized their identities as individual economic and religious actors, even as cooperation was held up as a supreme value. In this way, the tensions between liberationist Catholicism and its more contemporary iterations, and the role of such tensions in the life of the cooperative, become visible. Liberation theology in a neoliberal context is a domesticated theology, one enacted in private spaces and one that privileges individual commitments over systemic change, even as it retains values such as "cooperation."

FOUR

Las Juanes

Charismatic Catholicism, Women, and the Market in Chillanes

The arrival of Charismatic Catholicism not long after the Virgen de las Nubes Cooperative began cheese production introduced new modes of being Catholic into an already complex amalgamation of attitudes, practices, social structures, and beliefs. Although no woman in the group and no one I interviewed in the surrounding community made the direct association between charismatic modes of Catholicism, neoliberal capitalism, a rising middle class, and the group's economic failure, ideas of "religious change" and "the market" did permeate conversations in deep and significant ways. This chapter explores Charismatic Catholicism in Chillanes as a new mode of social capital, one that emphasizes emotion, individuality, charity, sacraments, and interpersonal relationships as much as if not more than community development and group cohesion. Like many treatments of Pentecostal and charismatic Protestantism in Latin America, I focus here on its specific entanglements with economic structures.[1] I do so, however, not to argue for a rational choice model of religious identity. I do not believe that Charismatic Catholics in Chillanes are opting for this version of Catholicism as a more direct road to healing, change, or financial success. Rather, I explore the increasing popularity of Charismatic Catholicism in Chillanes as a form of religiosity that offered cooperative members new and laterally relational ways of imagining Catholic identity and action outside of historical institutional models at the same time that economic conditions and possibilities were realigning other relationships—in homes, communities, and between people and the state.

The noted Latin American religious historian Edward Cleary traced the roots of the charismatic movement within Catholicism to Holiness and Pentecostal churches that sprang up in early twentieth-century North American locations, specifically Topeka, Kansas, in 1901 and the 1906 Azusa Street Mission revival in Los Angeles. Events in these locations generated the Assemblies of God, the Church of God in Christ, the Church of God, and Aimee Semple McPherson's Church of the Foursquare Gospel. These in turn spawned countless independent Pentecostal entities, from stand-alone storefront churches to international organizations such as the Universal Church of the Kingdom of God, which is based in Brazil but claims followers on every continent.[2] Pentecostals have been particularly successful in Latin America. According to Pew Research Center data on religious affiliation in 2014, 69 percent of Latin Americans identify as Catholic, down from close to 90 percent, a number that held steady until the last decades of the twentieth century. Of those who identify as Protestant, 65 percent identify either individually as Pentecostal or with a Pentecostal denomination. Eighty-four percent of Latin American adults identify as being raised Catholic, meaning that 15 percent have converted to Protestant Christianity the majority of whom have converted to Pentecostal versions of Protestantism (Pew Research Center 2014).

This broad overview does not account for charismatics, Christians who embrace at least some Pentecostal practices and beliefs within previously existing and generally noncharismatic denominational organizations. Charismatics are commonly identified as "second wave" Pentecostals who differ from their more classical predecessors in institutions such as the Assemblies of God and from more recent "third wave" Pentecostals such as those in the Universal Church of the Kingdom of God and many independent churches. Scholars generally trace the charismatic movement to an Episcopal priest, Dennis Bennett, who claimed to have been baptized in the Holy Spirit while in the pulpit of his Van Nuys, California, church during a 1960 sermon. Bennett and his wife, Rita, left the Van Nuys church and went on to found the Christian Renewal Association, an organization that focuses on charismatic themes of the work of the Holy Spirit in daily life, especially in areas of health and healing.[3]

Bennett's experience and ministry, which focused on direct experiences of the Spirit in healing and ecstatic forms of worship, was replicated to greater and lesser extents in several Protestant denominations in the United States, Canada, and Britain in the late 1960s and early 1970s. Evangelical Protestants began adopting charismatic practices in the mid-1980s, when many congregations embraced Pentecostal forms of worship, once again focused on ecstatic forms of worship and healing. Today's Vineyard Church, Joel Osteen's ministries, and T. D. Jakes's Potter's House are all examples of this evangelical form of Pentecostal practice that emphasizes gifts of the spirit and direct experiences with God.

Charismatic Catholics trace their lineage to two events early on in this charismatic ascendency. In North America, students on retreat at Duquesne University in 1967 reported intense spiritual experiences, including baptism by the Holy Spirit and speaking in tongues. This group would later go on to found the Catholic Charismatic Renewal (CCR), now an officially sanctioned body within the Roman Catholic Church. At about the same time as what would come to be known as the "Duquesne Weekend," students in Bogotá, Colombia, reported a similar experience. The CCR in the United States and Canada gained several million followers during the 1960s and 1970s, though it has been in decline in the decades since (Cleary 2011, 10). This has not been the case in Latin America, where roughly 40 percent of all Catholics reported being charismatics in 2014 (Pew Research Center 2014).

Most accounts of the Charismatic Renewal among Catholics in Latin America credit Francis MacNutt, a North American Roman Catholic priest who combined a gift for the dramatic arts with an interest in spiritual healing, with helping to spread the Charismatic movement on the continent. MacNutt traveled widely during the early years of his ministry, founding the Association of Christian Therapists, a group dedicated to bringing spiritual gifts into medical practice. After renouncing his priestly vows and marrying Judith Sewall, a woman with whom he had collaborated in spiritual healing, he settled in Clearwater, Florida, where he and his wife founded Christian Healing Ministries. Now located in Jacksonville, Florida, Christian Healing Ministries includes a healing center and training center for what MacNutt calls "prayer ministry." Though MacNutt has stepped down from daily leadership, Christian Healing Ministries remains an active, international organization that promotes charismatic practice across the globe.

Cleary credited MacNutt and his followers with filling a void left by the institutional church in Latin America, where even the reforms of the Second Vatican Council and ensuing liberation theology movement could not overcome what Cleary characterized as "shallow" Catholicism in which laypeople were never invited to really interact with their faith, even in the context of the CEBs. Describing a charismatic movement in Bolivia in the 1980s, Cleary wrote:

> In discovering Charismaticism laypeople also discovered that they did not know much about the faith, either through the Bible or through orthodox Catholic teaching. They saw they were ignorant in ways they had never seen before. (If nothing else, the Charismatic movement holds up a mirror to ordinary Catholics to show them their deficiencies.) They felt deeply that they needed to fill this void and turned to educating themselves and to evangelization, the effort to educate others. (Cleary 2011, 44)

Although Cleary's analysis perhaps overemphasizes the degree to which lay Catholics were disassociated with Catholic identity and teachings before the advent of charismaticism in Latin America, he is correct in his assessment that charismatic groups demand large investments of time and active engagement with Catholic identity. They also continue many of the small group Bible studies started during the liberation theology era. As Cleary points out:

> In fact there have been small groups in the Latin American church for decades. Catholic Action and the League of Mary functioned through small groups through much of the twentieth century. Those groups had specialized categories of members, such as students or farmers, while contemporary small communities were made up of ordinary parishioners, often from the same neighborhood or rural village. Be they CEBs or Charismatic prayer groups, these communities are living cells within a parish. (Cleary 2011, 17)

Like the service organizations and neighborhood organizations before them, charismatic groups bring people together from the larger community to reflect and act on their faith commitments. As Thomas Csordas (2009, 91) describes it in his analysis of charismaticism as a global movement, such actions may be the effect of "reenchanting" or "resacralizing" a secular world.

This is certainly the case in Chillanes, where Charismatic Catholicism arrived in 2008 with a family returning to the area after twenty-five years of living in Quito. Elena Sánchez and her family were renting several rooms near Chillanes's central plaza as Elena worked long hours cooking meals for students at Chillanes's public high school. Elena and her daughter, Silvia Escobar, came to Chillanes after a period of active participation in Juan XXIII, a charismatic group that requires members to go on three-day retreats during which initiates are encouraged to examine their lives and shortcomings and surrender themselves to God, an experience that often includes a baptism in the Holy Spirit and other charismatic elements. After the retreat, members continue to meet regularly to sing, pray, share concerns, conduct Bible studies, and serve people whom group members describe as "the least among us," including prisoners, elderly people living in Chillanes's state-run nursing home, and families in need of financial assistance. In Chillanes, members of Juan XXIII also assist Padre Orlando in conducting yearly mission efforts, and many serve as catechists.

Juan XXIII, formally known as Movimiento de Retiros Juan XXIII (Retreat Movement John XXIII), is an early subset of the charismatic revival in Catholicism. Founded in Puerto Rico in 1973 by Nelson Rivera Beauchamp, the group emphasizes evangelism to people only marginally affiliated with, or even outside, the church. Entrance to the group is always initiated through the three-day retreats, and Juan XXIII is primarily active in Latin America and the Caribbean, with groups in Puerto Rico, Peru, the Dominican Republic, Ecuador, Honduras, the United States, Italy, and Spain. In its literature and other modes of presentation, group members are careful to characterize the movement as "apostolic" and "Catholic" and often emphasize that members support local priests in the work of the parish.

Such careful positioning is not coincidental. Speaking with me in 2009, one year after she had started a group in Chillanes, Elena described an attitude of suspicion among Roman Catholics who had not participated in the retreats toward members of Juan XXIII, people known locally as "retiristas" (retreaters) and easily identified by jackets, notebooks, and occasionally cars emblazoned with the movement's distinctive logo and slogan. "The slogan of the movement is 'Love, Surrender, and Sacrifice,'" she explained after talking about love being the greatest of these values.

ES: But here they see us as, they look at us with jealousy. They act that way in church as they aren't used to seeing us do this, that is, for example, we meet, we sing, we pray. And also we show that we're part of the movement by putting on long skirts and for that they look down on us. They're jealous.

JD: Why is that?

ES: It's that they say, it's that they say it's because they think we're separated brothers [*hermanos separados*] of another religion.

JD: Which religion, exactly?

ES: But we're in the mass, we're helping the padre, they know that John XXIII was a pope! But people are ignorant. It's because of ignorance.

Indeed, in the first several years of its existence in Chillanes, Juan XXIII faced resistance from Padre Orlando and non-Charismatic Catholics who worried that the movement was a form of non-Catholic Pentecostal Christianity designed to weaken the Roman heritage and identity of the church. As membership in the organization went from around 40 in 2009 to more than 150 in 2012, however, and as members began to regularly help Padre Orlando in providing music for masses, eager adults training to be catechists and a regular supply of missionaries, the priest has accepted the group, at least to a certain degree, and he regularly attends their Thursday night Bible studies and prayer sessions. The lay orientation of the group, however, continues to challenge institutional models of Catholicism that endow the institution of the church with more capital than individual parishioners. For women especially, participation in Charismatic Catholicism opens up new modes of gaining and deploying social and spiritual capital in channels very different from those offered by traditional liberationist projects such as the Virgen de las Nubes group.

LIFE MOVIES: THE ACCUMULATION OF SPIRITUAL CAPITAL AS SOCIAL CAPITAL IN CHARISMATIC PRACTICE

In a seminal 2003 article, Bradford Verter traces ideas of "spiritual capital" through the work of Pierre Bourdieu and Max Weber, seeking to distinguish spiritual capital as separate from Bourdieu's and Weber's more institutional forms. "If religious capital is conceived à la Bourdieu as something that is produced and accumulated within a hierocratic institutional framework," he writes, "spiritual capital may be regarded as a more widely diffused commodity, governed by more complex patterns of production, distribution, exchange, and consumption" (Verter 2003, 158). Whereas religious capital in its embodied, objectified, and institutional state is generally held and, to a certain extent, controlled by religious institutions, Verter argues that spiritual capital is more fluid and less institutionally based as laypeople produce and consume it in the space of their social lives. As such, spiritual capital is more potentially disruptive than religious capital, more potentially the source (or result) of conflict, even as it can be a powerful mechanism for creating what Bourdieu (1980, 53) called habitus: the social worlds that shape what people can imagine and enact in daily life.

For those participating in the Juan XXIII movement, the three-day retreats are a central site where people produce and consume spiritual capital in all its forms. Though specific details of the retreat are reserved for participants, retiristas in Chillanes were generally enthusiastic about sharing their experiences in broad strokes, though they all cautioned that one has "to live it to feel it" (*hay que vivirlo para sentirlo*), a phrase that captures a pervasive theme of personal transformation they emphasize as they talk about their retreat experiences. "To go on a retreat is to have a personal encounter with Christ," explained Silvia Escobar, Elena's daughter and one of the founding members of the movement in Chillanes. "And it's like making a photocopy of yourself. It's like going to the doctor and asking what kind of illness I have. One encounters Christ again. Like I told you before, you have to live it to feel it. It's an emotion, it's an encounter with yourself. But you also share with others, with the people you meet there." Silvia's image of the copy machine and focus on the emotional impact of the retreats were repeated by others in describing their retreat experiences. Rosita Quinatoa, a woman who had completed the retreat and joined Juan XXIII several years before our 2012 interview, described the first day of the retreats (usually Friday) as "the movie of our lives," a phrase her husband, Juan Quinatoa, then repeated.

RQ: There are different days, for example, Fridays are about—they're about the movie of our life.
JQ: The movie of our life.
JD: The movie—so you're thinking about how your life is?
RQ: Yes. Then Saturday is for forgiveness, and Sunday is for thanksgiving, and for receiving the Lord.

Elena Sánchez, one of the founders of the movement in Chillanes, described the retreat as a process of recognition and liberation.

> My life changed when I encountered the word of God [on a retreat]. Because before, I lived badly, I was living terribly. But after I encountered my God, Father God, I don't have material wealth, but I live well. That is, I don't fight with my husband, I don't behave badly, I don't get along badly with my in-laws. We live in harmony. . . . God gives us liberty, but we bind ourselves up with things that do harm. . . . To be Catholic isn't just to say that one is Catholic, no, no, no! I was like that. I was a catechist, for many years I was a catechist, but in reality I wasn't. I didn't understand the plans of the Lord, which make me free, free, free. To be free, free, free is to be happy. It's what I think people are meant to be.

The retreat allowed Elena to examine her life, ask forgiveness for her perceived sins, and then enter into a "personal relationship with God" that has improved her home life and led to an enhanced quality of spiritual, if not material, existence.

This element of self-examination in group settings is repeated in weekly meetings, which take place after Thursday evening masses, to which members of Juan XXIII regularly contribute music, readings of scripture, and flowers. At the meetings, members gather to sing, pray, read and reflect on Bible passages, share concerns, and continue the practices and commitments they encountered in the retreats. Held in a room in the rectory next to Chillanes's church, the meetings are intensely personal. Twenty or so Juan XXIII members come together, sitting on chairs they have placed in a circle so that everyone is visible to everyone else. Unlike the liturgy in the regular mass, the meetings are free-form, though they generally start with standardized Catholic prayers, including the Our Father, a Hail Mary, and the Prayer to the Holy Spirit.[4] A group member then reads a preselected passage from the Bible, offers a commentary, and asks other members for their interpretations and reflections. It is in these reflections that members often refer to the retreats and themes that were important to them, especially as they relate to family and perceived inadequacies among group members.

At a July 2012 meeting, for example, Silvia Escobar, president of the group at the time, began the meeting after the prayers by reading the passage from Matthew 11:28–30 in which Jesus invites those with heavy burdens to come to him, for those who do will find their burdens are light: "Come to me, all you who are weary and burdened, and I will give you rest. Take my yoke upon you and learn from me, for I am gentle and humble in heart, and you will find rest for your souls. For my yoke is easy and my burden is light" (NIV). Following a typical pattern, she then asked what group members thought the passage meant and after entertaining a few genera responses about being free to follow Jesus, narrowed the focus of the conversation by asking how many people in the room had ever been tired. "All of us have burdens," she continued and then focused on the domestic sphere. Being married can sometimes feel like one is "sleeping with the enemy," she said, though she assured the group that "happy marriages" were the result of "not giving up" and of letting Jesus carry the load.

The group continued the conversation, which wandered from the nature of burdens to the need for gratitude and eventually came to a discussion of prayer that focused on prayer not as recitation (*rezar*) but as direct communication with God (*orar*). "We need to pray *all* the time," Silvia affirmed after a young man commented that it was important not to pray only at home or in church but in wild places that showed God's creation. Praying, she went on, must be mindful, with attention and intention. It is the only way to develop a proper frame of mind in relationship to God.

As was typical in Juan XXIII meetings, members continued to chime in, changing the focus of the discussion to issues that were important to them and frequently referring to the framing of their retreat experiences. On the same night the group was discussing burdens and prayer, a woman wondered about the limits of forgiveness, unsure about her ability to forgive someone who had done something truly terrible. Silvia was in the midst of explaining that God is the ultimate judge when a woman related a story about encountering a man on the street who had committed a wrong against her mother. She described making a conscious decision to be nice to him, even smiling when she encountered him, an act that was met by apparent surprise. Another man then spoke up, saying that moments like those are why "mass is so important. It's what we learn at the retreat." This led to a general, vocal affirmation by several people that "the most difficult thing to overcome is oneself." Indeed, this is the point of the weekly meetings. "We have a beast inside each of us," a man commented, "and the hardest time is one, two, three years after the retreat." "The answer," he continued, "is here in this room, where 120 brothers should be."

The meeting concluded with songs, during which people raised their hands to heaven in classic charismatic style, and personal prayers, which included petitions on behalf of those in the state-run home for elderly people, whom the petitioner described as "abandoned," those who were unemployed and sick, and those who were not attending the meeting.

The personal focus of the retreats, the meetings, and the movement more broadly makes Juan XXIII markedly different from its progenitor. Though the movement is focused on sacraments, and most members serve as catechists, missionaries, or both, the focus on what Elena Sánchez described as a "personal relationship" with God creates a space for lay experience and authority in ways that do not require institutional authority. For this reason, the group was initially regarded by many in Chillanes as disruptive, or even as some kind of Protestantism in disguise. Padre Orlando was originally skeptical of charismatics in the church, worrying that they were "nothing but alleluias" (*puros aleyuyias, no más*) in a 2012 interview. Several other community members commented that the group appeared divisive in the immediate aftermath of its arrival, especially as members were perceived to consider themselves "purer" than run-of-the-mill Catholics in town. At the evening masses before Juan XXIII meetings, group members occupied very public roles: they provided guitar accompaniment before and during the service, they often read biblical passages before the sermon, and they notably took communion on a more regular basis. As in much of Latin America, Chillanenses typically do not take communion during weekly mass as most take a conservative stance that requires full confession and ritual purity before taking part. In a typical Sunday mass, which usually draws between 120 and 200 people, 17 percent of those attending take part in the Eucharist. Thursday nights, the second most popular mass offered in Chillanes's central church every week, an average of one hundred people are in attendance, with 20 percent of them participating in the rite. Most of those partaking are Juan XXIII members who then join in the weekly meeting.

This kind of public participation in church life, reinforced as many Juan XXIII members act as catechists and participants in yearly mission efforts and amplified by their branding with a distinctive logo on stickers, meant for automobiles, which many members wear on jackets and put on Bibles that they carry with them to mass and to meetings, has made the charismatics highly visible, even as their number remains relatively small, about 150 members as of 2015. To be part of Juan XXIII is to be noticeably different from Roman Catholics who have not been through the retreat experience, who have not "lived it to feel it."

As a lay movement, Juan XXIII is also distinct from non-Charismatic Catholicism in encouraging direct experiences of the divine, without the necessary intervention of the church hierarchy. This is one of the reasons that Orlando met the group with skepticism when they first arrived in his parish and that drives his continual involvement and oversight, though much of what happens in weekly gatherings is still beyond his immediate control, despite his attempts to maintain a watchful eye on the group. In typical meetings, it was Silvia Escobar, the energetic young woman who served as president, who led the meetings, read the scripture passage for the day, and interpreted that passage for general discussion. While Orlando often arrived for the second half of the meetings, and was sure to give his own, sanctioned interpretation of the passages under consideration, as well as historical or other context that Silvia did not typically provide, the tenor of the meetings changed when he entered the room, generally moving from robust discussion to muted endorsement of the priest's claims. Indeed, in 2011, soon after the establishment of Juan XXIII in Chillanes in 2009, several members of the group petitioned the diocese to have Orlando removed to a different parish, claiming he was obstructing progress in the local church. Supporters of Orlando filed a counter petition with more than twelve hundred signatures, resulting in his more or less permanent assignment to the town. The fracas led to greater cooperation between hierarchy and the lay group, but Orlando is always careful to qualify his support by reminding charismatics of the importance of church history, authority, and teaching. Charismatics may have gained social and spiritual capital, but they must deploy it within the system, at least in formal group settings.

These tensions between Catholicism as a hierarchically organized religion and vehicle to charismatic personal experience reflect broader economic and social realities as Ecuador has embraced leftist leadership at the national level at the same time that its economy has become more neoliberal in its focus on private capital and global markets, and as Ecuador continues to experience a growing middle class. "Los Juanes," as those involved in the Juan XXIII movement have come to be called in Chillanes, reflect larger shifts away from centrally controlled hierarchies and toward a politics, and an economy, of individualized, privatized experiences that may be shared in group settings but that are, at the end of the day, one's own.

ACCESO: THE RISE OF THE ECUADORIAN MIDDLE CLASS

There is no question that Ecuador's middle class, measured as households with access to between US$10 to $20 per capita per day, has grown significantly between 1995 and 2014.[5] Pew Center and World Bank data show that while 8 percent of Ecuadorians were middle class in in 2001, by 2011 that figure had risen to 21 percent, placing Ecuador slightly ahead of Latin America as a whole (Kochlar 2015, 24). The growth has come from upward mobility, with most new members of the middle class having been classified as "poor" in previous surveys (Ferreira et al. 2012, 3).

The contours of this economic mobility are variable and highly localized, though analysts have identified that more years of education, as well as stable government spending on health and education programs, correlates with upward mobility into middle-class incomes (Ferreira et al. 2012, 6). Certainly this is the case in Chillanes, where government services ranging from the local public hospital to a branch campus of the state university to national and municipal records offices to the privatization of phone services and collection of sales taxes have reoriented many of the ways in which people do business with the state and with each other. Another factor has been the steady decrease in interest that banks, both private and national, charge for loans. In 1996, the average annual rate for loans, as set by the Central Bank of Ecuador, was 54.5 percent. Rates fell significantly after Ecuador moved from the sucre to the U.S. dollar in 2000 and then more after Correa's government included banking reform in the 2008 Constitution and worked on more general financial reform in the country. By 2013, lending rates were at 3.85 percent (Banco Central del Ecuador). In addition, the Correa reforms defined the financial sector more broadly than did previous governments, expanding to include cooperatives and member-based organizations. The *Programa de Finanzas Populares*, established by the Correa administration in 2008 to expand lending to smaller financial cooperatives, had the goal of increasing popular access to lending. It also had the goal of increased regulation of banking practices such as maximum fees on transactions, taxes on capital leaving the country, and new regulations designed to limit the economic and political power of the financial industry in the country. Prior to the 2008 regulations, for example, banks owned most of Ecuador's major television stations (Weisbrot, Johnston, and Lefebvre 2013, 3). All of these reforms, in addition to a housing program (MIDUVI) that allowed many to own a home for the first time, and continuing remittances from Ecuadorians who had left the country to work in Spain, Italy, the United States, and other locations during the financial crisis of 2000, contributed to an ability to obtain and invest capital that was previously unimaginable in places like Chillanes.

One compelling example of the growing middle class in rural Ecuador is the Lucio family. Mercedes continues to pursue agriculture as a primary economic activity, growing corn, beans, and blackberries on lands she owns and rents close to town and raising livestock for slaughter and sale. Mercedes's two sons are police officers, providing them with salaries that are steady and allowing both men to marry. In recent years, and as a result of the economic reforms that have made low-interest loans available, both men have also purchased private vehicles for their families. Ligia has also taken advantage of lower interest rates, investing in a copy machine in 2000 that drew local high school students into the family dry goods store that occupies the bottom half of their house in droves to reproduce workbooks and other school materials. In 2008 Ligia purchased four computers and a modem and set up one of Chillanes's first internet cafés. When broadband arrived in 2012, she upgraded her equipment and continues to do good business renting computer time to kids who want to game or surf the web, adults who need to craft presentations or reports, and community members wanting to video chat with relatives abroad. Her computer business is far more profitable than the flour, candy, and party decorations that sustained the family, along with Mercedes's agricultural endeavors, in the decades before.

When Ligia decided to marry in 2009, she and her fiancé, Alfaro, along with Ligia's daughter, Sofia, departed for the civil ceremony on Alfaro's motorcycle, a considerable luxury at a time when there were few private vehicles, and no taxis, in town. After the church ceremony several days later, the family held a large celebration in a vacant cement house that had been recently purchased by one of Mercedes's sisters who continues to live in Spain. When Ligia and Alfaro had their first child in 2012, they went to the hospital in their own truck, a purchase made possible by Ligia's growing business and by Alfaro's employment driving heavy machinery for a private company contracted to build a road connecting Chillanes to the coastal city of Guayaquil and then for the Municipio de Chillanes. Though the couple owns land outside of town, it is notable that they do not make their living primarily in agriculture, and neither do most young people who grew up in the region. In the smaller communities around

FIGURE 6. Riding to the Wedding

Chillanes, many houses are abandoned, and the population of the province continues to shift as young adults seek salaried positions in more urban areas such as Guaranda and outside the province in cities such as Guayaquil, Quito, Cuenca, and Riobamba.[6]

Ligia and Alfaro's story, including the fact that they could afford the church wedding and the large celebration that followed, points to the many ways that a changing economic environment affects the ways people engage with the communities in which they live, including religious communities. Access to capital from remittances and favorable banking conditions, as well as to global information streams from internet media sources and relatives abroad, has reoriented horizons of possibility in significant ways. This is especially true for women. Market women in Chillanes are no longer the only ones selling agricultural goods on the days designated for such exchanges. As the market has expanded, so have opportunities for women to interact more directly, and more individually, with it. Women are shop owners, entrepreneurs, and actors connected directly with clients and customers. With more access to credit and to markets via privatized transport and virtual networks, structures such as the Virgen de las Nubes

Cooperative are less necessary than they used to be. The social and spiritual capital of the church can be harnessed by individual women in ways unimaginable previously or outright impossible.

As women are negotiating new roles in an increasingly middle-class economy, they are doing so in ways that often mirror the more individualized style of the Catholic charismatic movement, and the movement itself is home to several women who own small businesses or are otherwise actively participating in the new economy. Unlike the cooperative model, which attempted to leverage collective social capital rooted in gender and religious identities in order to create a cooperative economic engine, the approach to poverty reduction in Charismatic Catholicism is more individualized, focusing on charity rather than collective production.

PRAYING FOR ADVANCEMENT: CHARISMATIC APPROACHES TO POVERTY REDUCTION

There are many reasons Juan XXIII members are drawn to the movement and diverse ways in which members interact with the larger group, with each other, and with the institutional church once they have gone through the retreat experience. For many in Chillanes, the decision to try a retreat and then become actively involved with charismaticism was sparked by a desire to improve their circumstances, which they described as better health, family relationships, economic standing, or rectifying a perceived distance from God. In many instances, joining Juan XXIII was a step people used to keep a *promesa*, a promise made to God in exchange for divine favor.

Elena Sánchez, for example, joined Juan XXIII not only to improve herself, but as an act of hope for curing Silvia, who had been ill as a child, a story she related when I asked why she had decided to participate as a missionary with the church in Quito.

> First it was because I asked of God, well, it wasn't that I asked him that way, as I was going to tell you, it's just that—ah! The better question is, why did I join God? It was because my daughter had a serious illness when she was nine. And it was going to turn out badly. We had to treat her for a year and then see how it would turn out. So it was in desperation. God! Who else can help me? God, God can help me! And so I joined. Or rather, we glued ourselves to God [*apeguémenos a*

Dios], we glued ourselves to God. We started going on missions with the group [Juan XXIII].

After Silvia was cured of her illness, Elena was determined to remain glued, commenting that it "makes no sense to distance oneself from God, who has everything."

Rosita Quinatoa recounted a similar story, though she turned to God to remedy extreme poverty rather than illness. Because she so succinctly describes the conditions that make leaving poverty so difficult in Ecuador's rural economy—and also a close alliance between mystical events and economic advancement—it is worth taking some time to consider a lengthy story she told me one afternoon when I went to ask about her involvement with the Charismatic Catholic movement.

Rosita was in her forties at the time of the interview, married for several decades, and the mother of several children who were either adults or teenagers. The interview took place in Rosita's living room, a large space furnished with a mass-produced couch, several chairs, and a table. The living room was connected via a small window to a modern kitchen with a gas stove and refrigerator and to several smaller rooms and a bathroom via a hallway, a configuration indicative of the house's recent construction date and of relative wealth. Older houses in Chillanes typically do not have indoor plumbing, kitchens with space for refrigerators, or open designs that allow for easy passage between kitchens and living areas.

The day of the interview, Rosita invited me in, offered me some tea and bread, and then nervously settled in as I asked questions about what she did in a typical day, who lived with her and did what job in the household, and how long they had lived in the house. Then I turned to what became the main subject of the interview, her involvement in Juan XXIII and her experiences as a Catholic in rural Ecuador.

JD: You're a Catholic?
RQ: Yes.
JD: And what do you do as a Catholic?
RQ: I give catechism to children. For example, on Sunday, as I was telling you, you need to go for the confirmation service at the church. Because my students will be there, three groups of them. And tomorrow I have a meeting with their parents. We're going to do the confirmation in groups of students.

JD: I see. And for how many years . . . ?
RQ: It's, let's see, it's going to be ten years.
JD: That's quite a bit.
RQ: Yes, thanks be to God, little by little I've been learning it.
JD: What made you decide to be a catechist?
RQ: It's as I've been telling you, I had a miracle.

Rosita then proceeded to tell her story.

Yes, you see, it's that we were poor. Really poor, you see. And my husband was still in high school, and I was only in my fourth year of high school [out of six years in the Ecuadorian system]. Imagine! And I got married. And we didn't have—I worked as a cook in the nursery school. The people were bad, I tell you. The cooks ate the food and didn't give any to the children. Staff took things. We didn't have anything. It was really complicated. The children, one of them cried, and another—Holy cow! It was really complicated. And we didn't have, we didn't have any place to live. I lived in a rented place, and my husband worked making pants, as a tailor.

When I finished high school my son was three years old, and I filled out the papers. I filled out the papers to send my husband to the Police Academy [giggles]. He had graduated from high school, so he was eligible. And so I went to the church, and I got on my knees, and there were all the saints, Santa Rita, all of them. And I knelt and asked their favor that they would perform a miracle and help me with my husband. Because he was of age, he was already twenty-eight. He was old, older than me by three years. And I said, "My God," I said, "Help me, Lord. You have to help me. If you help me and my husband goes to the Police Academy, I will help you by teaching catechesis."

And it wasn't quick, no, it wasn't quick as my children were still small, but one night, when we were living in the upper part of town, renting a room. One night, I was sleeping, and God helped my husband. He had a broken leg and he was praying that nobody touch him [during the police physical], not anywhere on his body, so they wouldn't feel his leg. And it's because blessed Santa Rita told him, "Go ahead and go," that from the moment he started at the academy, no one laid a hand on him. "Go ahead and go," she told him. He broke the leg because he was drunk, he was fighting. He was a young guy, seventeen years old, and someone kicked him and broke his leg. And blessed Santa Rita, it's as I told you, the man checking recruits, he checked without feeling, but only by looking, and Santa Rita blessed it and nothing happened.

After that, one night I dreamed of Jesus. I dreamed of my Jesus. And I had put a hanging over a doorway, and I tell you that I saw an image of Jesus on the hanging. And that made my head spin. I put the hanging over the door, on the wall. I had it there because the door was old and black, black, black [with smoke from cooking fires]. I hung it with a nail here, a nail there, because the tiny little living room was very close to the little kitchen because in there, in the little room, we also had the bed, and the stove. We were very poor and couldn't rent an apartment. We were very poor and didn't have enough. And I tell you he, my Jesus, helped me. And so I started helping with catechism. And on the night I decided it was time to start, I was sound asleep, and he appeared to me on that painting over there [large intake of breath to show amazement]. I said, "Oh, Oh! Clearly it's the promesa I made, and I have to respond. I have to help with catechism." So from then on I started helping with catechism, and I also put my children in the classes, all the way until my son also entered the Police Academy. And how that made me tired, to the point where I was about to retire from being a catechist. And that's when the brothers of Juan XXIII asked me, "Do you want to go on a retreat?" I said yes, but I was going to let teaching catechesis go. And there [on the retreat] is where I started thinking more about God, I started thinking more about God, and there I said, "No." When I die I will quit teaching catechesis. That is, it was in the retreat that I lived. It was so nice. How beautiful that I lived that day for God. And so now I have decided that no, no, no, no, I am not going to retire. I will help in the church. And so that's why I help, and I ask God that nothing happens to my children.

My son also drank every time he came home, my eldest son. And look, now he has a salary. He was drinking every time he came home. He drank with his friends, they would come and call him. And so I asked my God to take him into the movement. He went on a retreat, and he stopped drinking. And I asked God to make him study, because he didn't want to know anything. But now he works as a police officer. He studies. I asked my God, he needed to prepare himself. Because I'm old, it's a different thing. But because he's young, he has to defend himself. And so it's because of God that he's studying.

So yes, I'm very happy, and I tell you that God has helped me, blessed me. Because I was poor. My husband was also poor. And I tell you that working that way, in other people's houses, even with me helping, we couldn't make it. And because I received that miracle, my son, my husband, became police officers. My son became that because, from the time he was little, he wanted to be like his father. And it hurt me. Imagine, a tailor! Without a car, without a house. Tailors live that way, poor and growing older without anything. And God helped me, and for that reason I have this house. Because with a tailor, no one was going to give me a loan. But with a police officer, we could get a loan. And with a loan we built my house. With a loan we've bought a little piece of land over there, we have it planted in sweet corn, with the loan. With the loan we've bought a car, we can go on trips. And a cow. Who's going to give a loan to a tailor?

Rosita's story highlights the ways Charismatic Catholicism allows for shared, yet individualized experiences of the divine as it intersects with financial and social concerns. As is common in classical Latin American Catholicism, she made a promesa, a promise to God, often through a saint, to serve the church or commit an act of penance in exchange for a specific favor. For many Catholics in Chillanes, promesas are fulfilled by making an annual pilgrimage to Guayco, a local shrine dedicated to an apparition of the Virgin Mary, or to the southern Ecuadorian site of Cisne, where pilgrims engage in a three-day processional that moves the image of the Virgin from her home in that small town to the cathedral in Loja, the provincial capital. Indeed, many promesas are requested and fulfilled at pilgrimage sites, which are often filled with petitionary cards and other objects left in gratitude for requests that have been granted.

What is striking about Rosita's story, then, is not that she made a request of God through Santa Rita or that she promised to become a catechist in the church if God saw fit to deter the searching hand of a doctor at the Police Academy physical. Rather, it is the way her narrative reveals how charismatic modes of being Catholic circumvent the more formalized, institutional forms of the church by allowing the accumulation, dispersal, and linkage of spiritual capital to larger economic realities. The Jesus on the wall of Rosita's house—the house built with a loan procured because her husband is no longer a tailor but enjoys a salaried position with the police force—did not appear there at the behest of the church, or the spiritual capital accumulated in its offices. The miracle, and its attendant goods, was personal and did not require the mediation of the institution, even in so much as a procession or shrine.

This is an important shift in the way that many charismatic individuals negotiate religious worldviews, economic realities, and what might be best described as middle-class aspirations for social advancement. As John Burdick, Virginia Garrard-Burnett, Andrew Chesnut, and other scholars have argued, Pentecostal forms of Christianity offer ways of negotiating social realities linked with poverty that are not dependent on changing a broader system. Unlike liberation theology's emphasis on social justice and societal and political change, Pentecostals, especially those in Latin America, often name poverty, drug addiction, corrupt governance, or domestic violence as demons in need of exorcism rather than inequality. Rosita's story does not name demons, but it does point to individualized solutions to the reality of structural poverty and to religious explanations for those individualized solutions. Jesus appeared on her wall; the promise she made was hers alone to keep, even if she fulfilled that promise through the institutional mechanism of catechism classes. The risk of the promise, in other words, was hers alone, as was the reward for a promise well made and well kept.

This is not to say, however, that Rosita and other members of Juan XXIII do not experience Catholicism, or their particular form of charismaticism, in isolation. The retreats are powerful for people because they focus on individual experiences but then amplify those experiences in relation to others as they share them in an intimate group setting. After the retreat, the small group meetings continue to encourage members to share personal stories and to reflect on divine gifts with each other. The intense experience of the retreat and the support of the group are key for members as it frames Catholicism as something to be experienced, powerfully and most important at the individual level but then shared and reinforced laterally and in relationship to peers.

The nature of spiritual capital is thus quite different between liberationist projects such as the Virgen de las Nubes group and charismatic organizations such as Juan XXIII. In the Virgen de las Nubes Cooperative, spiritual capital was collective capital, described using collective terms ("woman," "Catholic"), and used to define and uphold the collective economic project. The risk of failure in that project was a collective risk. While there is still a clear and powerful group identity among the Juanes ("Catholic," "Apostolic," "Brothers"), members' individual relationships with God, with family, and with society are the focus of every meeting. One risks one's own identity as he or she goes on retreat and sees the movie of his or her life, but there is not a sense of group capital or group risk. Instead, the experience of charismaticism is one of shared individualism rather than collective effort or hierarchical response. One has "to live it to feel it," not, as the cooperative members may have put it, "shared it to earn it."

The charismatic approach to poverty and other forms of suffering is thus one that focuses less on structural change and more on conversion, deep faith experiences in sacrament and liturgy, and charity. Members of Juan XXIII are commonly catechists and missionaries, and the group also organizes trips to the Chillanes jail and retirement home to visit prisoners and the elderly. Missions regularly feature community works projects such as church painting or help with individual residences. In addition, members often share personal financial concerns in meetings, and in one instance banded together to help a member who was in imminent danger of having his land taken by the state as the result of a tax dispute. It is a project of no project, focused on immediate needs and right relationships with God rather than long-term structural change.[7]

It is this focus on charity over structure and a lack of consideration for broader systems of oppression that characterized liberation theology that make Juan XXIII and other forms of charismaticism easily cognate with Ecuador's burgeoning neoliberal economy. When Rosita speaks of bargaining directly with God for the economic advancement of her family as she prayed for her husband's entrance into the Police Academy, and thus a chance at middle-class existence including a salary and financial viability in the eyes of the banking system, she was not criticizing a system that values tailors less than policemen or that makes sufficient housing difficult to come by. She was not asking banks to give loans to tailors. She did not ask for an education system that might provide more for her potentially errant son. In a similar manner, members regularly prayed for healing from physical illness but never that the small state hospital in Chillanes be improved or that access to the regional clinics may become easier. In the project of no project, each crisis is to be handled in isolation, using flexible means—prayer, private funds raised on an ad hoc basis, social capital within the group, and, on rare occasions, the resources of the institutional church—to solve the problem at hand. Calling such an ethic "Catholicized neoliberalism," Andrea Muehlbach (2013, 455) explains it as a "moral style, . . . an ethic or cultural sensibility that is less ideology than diffuse disposition, less explicit doctrine than 'collective psycho-moral stance' (Appadurai 2011, 519)." In focusing on charity rather than collective work or social change, charismatics in Chillanes adopt such a moral style. While they base it in biblical contexts more than Muehlbach may account for, often having long conversations about biblical texts and teaching, the fact that such discussions happen among peers, with only occasional clerical oversight, supports her description as less explicitly doctrinal and more in conversation with the cultural contexts in which it takes place.

One explanation for the rapid growth of Charismatic Catholicism in Latin America broadly, and in Chillanes specifically, is thus that it reflects the changing social and economic realities, the moral styles, in which it operates. As Chillanes, along with other localities in the country and the continent, begins to develop a middle class that allows some people to move ahead economically through entrepreneurship supported by newly available loans and more stable currencies, Chillanenses may be less likely to want or need the "projects" of the liberationist or international development eras, when such individualized action was virtually impossible and almost never profitable. New ways of being Catholic are tied to new ways of being Ecuadorian, which are, in turn, tied to new access to credit, new chances of upward mobility, and new expectations about living standards tied to consumer goods that range from cell phones to private vehicles.

THE FAMILY THAT PRAYS TOGETHER: GENDER IN JUAN XXIII

In her seminal 1995 book, *The Reformation of Machismo,* Elizabeth Brusco detailed the ways in which evangelical Christianity encourages a reformation of male roles in the household, establishing a culture that encourages men to attend to domestic tasks and responsible roles as fathers and spouses. As Brusco notes, however, the reform is one-sided, and women are not likewise encouraged to take on public leadership roles, though she does argue for its revolutionary potential.

> The outcome of conversion [of men, from an orientation to the street to that of the home], then, is that the boundaries of public (male) life and private (female) life are redrawn and the spheres themselves are redefined. The relative power positions of the spouses change. That is not to say that the women now have more power over their husbands. In evangelical households the husband may still occupy the position of head, but his relative aspirations have changed to coincide with those of his wife. I believe that this last fact constitutes a change of revolutionary proportions. (Brusco 1995, 137)

At least in its incarnation in Chillanes, Charismatic Catholicism appears to come closer to a complete reformation and more realized revolution as women take on powerful leadership roles and both men and women are encouraged to focus on improving what Pope Francis calls the domestic church by establishing loving, respectful relationships at home.

Those relationships were often the focus of the Thursday meetings held by Juan XXIII members, which averaged about twenty-five participants, usually slightly more than half of whom were women. On most evenings, two or three married couples came together, usually sitting next to each other in the room. As noted previously, Silvia Escobar generally ran the meetings, read the scripture, and then framed the discussion. Members generally looked to her for guidance not just on meeting logistics, such as which passage was to be read; they also seemed to accept her commentary on scripture as instructional and authoritative. When she spoke about the various burdens akin to Jesus's cross, for example, no one sought to challenge her interpretation of Jesus's words but rather joined in the conversation, augmenting her comments and expanding on what she said. Until Padre Orlando came into the room, she was firmly in charge, occupying a position of authority on which several members commented positively. She was frequently described by Juanes as "enthusiastic," "smart," and "passionate," and I never heard anyone question her legitimacy as a leader for the group, despite her gender, relatively young age, or status as a single woman. In this lay context, which encouraged men and women to meet together after the gender-segregated retreats, female leadership appeared to be expected, even invited, especially as it led to frequent discussions about the domestic church and God's wish for harmonious and prosperous families.

On the evening the group talked about heavy burdens, for example, and Silvia mentioned that many marriages were like "sleeping with the enemy," the conversation continued with suggestions for improving spousal relationships, with members talking about "respect" and "understanding" as key components in good marriages. Notably, these attitudes were expected of both men and women and contrasted to a perceived popular culture in which women were presumed to be overly subservient and blind to their own needs. In another meeting, members discussed closeness as an important element in relationships, and one meeting attendee related a story about a couple who used to view pornography together as a means of cultivating closeness until they felt that God would not approve. This led to a lengthy conversation about media influences in the home, especially on children, and the dangers that popular culture presents to solid relationships through ideas such as "friends with benefits." The group roundly criticized such ideas and ended the meeting in a discussion about closeness, sharing household chores, and the need to be fiscally responsible. Again, these values were contrasted to what many saw as majority Ecuadorian values that might allow men to work less in the household, to spend hours away from home with friends, or to spend money freely on alcohol, gambling, cigarettes, or a partner outside the marriage relationship. In this particular discussion, someone wondered if Protestants might be worth emulating as they seemed to prohibit such things more aggressively. Silvia and then Orlando both emphasized that Catholics also discourage such behavior, even more, and that the real goal was to live as God intends, especially when it comes to things like fiestas.

In all of these discussions, women spoke frequently, and men often offered additional comments that responded to and supported what the women had to say. Many suggested that a greater commitment to home life, including more attention to household roles, was part of being a retirista. Indeed, one hermano found himself shunned from the group when he fathered a child with a mistress, an act that several people told me about, emphasizing that he had done so *after* the retreat, making it harder to forgive. One retirista talked about home life and the difficulty of making complete changes in it after joining the movement.

Retirista: My life changed completely. Before, I was distant from the church. It was over there. I would hear the bells ringing, good, good. Now, no. Now I attend, I like going to church. If I need to take communion, I do so when my conscience is clean. If I need to help the priest, I read the lectionary. So my participation, my closeness with the Lord, is completely improved. Mine and my husband's.

JD: Really.

Retirista: My mother as well. She's been Catholic her whole life, and now she's a retirista.

JD: So the whole family is involved.

Retirista: More or less, yes.

JD: And has your home life changed?

Retirista: [small hesitation] I wouldn't say 100 percent, because it's a process. It's not a 180-degree change. It's a process. And in this process there are traps, there are criticisms. You encounter a little of everything on the journey. But that's where you have to stand firm in the faith and follow what you learned on the retreat. You have to let the Lord call your faith on fire so that it grows. Don't put it out! We look for that, a faith on fire that doesn't go out but that burns. And we owe all our days to the Lord, to our Holy Mother. We ask the Lord and our Holy Mother to intervene in any difficulty. That's the way it is.

Group members, both men and women, frequently highlighted better home relationships as a benefit of being a retirista, often through the group's ability to focus on what its president, Silvia Escobar, described as "gender equality" or what one retirista, Walter Ayala, spoke about as "improved family relationships." In a lengthy interview, Silvia described her role as president and the parallel nature of her position and the parish priest's.

SE: My responsibility [as president] is to try to have all the members [*hermanos*] come to meetings, or also to visit them in their homes. I also bring information, and help people get into the retreats. I also look for ways to help individuals, communities, all of that. I also support the parish, though this is difficult because they have so many activities.

JD: And this takes a lot of time?

SE: Yes. For example, when I go on a retreat it's Friday, Saturday, and Sunday.

JD: You go to all the retreats?

SE: When I don't have extra activities. There are times when I have classes and I can't go because my university doesn't allow me to miss. I can't then. But in general, I try to be at as many activities as I can and to bring as many people as I can.

JD: And I've noticed you direct all of the [weekly] meetings.

SE: Ah, yes. I do direct the meetings a little. I try to make things run smoothly. I want to be the person who thinks and believes the same things in my house as I do outside. I try to live that in my personal life. As I am in my house, I am in public. Because I'm not going to know a live Christ outside and a dead Christ inside. And so this is what I try to do in my community, in my parish—to live that.

JD: And what's the best thing about being a member of Juan XXIII, of being president?

SE: The nice thing about being president is that I get to travel to various parishes, to get to know many places. The part that's also a big responsibility is that I help, or at least contribute to, the brothers and sisters in the movement. I try to give counsel, a message, make visits, do social work. I try to work with that perspective. It gives me a little advantage, you could say. Because when you are genuine, people will listen. Sometimes, for example, people are fighting in a household. I go to visit as president, and we talk, and we come to a happy conclusion. God put us in this world to be happy, not unhappy! . . . I encounter a lot of different situations, but it's a good experience. . . .

JD: It seems like you have many of the same responsibilities as the priest.

SE: [laughs] Not exactly, but more or less! I'm not going to get rid of him, though.

After assuring me that Padre Orlando remains firmly in charge of teaching as he "guides" the lay movement and that this is why she immediately hands control of the weekly meetings to him when he comes in after she has started the discussion and led the prayer, Silvia went on to reflect on the ways the movement is changing gender roles for both men and women in the context of greater changes in Ecuadorian society. Noting that slightly more than half of Juan XXIII members are women, she went on to reflect on the reason for this.

SE: Men work, so it's harder for them to attend meetings, and sometimes men are more reluctant, too. There's a little machismo here, and we carry that a bit. We're leaving that aspect behind little by little, and we try to maintain gender equity, as we call it today. But we still carry a little machismo.

JD: While we're on the subject, how are the lives of women here, in Chillanes, in Ecuador?

SE: In reality, the women, we're harder workers [laughs].

JD: You work harder?

SE: It's that women, you could say, are responsible for the household. They're the head of the household. I know that husbands work, physically maintain things, and all that. But women form the household. They have greater responsibility for the formation of children, of the household, and maintaining stability, though this depends on the husband also. Because, as I was just saying, machismo still exists, when in actuality it is the woman who is also working [outside the home].

JD: Yes, I think more than before.

SE: So it's changing a little bit. Because before, it was the woman in the house and the man at work. And I don't know if you've gone out sometimes to the plaza on the weekends and seen some husbands drinking or gone during the week when women are carrying heavy sacks of goods while their husbands hang around the stores. This has been changing gradually, and now women are the administrators of the home. It's starting to change here because generally in the city women are independent, and each one can do what she wants. But here we still carry stricter notions about what men and women can do.

JD: That can be difficult.

SE: Yes, and it's a little complicated because women are not generally free because sometimes husbands are very machista but can be impotent or ineffective at home. I've seen this, too. But little by little—for example, in the group what we're seeking is that men and women are equally free and that that they have equality, that they have the same responsibilities and deserve the same respect.

Several things are notable in these remarks. First, like the recent pontifical emphasis on the domestic church, Silvia and other members of Juan XXIII make the home a central part of religious life and begin with the assumption that a happy home, free of conflict, is a godly home. In identifying women as the "head of the household," however, and explicitly mentioning women's roles working outside the home, Silvia broadens the scope of the domestic church in ways that allow for its direct interaction with larger economic and social realities. Like the reformation of machismo that Brusco identified in Protestant movements in the late 1980s and early 1990s, Silvia and other members of the charismatic movement seek to redefine masculinity in a way that includes the home as much as if not more than the streets. Unlike Brusco's reformation, however, Silvia's vision for equality also includes women who leave the house to work and lead organizations and gives credit to women as "administrators" in the domestic sphere.

The model of gender crafted by Juan XXIII in retreats, meetings, and other activities is one that in many ways addresses inequalities for women in the home and to some extent in public life. In meetings and other private and public venues such as the mass, women are encouraged to take leadership roles, even as men are encouraged to become more cooperative and active at home, in church, and in the larger community. These cooperative roles are coded as godly and as one's duty as a loyal Catholic who has had a direct encounter with Jesus as savior during a retreat. In this way, spiritual capital that begins with an individual religious awakening can, ideally, support evolving visions of gender equity and cooperation in homes, communities, and the church more broadly, though, as the retirista interviewed above points out, such change is hard to come by "100 percent."

The introduction of Charismatic Catholicism to Chillanes offered new ways for Chillanenses to negotiate religious, gender, and economic identities that were, and are, markedly different from those offered by liberationist projects such as the Virgen de las Nubes Cooperative. In the charismatic model, individual encounters with the divine are the basis for the reformation of self and society. Juan XXIII offers members a chance to have a direct encounter with Jesus such that they reform their lives, dedicating themselves to charitable acts, better and more equitable homes, and renewed participation in traditional church activities such as the mass, catechisms, and the burgeoning mission movement. In this model, social change comes through charity rather than through cooperative projects, a system that resembles many Ecuadorians' experiences in an economic system that has privatized and supported increasing numbers of middle-class citizens. Private capital, spiritual and financial, once difficult to come by in banks or the church, is now offered by both. For participants such as Rosita Quinatoa, to embrace one has been to reap the rewards of the other as she credits her dedication to a more individualized and, by her account, realized Catholicism for her relative economic stability and upward mobility. In a similar manner, charismaticism's emphasis on cooperative and peaceful home lives that involve the individual efforts of men and women has opened at least some space for men to be more active in domestic spheres even as women can claim to be in charge there and, to a certain degree, in official church leadership roles as they participate in things like weekly meetings. This kind of flexible social production, not dependent on outside organization or cooperation led by an organizing authority, has adapted a neoliberal emphasis on individualism, self-reliance, and independence that reformats earlier Catholic emphases on social justice, moving liberationist concerns from the political and structural into the private spaces of the home and the heart.

In contrast, the Virgen de las Nubes Cooperative remained collectivist, often subventing the role of individuals as it held up values of cooperation and group identity rooted not in individual religious experience but in shared religious tradition and in a shared gender identity that allowed for discussion of home spaces, and even replication of them, without an overt mission to reform them. Because men were barred from the organization, women were encouraged to reform their status as breadwinners in a changing economy without necessarily reforming home relationships, roles, or understandings. The cooperative was a space where women "de-stressed," often finding refuge from difficult home situations, but the exclusion of men from formal meetings, activities, or visions of success as laid out by the parent organization meant that reforming economic roles was women's work, work to be undertaken as a class through economic means. The domestic church did not factor in, often to the frustration of women struggling to work in the cheese factory as they continued to be responsible for children, chores, and agricultural tasks at home. The demands of the domestic church, along with a cooperative market life, did not align neatly, or successfully, with Ecuador's changing cultural and economic realities.

Finally, the introduction of Charismatic Catholicism in Chillanes raises the specter of emotion as an important component of social capital in religious and development processes.[8] When Charismatic Catholics in Chillanes describe the retreats, and their relationship with the church (or tellingly, with God or Jesus) after the retreats, they do so in emotional terms. Rosita describes herself as "very happy" because her life improved after her retreat experience, and Elena's exhortation that one "has to live it to feel it" emphasizes the emotional nature of the charismatic experience. In meetings where singing, public confession, and shared prayer are commonplace, emotions are much more on display, and much more central, than in more conventional Roman Catholic services, something charismatics value highly as they speak about the emotional nature of the retreats and the emotional connections they form in the group as they continue to meet, pray, work, and support the church together. While emotion is present, however, Padre Orlando's fear that the group would become entirely based on emotive responses to church teachings (*puros aleluyias, no más*) does not seem to have been realized as retiristas continue to attend regular mass, serve as catechists, and engage in charitable work in the community. Where third wave Pentecostals have been widely criticized for shifting responsibility for problems of poverty from the state or social structures onto the shoulders of individuals deemed "possessed" by demons, Charismatic Catholics walk a middle road. They are open to an emotional spirituality that recognizes healing and hardship but one that does not blame the supernatural for life's daily problems or rely entirely on it to solve them. Emotions—joy, sorrow, frustration, fear, gratitude—are channeled in charismatic worship and practices to build a network of meaningful relationships, which are then presumed to spur positive acts and attitudes in the world. Change starts from within, working its way out. In this way, Charismatic Catholicism is a hybrid space where it is possible to have and express emotions without many of the facets that early Latin American Pentecostalism exhibited. In the Chillanes church there were no demons, few alleluias, and Juan XXIII retained some sense of community involvement. By choosing a project of no project, retiristas are not choosing the almost entirely individual focus exhibited by third wave Pentecostals but are instead retaining a Catholic character, even as the movement is more neoliberal in its emphasis on individual experience and charity over widespread structural change. In this way, Charismatic Catholicism appears to be a good match for Chillanes's growing middle class, which is less reliant on state programs or cooperative economic efforts and increasingly benefiting from individual, small business ventures made possible by individual loans and more access to education, transportation, and virtual networks.

This embrace of emotion as a positive force for action did not manifest in the daily operations or orientation of the Virgen de las Nubes group. Even where shared gender or religious identity was identified as a source of social strength, these were not considered emotional bonds but rather shared positionality that would lead to mutual understanding and heightened likelihood of cooperation. Indeed, when the women expressed emotion in group meetings, usually in times of tension, they were criticized by local administrators, and sometimes among themselves, for not being professional or for not "cooperating" to the degree expected. As a liberationist project, the cooperative sought to address injustice and create change by means of economic mechanisms first, a structure presumed to lead to emotional fulfillment and general improvement in happiness and fulfillment. While socias often described the group in emotional terms—as a place of camaraderie and relief from stress—such emphases were not repeated by administrators, who instead spoke frequently about the power of solidarity around issues of gender and economic success.

The collapse of the cooperative just before the introduction of Charismatic Catholicism in Chillanes and at the same time that a middle-class economy was beginning to be established highlights changing relationships between religiosity, identities, and economic realities that have influenced the way cooperative members interpret their experiences and the ways those experiences are linked to ideas about being Catholic and women. It is to those interpretations that we now turn.

FIVE

"We Are Also Outside"

Religious and Gender Identities When Development Fails

Field Notes, June 28, 2006

The time had come, 5:30 on a Wednesday evening, for the remaining socias of the Virgen de las Nubes quesera project to figure out what to do. We gathered at Josefa's new house, complete with plumbing but not yet endowed with electricity, sitting in the yard to take advantage of the remaining light. The women took stock of the situation. In an informal count of membership, they could think of eighteen remaining socias, though three have announced their intentions to resign from the group. That left fifteen, of whom nine were in attendance.

The meeting was run by Josefa, who began by saying, "Today we're going to fix things. That's why we're here." She kept the mood light but explained that she and Jesus had gone to see Padre Mateo about the quesera's debt, and he had said they needed to hold a meeting and decide what to do. They could try and find a way to keep the quesera and work their way out of debt, or they could sell it, pay off their creditors, and divide whatever remains [the land and building were deeded to the cooperative by PH in 2005]. *She presented the options, let silence come over the group for a moment, and then made it clear that she doesn't want to sell it as it was "too much work" to purchase the land and construct the building and the business in the first place. Jesus echoed those sentiments, saying that she, too, would like to keep the project going. She was joined by Magdalena, who said that they have "always collaborated."*

This seemed to be the sentiment of the nine who had gathered, so Josefa then proposed that they figure out who was really a socia. "To be a socia you have to come to mingas [group workdays]*," she emphasized. Again, Magdalena joined her by saying, "We're completely adults. It's in our hands."*

This comment sparked Josefa to reflect on how they got into such dire straits. She said, "This is our fault, too [e.g., not just accounting mistakes made by a past president]. *We need to keep better books."*

The problem, the women decided, was that they had the administration of the plant confused with the accounting wing. Whoever runs the plant should not be in charge of the books. They took full responsibility for the setup. As one woman put it, "Nadie se puede tocar todo el orquesta. Es falla de todas" (No one can play every instrument in the orchestra. It's everyone's fault).

This meeting was the first of several over a three-year period during which the remaining Virgen de las Nubes Cooperative members struggled to find a way to pay off their debts, restart cheese-making operations in the quesera, and continue as a recognized women's group. The meetings exposed the financial reasons for the group's failure, which this chapter treats. They also reveal the ways the women and the leadership at Promoción Humana and FEPP viewed the failure of the cooperative in light of the religious and gender identities and values it was designed to promote. A full time line of events, reconstructed from legal documents, the Libro de Actas, and interviews with group members and community members, is available in the appendix.

Rather than focus exclusively on specific failures in accounting, leadership, or training, though these are certainly important, my emphasis throughout this chapter is on how such failures were experienced and internalized by cooperative members, an analysis that allows for an assessment of the risks and rewards of social capital as a development strategy. It also allows for an evaluation of development projects such as the Virgen de las Nubes Cooperative that attempt to harness religious values and perceived gender strengths alongside capitalist markets. What happened to the Catholic identity of the socias who claimed that the Catholic values of the group, especially those of solidarity, cooperation, and respect, were an important reason for the group's early success? And how do these same cooperative members, many of whom found the group even more important as a place to de-stress and harness support they did not necessarily encounter at home, talk about being women after the cooperative failed? What is at risk, in other words, when social capital of this kind is invested and lost?

WHAT HAPPENED: THE ANATOMY OF A FAILURE

After almost a decade of relative success making sweaters and other knitted goods, Eugenia Montero, the Promoción Humana promoter in charge of the Virgen de las Nubes group, approached the women at a regular meeting. According to the minutes recorded in the Libro de Actas, on October 16, 1997, she asked the women to consider buying a plot of land made available by a failed men's confraternity after delivering a reflection on John 7:37–39,[1] asking the women to "follow God" and "put into practice good communication among yourselves and to others, avoiding falling into evil, and practicing the Word of God in your spare time" (Libro de Actas 4). This was followed by a proposal on November 13 to buy the land so that they would have a place to make jams, have a community garden, and perhaps pasture animals. In the next meeting, she followed up by asking the women to "leave their selfishness behind, maintain their focus, seek out new activities, and always pray to God" (5). At the next recorded meeting, March 12, 1998, the group made a decision to buy the land for 25,000,000 sucres (about $5,555), a decision recorded this way:

> At 4:30 in the afternoon on the twelfth of March, 1998, an extraordinary meeting was called with most cooperative members, minus two—Jesus Galarza and Olga Tipan—attending. In this way, the decisions that were made were binding. The meeting was also attended by Eugenia Montero. We took up the issue of buying the land, and heard the opinion of Padre Mateo [Panteghini] about the Quilayacu land that is available for purchase. It measures 5,000 square meters and is valued at 25,000,000 sucres, which might be discounted. The proposed ideas [for the land] are as follows: implement a cheese-making project with the support of Padre Mateo. He will train us and facilitate the construction of the plant and support the buying of implements necessary

> for cheese production in the form of the Salesian operations for one year, teaching us [to make the cheese] in the same way as our colleagues have been taught. He will also assist with learning to buy the milk and with helping [community members] understand the benefits, such as bringing in milk and taking away whey. This is a way of working in the organization, and in addition it could also offer bigger projects for collaboration. We are in agreement with the proposal, and for this reason the signatures of all the cooperative members are here promising to go forward. Sra Magdalena Estrada, Sra Jesus Galarza, Sra Mercedes Huilca, Srta Estela Huilca, Sra Carmen Rodriguez, Sra Martha Manzano, Srta Silvia Samaneiego, Sra Julia Guamán, Sra Olga Tipan, Srta Silvia Moyano. (Libro de Actas 6)

The rest of the entry is a list of financial transactions made by the cooperative, including yarn purchases, payment of interest on microcredit loans, payment toward communal food used for meetings, money earned for the sale of sweaters and other knitted goods, and a summation of money owed the cooperative on the microcredit loans given through the community bank wing of the cooperative. At the end of the meeting, Eugenia Montero reminded the group that they need to give an annual report to PH in which all such transactions were to be recorded, explained, and balanced.

Having made the decision to move forward, the socias then elected two women to receive training in cheese production. Dora Quinaloa and Julia Guamán went to Salinas to learn cheese making. When they returned to Chillanes in 1998, the group started production in two houses in San Juan Pamba, gathering the milk required from local farmers and selling their product back to the consortium in Salinas. Meanwhile, the group made an agreement with Promoción Humana that allowed them to contribute half of the capital needed to purchase the land and build the quesera, most of which they would provide in the form of labor. This led immediately to questions within the group about how to value the labor of group members and if the spouses of socias should be hired preferentially as laborers or compensated for their work. At a meeting on October 3, 2000, after a discussion of cheese prices set by the consortium, a reminder from the group president that they still owed 50 percent of the construction costs to Promoción Humana, and a discussion about how the plant would obtain water, a socia took the floor and commented, "We should give opportunities for work to our spouses because they don't have many opportunities." According to the minutes, Eugenia responded to the request for preferential treatment by explaining that the craftsmen in charge of construction "have the authority to select whomever they want to work in accordance with their ability," going on to suggest that hiring spouses might "slow down the process" (Libro de Actas 19). There is no recorded response on the part of cooperative members, but as construction continued, several spouses did contribute labor and materials, resources for which they expected to be compensated but which were only vaguely noted in the financial sections of the Libro de Actas or were tallied as part of socias' contribution to the project (part of mingas) rather than as labor to be billed out. Thus while the cooperative's books did not show debts for the work, the men would eventually bill for their services, leaving the group with unpaid obligations, both fiscal and social.

Other early challenges included paying women who were already engaged in production work as the group began to make cheese on a regular basis. In a meeting held on November 16, 2000, with Eugenia Montero, after discussions about purchasing equipment, how to keep the cheese refrigerated and then move it to market, buying equipment, and painting the quesera, Julia Guamán asked to speak. "The workers request that we are paid more because the work is hard and leaves us alone, but we're only paid one dollar a day, and we end up paying that dollar to someone else who helps us [at home]," she said. Dora Quinaloa then added that because production was increasing and the cooperative was bringing in more milk, "We have to work more because there is so much milk. This requires us to get up very early, sometimes we get here as early as 3:00 a.m." (Libro de Actas 21). The minutes do not record a response to this request, though the next meeting with the PH promoter started with a reflection on Mary as a figure of humility and ended with a lengthy discussion of how the socias would pay the debt, especially as not all members appeared to be contributing equally to mingas and other aspects of the work. Again, those working in cheese production spoke about their long hours, and Eugenia ended the meeting by asking the group to revise their accounting practices such that every sale and payment was recorded, something she noted was not being done (Libro de Actas 22).

And indeed, as things went forward, opening biblical reflections focused on themes of unity, cooperation, and "being good" (*ser buenas*), even as the business portion of the meeting continued to address uneven participation among cooperative members, how to bring electricity and water to the new building, and how and when to pay the *lecheros*, the local farmers who were providing the milk with which the cheese was made, as well as how to compensate for the transportation of that milk to the production locations. Once a month, the cooperative president gave an overview of the financial status of the cooperative, which included small loans made out as part of the banco comunal, as well as continued orders for sweaters and other knitted goods and purchase of yarn to make those goods for the consortium. After a decision on December 14, 2000, to create two classes of cooperative members, one for the quesera and one only for knitting, after multiple complaints that not all cooperative members wanted to make cheese, all of these accounts were kept in several spiral-bound notebooks (Libro de Actas 22).

By the time the plant opened on October 22, 2002, the group had added guinea pig and pig production to their revenue stream, raising the animals for sale in the Chillanes market, and had planted the land around the quesera with corn for sale. These activities were meant to generate cash flow to cover debts for electricity and water that the cooperative had incurred in building the plant but had not paid off in the course of finishing the building. In 2005, the group received $2,500 from visiting American college students,[2] money they used to open a store in Chillanes's central plaza area where they hoped to sell their cheeses without having to move them to another market and where they also sold a few knitted and crocheted items. The majority of the cash infusion was used to purchase refrigerated display units necessary to keep the cheese in the store and to purchase a calf the group hoped to raise for sale but which died soon after purchase. The store was never successful and shut down a year after it opened. Silvia Moyano worked with the provincial government to secure funding for a new building for yogurt production, which was completed in 2005 and used briefly. Hopes the group held that yogurt, which is faster to make and which was to be marketed only in Chillanes, would bring in enough cash to cover their debts turned out to be overly optimistic. The quesera effectively ceased operations in 2006 with the group owing more than $5,000 to local farmers who had provided milk on credit, as well as to power and water companies. Yogurt production ceased at the same time, before the group was able to obtain the *registro sanitario* necessary for retail sale of their products on a larger scale. The plant went into receivership with Promoción Humana in late 2008, after Mateo Panteghini paid the rest of the original construction debt, and both buildings were locked, becoming inaccessible to cooperative members.

From 2006 to the end of 2009, Promoción Humana attempted to revive the cooperative, insisting that the women elect a board of directors and sending Eugenia Montero or another promoter to meet with the remaining socias on a regular basis. These meetings, often held in the field outside the quesera since the women did not have the key to access the building's second-story meeting room, focused on strategies to obtain enough regular milk deliveries to restart cheese production, arrange long-term debt repayment, and repair the relationships, both internal and external, damaged by the failure. Two of the last of these meetings, held on July 24 and July 30, 2009, are emblematic for the way they touched on the economic and social causes of the failure, the difficulties the socias faced restarting production, and the competing visions of success between the remaining socias and Promoción Humana.

The July 24 meeting started with a prayer asking God to bless the work of the women and PH more broadly, as well as an Our Father and Hail Mary. Eugenia Montero then explained why she wanted to see the women revive the quesera. "We don't want, we can't abandon the buildings," she told the women. "That would be just too great a loss. What I want is the cooperation of all of you so we can move forward. I need your help. I know that nobody here believes in you, but with your help, we can continue." After reading the agreement the group had signed with PH and Padre Mateo in 2008, in which PH paid the outstanding utility bills in exchange for control of the buildings, she pointed out that nothing would prevent the group from retaking control of the quesera before the five-year deadline outlined in the agreement if they could prove themselves capable. She would be willing, she promised, to work closely with the group with that end in mind. As she was talking about this kind of support from PH, she also harkened to the past, reminding the group that they were the "first [all female] quesera." What she had admired, she said, wasn't just the cheese, but the example they had set. "You were a family," she said. "When there are problems at home you can talk about them here." She also reminded them that the community bank came out of the group. "What is in the past is in the past," she continued, "and we have to leave it," cutting short several of the women's objections that the cooperative had failed because of the decisions of previous administrators. When group members asked about the specifics of restarting cheese production with mozzarella, something they thought might be better done in the winter months when more grass, and thus more milk, is available, Eugenia imposed a six-month deadline and called a meeting for the next week to which milk producers were to be invited. Group members also asked about the "benefits" of restarting, wondering what those would be. "Work *is* the benefit," came the reply. Though the women had mentioned going back to being only a knitting cooperative to me in interviews, none of them broached the subject with Eugenia. The current president of the cooperative resigned her position at the end of the meeting, citing the requirements of a job she had recently obtained that would make working in the quesera impossible.

This kind of slippage was also visible in the meeting held the next week, on July 30. After starting without any kind of biblical reflection, something several women noted had fallen away as regular practice in the group, Eugenia chastised the women for not bringing any milk producers to the meeting, which she had requested in order to bring them into negotiation to repair and resume relationships between them and the group. She said she wanted to continue the meeting nevertheless, "so the buildings won't remain empty." She brought Edgar Vásconez, an expert in cheese production working for PH, to the meeting so that he could act as a consultant for the resumption of work at the quesera. My notes from the meeting, slightly abridged, are reproduced below.

> *[Eugenia] then turned the meeting over to Edgar, whom she promised would talk about prices, production, the best kind of cheeses and/or yogurt to make, and the like. Edgar started with production, saying that production of milk was not the issue. Rather, he said, the group would have to collaborate, and if they didn't, nothing would be possible. He talked about his history with the group, and with the queseras in the province in general, and said that having this building here, and empty, is "ugly." He also reminded the women that the "benefit isn't for Promoción Humana but for the community." He then talked about Eugenia's and his own contributions and work with the group, lamenting that it had come to naught at the moment.*
>
> *Eugenia took back control of the meeting and asked if the women had talked to any of the milk producers in the area. The answer came back with some scattered affirmative answers, though none of them was overly enthusiastic. Jesus said that she had talked with Rosa, who had offered a few liters a day.*
>
> *The conversation then turned to how many liters the group will need in order to start production of something. In Edgar's opinion, 250 liters*

would be the minimum number. Eugenia immediately started pushing for less, something like 100 liters. At this point, Jesus jumped in with what would become the main concern of the group, that starting in the summer would be a problem due to the lack of fresh grass and also the fact that this is a time when many cows are pregnant and therefore dry. Again, Jesus said that Rosa had talked to some lechero, but expressed doubt about the numbers proffered as it is summer. As a group, the socias wondered if it wouldn't be better to wait until winter. Again, Eugenia said that she wants to start NOW. She thought it would be possible if they could start with 20 liters of yogurt on Friday and then queso fresco on the weekends. These products require less milk, and less work, than does mozzarella or parmesan. Eugenia also mentioned the plaza store, saying that they would need it in order to make local sales, especially of the yogurt.

The talk moved to specifics, and Edgar gave a range for the price the group would need to pay producers for the milk. At the moment, fresh milk sells for 50 cents/liter in stores. Eugenia pointed out that this is a retail price and said that wholesale prices would be lower. The group would have to ask the lecheros for how much they would be willing to sell their milk. Edgar said that the going rate in Salinas is 34 cents per liter, though others are selling for 18 to 32 cents. At the national level, he continued, there is an overabundance of milk, so much so that the government has shut down the import of milk in powder (e.g., from Nestlé). A kilo of queso fresco, which takes 3 liters of milk to make, is currently selling for about $1.75 in stores, and mozzarella is selling for $3.80/kilo. Ten liters of milk go into a kilo of this cheese. To set the price, Edgar reminded the women, they had to think of not only the cost of the milk, but of salaries, electricity, water, transportation, etc.

This opened up a conversation about the problems with transport of milk, something that has apparently been an issue for some time. Edgar and Eugenia reminded the group that PH has never paid for transport of milk and that they do not do so in Salinas, where people bring milk in buckets and on animals. The group will need to buy local or pay less for milk that they pay to transport. Related to this issue, Eugenia stressed that they needed to maintain quality and not use old milk to make cheese. Edgar, she said, would come to do tests to be sure they were producing the cheese correctly. Eugenia then articulated that the group should pay less, substantially less, for milk if they had to pay to get it to the factory. "No es negocio pagar el caro (It's not profitable to pay for transport)," is the way she put it. Edgar then chimed in by saying, "You [the socias], set the price [for the milk]. You are the owners, the accounting is in your hands." When the women suggested paying even 35 cents for a liter, however, he told them that this was out of the question.

Eugenia went on to ask about other sources of income using quesera resources, including the pasture that is currently rented out to a sharecropper and is planted in choclos (sweet corn). She talked generally about finances, and suggested that the group pay producers every 15 days. Going back to themes related to the land, and to the group, she said that her idea is to start with quesos, and then get back into gardening and other activities the group used to have. "La idea es retomar los otros trabajos [the idea is to "retake," e.g., restart, the other work]," she stated. She then referenced the group as one of the first and best in the province. She wants to see them that way again.

Jesus wanted to know who would work at a newly functioning quesera. And who would put up the capital to get going again?

Eugenia responded that PH would do it but that she needed a firmer idea that they had the milk they would need to start production again. She asked for commitments from the women gathered. Greys said she could provide about 10 liters, Teresa had 15, Rosa Tomama had 2 and promised to talk to Narcisa Inca about more. Dolores, the young new socia, promised 10 liters. Rosa Galarza's mother, not present at the meeting, also appeared to be good for about 10 liters of milk. These, figured on the high end, and some other scattered promises led Eugenia to figure they had about 51 liters of milk, a good 50 liters of the 100 liter number she had opted for. She then fixed the price at 34 cents and emphasized that this was a fixed price, not to fluctuate with the season [e.g., right now cheese prices are high due to the choclo harvest in progress].[3]

Edgar then talked about improving pasture and the herd stock but said that it made no sense to think about these things at the moment due to a bovine virus that is going around. This led to talk of swine flu, which has apparently made an appearance in Guaranda and San Miguel. Teresa chose this moment to ask if it might be possible to offer 40 cents per liter of milk, an idea that Edgar and Eugenia dismissed immediately as impossible. They said it might work if the group was only selling yogurt but never for cheese production.

Edgar continued by asking about the registro sanitario, to which the group responded that they didn't have one, a perpetual concern. Eugenia countered by saying that they had to open first in order to get the registro, as getting one requires samples from an operating plant. This led to talk about the lack of confidence on the part of the local lecheros and also ongoing prob-

lems with the SRI, the Ecuadorian version of the IRS. There are outstanding taxes to be paid [all of them on the personal account of a previous president of the group], *something of which Edgar was keenly aware and an issue that he himself raised.*

The talk then returned to the chagra *(the land around the quesera), and how much the group was charging the sharecropper, and where the money was going. Rightfully, it needs to go to PH as they have taken control of the plant, and Eugenia wants this regularized. She mentioned regularizing accounting so that accounts such as this would be due at the end of every month. This led Jesus to talk about problems with the sharecropper and the fact that he planted his choclos very late this year. If they don't rent it out, Eugenia wanted to know, what would the group put there? Greys opted for grass so that the group could keep its own milk cow on the property. She then asked if PH had improved grass stock that she could get. Greys's pregnant milk cow, it should be noted, was grazing on the property as we held the meeting.*

Eugenia started to wrap up the meeting by relisting the milk suppliers and by asking who else the socias were talking with about getting milk. She said, "Tenemos que irnos rápidos" (We have to move quickly), and suggested that the group do an initial cleaning of the plant to see what they have and what they need to restart production. She also asked for a fixed day for a monthly meeting, a suggestion that went totally unanswered.

The talk then turned to who would actually work in the plant if/when it reopens. Teresa said she has a neighbor who wants to work, leading Eugenia and Edgar to lay out that whoever works in the plant must be a socia, and must be available for two weeks for training. If no one in the group is willing to do it, then PH would send someone from the outside (though a member of PH).

This led Agustina to observe that the problem the group had had in the past was that they would train someone and then she would leave, as in the case of Dora, Julia's cousin. Edgar then repeated that PH would train one person, sending her to Salinas for the training. Lucia offered that if the group was going to make parmesan or mozzarella, they might need a man to work in the plant. Eugenia brushed this off with the observation, repeated three times, that women are the stronger sex. "Are you saying that men are stronger?," she asked. "Women are stronger!" Someone else agreed, and diverted a bit by saying that when men get a cut on their fingers, they cry and whine. Dolores, the new young socia, stopped this conversation by saying that she'd like to learn. This led the other socias to suggest that PH train two people, "de repente" (just in case). Dolores asked who would pay for the training, to which Eugenia and Edgar responded that PH would do it. Dolores then said that World Vision has offered to pay for capacitation, presumably in their cheese factory in San Simón. Edgar seemed excited about this and declared that he didn't care who did the training.

The meeting ended with Edgar, Eugenia, Dolores, Jesus, and a few other socias taking the PH truck into town in order to talk to World Vision. I walked up the road with Agustina, Greys, Lucia, Cecilia, Teresa, and a couple of others. Greys and the others thought that the general plan was good but are frustrated with the pace. Better to start in November, they said, when there is grass. They seem to feel that the plan is doomed to fail if started on Eugenia's time line. There was also some talk about gender roles, put in the form of a question: "Quién manda aquí? Las faldas o los pantalones?" (Who's in charge around here? The skirts or the pants?). Looking around, only one woman was wearing a skirt, though the women agreed that the faldas were the ones in charge around these parts.

In the end, the women, even with the support of Eugenia and Edgar, were unable to convince local milk producers, many of whom were still owed substantial sums by the cooperative, to provide enough milk to restart any sort of cheese or yogurt production. By 2015 the cooperative was inactive, and the women no longer meet in any capacity. Most women have returned to working in their homes, though some have attained the credentialing necessary to take up work as schoolteachers, and others, like Julia Guamán, have found work in other sectors or continue to operate their own small businesses. The social rifts that became apparent during the dissolution of the cooperative have solidified, with many of the women no longer speaking to one or the other of the past presidents of the group, who they blame for the failure and the "lack of benefits." The capital equipment used for cheese production and sale—the quesera, stainless steel vats, refrigerated display cases, and the yogurt building—remains unused behind locked doors, physical reminders of failure.

"SE FUE A LA QUIEBRA": NARRATING FINANCIAL LOSS

When women involved in the cooperative spoke about why it failed, they usually started by reflecting on financial mismanagement, something they generally summed up with the phrase "mala administración," "poor administration," or weak management and accounting practices. In 2009, after explaining that "we haven't studied and we can't work" because there are no jobs available for women locally, Jesus Galarza blamed the failure of the quesera on the initial lack of pay for the women who worked daily to make cheese in conjunction with poor financial oversight on the part of the cooperative member tasked with daily operations. "We worked and we worked," she explained when I asked why the quesera was no longer operating.

JG: We worked, but there were no benefits for us. She [the plant manager] is the problem, but also the spouses, some of them started asking, they were saying, "You're leaving us here in the house, going to work there, and what are you getting out of it? What benefit?"

JD: And so the problem was there was no one to do the work at home?

JG: Yes, that was it. The problem was that some socias had to quit, and they no longer wanted to work. And then the administration changed, and everything was destroyed. And that's how the quesera went into bankruptcy. Yes, that's what happened. It was because of poor administration.

Mercedes Huilca, a past president of the group who worked full time in the quesera, gave a similar account.

JD: What happened to the group? Why isn't it functioning anymore?

MH: They say poor administration is what sent it into bankruptcy. From the administration. [The administrator] was in charge of everything. She was in charge of the cheese, the knitting, of the store we had opened, she did everything. And without doubt, it all went bankrupt.

JD: Was it a lack of accounting? What happened?

MH: When we say poor administration, this can be a lack of accounting.

JD: And how was this? Did Promoción Humana provide oversight?

MH: I think Eugenia [Montero] left, and another woman came in.

JD: So it was that?

MH: Neither one of them really oversaw the administration, but I don't know. I really don't know what happened there.

Rosa Galarza also blamed poor administration, though she put poor accounting practices in the context of a weak educational system. She began by talking about the store.

> RG: I worked there for three months, with another women, three months, and they didn't pay anyone. They didn't pay me. So I took some yarn and some needles so at least I got a discount. And from there, we were left with an inventory that some people have been selling. Yes, some are selling, one here, one there [claps her hand].
>
> JD: So there was a lack of accounting?
>
> RG: It's because we don't have it here. They haven't offered accounting classes here. This is something that was good before. [Promoción Humana] trained five people in accounting. This was good. Two had almost finished, but they didn't have much education. It was good that they offered us a course so we would have at least something, so that we could compete [*defenderse*]. But imagine, now no one is learning. That's what happened.

What is striking about the women's comments is not so much that they agree that irregular accounting procedures and administrative practices that appeared to concentrate business decisions in the hands of one or two cooperative members led to economic collapse but rather the way they locate those realities in broader social contexts. Going bankrupt describes an economic reality, specifically, significant debt as the result of poor accounting and business decisions, which, in turn, reflects the perpetual lack of opportunities in education and market participation. Going bankrupt was in many ways a return to an original state where profit was hard to come by. In this way, the women were commenting as much on market structures from which they were perpetually excluded as they were on the particular pathology of their experience in the group. "The market," as they had come to know it, was a distinctly hostile environment. "We have an agreement," commented Josefa Arteaga in a 2003 interview.

> For example, we bring mature cheese by order to Salinas. It's by direct order, and so they normally set the prices and everything, and it's all hard cheeses that need to go to Salinas. We don't have the right climate here. It's too humid here for the cheese to mature. With the soft

> cheeses we can just make them to order, put them in local stores, or sell them to individuals. We also sell them in the coastal sector, Babahoyo, Montalvo, Guayaquil, and in local markets. We aren't only in the consortium, we are also outside. Definitely.

Being outside the markets established by the consortium allowed the cooperative a certain flexibility but also meant a certain vulnerability as those markets were less regular, and more vulnerable, than the channels FUNCONQUERUCOM carved and maintained. Read broadly, Josefa's observation that the cooperative was "definitely" "also outside" points to the precariousness of markets in the cooperative structure. Those markets helped the cooperative to be profitable when they functioned well but contributed to failure when vendors did not pay the group for the cheese they brought to sell, something that happened with increasing regularity in 2004 and 2005, or when transporting cheese to the coastal locations became difficult because women did not have the time to travel or because the price of transport outpaced the price of the cheese as set by the consortium. The need to negotiate with local milk vendors using prices set by the consortium also led to tension, debt, and ambivalence on the part of the women who wanted to enter the market economy but continue to be rooted locally. Being "also outside" turned out to be a difficult, and in the end untenable, location for success.

Aside from their position vis-à-vis various external realities, socias spoke of "poor administration" as a prologue to more introspective comments about their perceptions that they had failed to uphold shared and important social values, often coded as Catholic values, including generosity, respect for others, and self-sacrifice. It is to these values, and their expression, that we now turn.

"BEING CATHOLIC WAS NEVER IMPORTANT": AUTHORING RELIGIOUS IDENTITY IN THE CONTEXT OF FAILURE

While cooperative members were swift to blame poor administration for the eventual collapse of cheese production, they also spoke frequently about individual and collective failures to live up to religious, specifically

Roman Catholic, values they perceived as vital to group success. In doing so, they crafted a narrative of Catholicism that divided the church into three distinct parts: institutional, quotidian, and sacramental. The institutional church included personnel and administrative subsets such as parish priests, Promoción Humana, and FEPP; quotidian Catholicism encompassed home practices such as prayer, child rearing, and relationships between spouses—roughly the domestic church; and sacramental Catholicism focused on sacraments such as baptism, confirmation, and the Eucharist, as well as attendance at mass. While these spaces may overlap, as in the example of officially sanctioned images that confraternities sponsor for individual worship in private settings, or the private repetition of prayers used in liturgy, the distinction between these modes of action became essential for the cooperative in narrating their relationship to the church. In telling the story of the cooperative's failure, socias identified sacramental Catholicism as the most important form, often downplaying the role of institutional Catholicism, which they associated in various ways with the poor administration that led to bankruptcy.

In a 2009 interview, Jesus Galarza noted:

> There's a difference between going to mass and [being in the group], but yes, being Catholic is important. We always did it, we had the habit of saying the Word of God and all that. We did that. But at times, we weren't really conscious of what that actually is, that religion is understanding the truth of the Word of God. It's trying to be better and change. But at times we didn't do that. I'm someone who has been around, and I've seen and experienced many things. I see a lot of people. I see people who are the most Catholic, the ones most involved in religion. They're the most involved in the Word of God. But they lead a life—I don't understand them because they are always concerned with the next person, with the people next to them and what they have. And that's not the Word of God.

Jesus's critique of the group's religious sincerity—there was Bible reading but not true comprehension that would be evidenced in greater group cohesion—was echoed by several socias as they reflected on the Catholic identity of the cooperative in light of its failure.

Rosa Galarza, for example, linked the failure to a lack of Catholic practice in group meetings.

RG: We used to begin with the Bible, a minute of reflection, and then we'd start other activities We used to talk about things. But now, no. Now it's totally destroyed, with some wanting this and some not. We used to have courage, but it's gone.

JD: But is the group still Catholic?

RG: Yes, all of us.

JD: Is it important that it's Catholic?

RG: No! It's not important that [the members] are Catholic. It's just that almost everyone here is Catholic. There just aren't people from other religions who want to be a part of the group. No, no. The priest is also a member. He's also a member. He has also tried to help us, but I think people said things to him, and he can't do much about the debts. But what's important is that a person wants to work, as Eugenia says, and that they're going to work. That's how we'll fix things.

Here Rosa values the sacramental church, specifically, the Bible reading and reflection that used to start meetings and create a community spirit, even as she points to the inefficacy of the institutional church as neither Eugenia nor Padre Orlando seems capable of righting the debt or the communal work ethic. Notably, where both the institutional and sacramental churches have failed, it is the sacramental failure that she deems more serious.

Julia Guamán made a similar analysis in a 2009 interview.

JD: How does religion work in the relationships between cooperative members, or in the community?

JG: Well, for example, speaking of the women and the group and religion, we are always together and in agreement that the month of May is the month of the Virgen María. Because we're very Catholic we organize, have meetings, pray the rosary. Sometimes we even get an invitation to pray in someone's house. It's very nice. When we were a group, when we functioned as a group, we sometimes invited the priest to celebrate a mass with communion and all of that, to share.

JD: Yes, I remember that.

JG: To share.

JD: You all used to say that you were united in that, that you were united by being Catholic.

JG: Yes, yes, that. We shared that, in that sense, yes . . .

JD: So it seems religion is important to you all.

JG: Yes, yes. You see, we maintain ourselves that way with a youthful spirit. One can be old, but one can feel young in this way. One can feel good. For me, I feel best when I'm serving actively in the church, which is my religion. I feel realized there.

JD: So when you say the best thing is to serve, do you mean serving people or serving God?

JG: Yes, of course. I feel good when I can do something, not of my own accord, but because of God. That's the thing.

JD: So when people say the cooperative failed because of selfishness, how does this work with Catholic values?

JG: No, no. What happened with, what you're hearing, was because there was a little of, I don't really know what happened economically, but it didn't have anything to do with religion. Nothing to do with it. Sure, we're human beings, and we make mistakes. We got a little off our feet and we ended up losing everything, but that doesn't have anything to do with religion, no. What's better is if we stay on our feet in spite of all the things weighing us down. There in the group, we're all believers. I'm going on a mission in three weeks!

Like Rosa, Julia downplayed the Catholic identity of the group as "not important" when it came to failure, though she continued to emphasize Catholic identity as important to women as individuals. It was not that the church failed but that individual women "got off their feet" in the administration of the project, a situation that she feels may be remedied by faith.

What Catholic believers do was characterized by cooperative members as a combination of sacramental and home practices that informed a set of values focused on respect for others. Cecilia Miño described her life as a Catholic.

JD: What do you do as a Catholic?

CM: We go to mass, to the fiestas.

JD: Anything else?

CM: We also have the practice of praying, when God can give us what we ask for.

JD: What values have you learned from your religion?

CM: For example, to be kind, to give what little I may have. In the church they say that peace is helping those who are lacking. It's good to be kind. And respecting others. I've taught my children to acknowledge and respect everyone, from the youngest to the oldest. They also pay attention in mass.

Cecilia keeps an icon of the Divino Niño on an altar in her home, a practice she describes as having "someone to accompany us and who passes our offerings on so God will be disposed toward us." When asked if people in Chillanes were faithful in their Catholicism, she said that they were as they regularly attended mass, though she commented that attending more than on Sundays was difficult because of the demands of tending to animals, a task that often conflicted with the services offered in the early mornings or late afternoons.

Other women also described quotidian Catholic practices such as prayer, offerings, and participation in fiestas and devotion to particular saints as the mark of devoted Catholics in the region, and they joined Cecilia in her emphasis on respect for others as a primary Catholic value. Jesus Galarza described her practices as a Catholic.

JG: We pray the rosary every night, things like that. And I like to share what I have, to be kind to older people, to help the poor, to help them know the Word of God, which is the truth. This is what one needs to do. As Catholics we need to have faith, and to do what God asks of us. This is what I have done and what I do, at least until now.

JD: And what values have you learned from your religion?

JG: That I will value what God asks of me. That we have to learn what God asks by learning to read the Bible.

JD: What do you think are the most important values?

JG: For me, to believe in God, and to do what God asks. To be meek and not be selfish. I get along with everyone. Every once in a while I may be without courage, but then I remember and I have courage again. I'm not capricious with other people.

Both Cecilia and Jesus ground Catholic values and practice first in home practice, the quotidian actions of prayer, Bible reading, and daily actions of respect for others that lead to a life well led. This kind of quotidian Catholicism was emphasized by every socia I interviewed, and each listed "respect for others" as the primary value she had learned from her religious practices. Like Jesus, most of them rooted this value in scriptural teaching. Learning to be Catholic, then, was based in daily practice affiliated with but apart from the institutional church, even as it was practiced in the sacramental church through actions such as teaching children to pay attention in mass.

Such segmentation of the church into these parts, however, was less apparent before the failure, when socias often spoke of an integrated church whose institutional components were important in supporting the group and other local economic development efforts. In a 2003 interview, for example, Josefa Arteaga credited God and the Catholic Church with being vital to group success.

JD: Do you think the religious aspect of the group has something to do with its success?

JA: Yes.

JD: And why is that?

JA: Because it has institutions that really and truly support poor people. There is a [church] organization from the U.S. that supports us with paying for staff and giving credit. And there is another, Catholic Relief Services, that helps with money. Also, there are religious in the church who support us, who give us money to invest so that we can help others, and the groups. And there's also another [Catholic] institution that supported us in the construction of the quesera, that we hope will keep helping going forward. That group is helping us. They know that we're strong, and that we won't do them wrong.

We also have a lot to do with the church because we are always with the Word of God. We are always giving thanks to God for what he gives us every day. And for life itself, not just for money, but for the life God gives us. Because without him, I believe that we couldn't move ourselves even a bit. So I am always supporting them [the socias], making them see that we are all the church, so we get along well. Yes, and you've seen that Padre Mateo is involved with us, he always visits us. He gives mass here. So does the priest here in Chillanes, and Padre Antonio [Polo].

> They come to different communities. Italian people from various places come to visit us as tourists. They say this is because of the work we're doing. So yes, there is a strong relationship between our success and the church.

In these comments, Josefa mentioned both the institutional and sacramental churches, especially in talking about mass as an important part of the service clergy brings to the group.

In 2012, however, Josefa was less inclined to give the Catholic Church credit for supporting development efforts in the Chillanes area and instead identified the work of the church as being rooted less in economic support and more in the sacramental form of reflection on Bible passages at the beginning of meetings sponsored by Promoción Humana, for which she worked as a promoter in the community bank program.

JD: What do you do as a Catholic on a daily or weekly basis?

JA: I go to church. Sometimes I go on Sundays, or sometimes I go in the communities when I go out, or at meetings in Guaranda. But our mission, the work we do, the mission of Promoción Humana is that every day, when I go out to work with a group, the Word of God is on the agenda. So when we go to meetings, we start with the Word of God. We read the Bible, reflect a little, and then teach people, little by little, that God exists. That without him, things cannot be.

And when we start with the Word of God, things go well. When once in a while we don't start with the Word of God, it isn't right. The Word of God makes us open. If we have two meetings, we put it in two meetings. If there are three meetings, we do three. They may be different reflections, but we do the Word of God. It's our mission. As Padre Mateo says, "It's not the salary we make. It isn't the interest on our money. It's that we come to the people." We teach them that the Word of God is very important, it's as if we're evangelizers for the Word of God, and until now, it's gone, well . . .

JD: And what is the church doing now in Chillanes?

JA: In Chillanes, we don't have much. As I was saying, there isn't much support. How do I say? Here, for example, in the parish, the priest that was here, he really didn't support us if we did

> something. If we were going to do something and asked him to be with us, he already had his appointments, a full schedule. They [parish priests] already have their days set and things they have to do. We don't count on that type of support.

Where the institutional church is unable to support community development efforts, it is the sacramental church, expressed in the Word of God, that keeps groups unified and Catholic in their identity. Where the institutional church has failed, the sacramental church succeeds and continues to fuel the kind of values ("getting along well") required for cooperative work.

In dividing the Catholic Church into three separate parts the women maintain a Catholic identity but one that is rooted not in the institution that established the project but rather in mass, scripture readings, and other sacramental practices that continue in spaces outside of cooperative activities. Indeed, when asked about values they had learned by being Catholic, "respect for others" was listed by the clear majority of socias as the most important. In this way, they have been able to retain a certain amount of spiritual capital that might otherwise have been lost as the project collapsed. If the sacramental church is the most important segment of Roman Catholicism, then the failure of the institutional church in the form of poor administration, or of the quotidian church in the form of failed social bonds, still allows for a continued, if altered, Roman Catholic identity.

AUTHORING GENDER IN THE CONTEXT OF FAILURE

Though cooperative members have been able to maintain a Catholic identity by dividing the church into constituent elements, a positive gender identity that allowed for the women to equate being female with natural success has been more difficult to maintain. In 2003 the women I interviewed uniformly credited the success of the cooperative, at least in part, to the all-female composition of the group, something that earned them accolades and attention from Promoción Humana, the provincial government, community members, and other aid and development organizations at local, national, and international levels. Recall that Josefa, for example, credited women with being "more grateful to God," as well as "more likely to save, more responsible, more likely to understand what's lacking in the house, responsible for children, spouses, for everything," as she explained why the Chillanes cooperative and other community banks were targeted at women. This kind of attitude was also reflected in the comments of Eugenia Montero in the more recent meeting detailed at the beginning of this chapter, as she declared that "women are stronger" in the process of trying to instill enthusiasm to restart production in the quesera. Taking a more philosophical stance, again in 2003, Silvia Moyano commented that the all-female nature of the group was important for the community: "Some people see us as an agency, but the majority, the majority are happy because we're an example of what women can be. There are many men's organizations or organizations with economic power that haven't been able to do what we have been able to. Many people see us as an example. Women can."

Language in the Libro de Actas also reflects the ideas that women are cooperative, more easily able to work in "solidarity," and will succeed if given the chance to participate in market structures, at least if they can avoid the pitfalls many associate with male behavior. The entry from November 5, 1997, records that after a reflection on having "clean hearts" that are "attached to God," Eugenia "asked socias to leave behind selfishness in the group, maintain focus, and search for new activities" before asking for an economic report (Libro de Actas 5). Other entries demonstrate the expectation that the women will expand their domestic roles to cooperative spaces. On March 10, 2003, Eugenia "suggested that we need to treat the workers [building the quesera] well, giving them food to sustain them as they are working far from home" (Libro de Actas 19). This suggestion was followed by the recommendation to also give the workers housing, but the group rejected this idea as outside the scope of their responsibilities.

While these comments and notes from meetings demonstrate a generally shared assumption that women are naturally more cooperative, honest, and responsible, reflections on gender made in the midst of and after the failure of the cooperative are more nuanced, and often include a focus on women's specific social contexts that goes unrecorded in the cooperative's early days. Lucía Alarcón, a socia who worked full time at the quesera for three years, described women's lives in Chillanes as "sacrificial" (*somos bien sacrificadas*) in a 2009 interview: "Yes, we get up early to cook, to wash, to clean the house, and we have various plants we need to tend to, and the crops. We do our washing. It isn't like, that is, because of the economy here, salaries are very low. You can't make much. Because of that we can't pay anyone to cook or clean. We have to do it all ourselves." Later in the interview, after listing "understanding" and "companionship" among women as the best parts of being a cooperative member and "lack of organization" as the reason for its failure, she continued to reflect on the hours required of women engaged in full-time work in the quesera and in yogurt production.

JD: So you worked in the quesera for three years. How many hours each week?
LA: We were contracted by the month.
JD: Ah, so about how many hours did you work every day, and how many days per month?
LA: Let's see, usually from about seven in the morning until about two or three in the afternoon. But when we were making that cheese, the parmesan, then we would work until five or six in the afternoon. Then when we started to make yogurt, sometimes we would work until ten or eleven at night so we could get the yogurt in jars the same day.

After a brief discussion about other work she had done with the cooperative, I asked if it was important that the group was female.

LA: Yes, it was good, but I don't know who—I don't know if it will continue. It was always—As mothers we couldn't always be there, we couldn't always keep working. We already had so much to do at home, and this made it impossible.
JD: Would it be possible to have a group with men and women?
LA: Of course! Yes, that would be better. It would be better to have men working in the plant because it's hard work for women, for people who have other jobs.
JD: Because you're also working at home?
LA: Yes, yes.
JD: When you were working in the quesera, who was doing things at home?
LA: My son was. And that's why I was telling you it was a little screwed up around here. At times the [cooperative] president would tell us to come, asking even for our husbands to come. That's how it was when I was working down there.
JD: It seems that for you all, how do I say? There isn't a tradition of women working outside of the house. Were there problems with that?

LA: Yes, yes, there were a few problems with that. There wasn't anyone to watch the children, so we ended up with problems. When I was working my son had to do a lot, to the point where we put him in night school so he could watch [his younger sister].

Despite all of this, Lucía still mourned the loss of the cooperative and concluded the interview by commenting that "friendship" and the chance to work for a salary were the things she missed the most, even as she mentioned, one last time, that women alone could not practically run such a large operation.

Lucia's observations, laced with nostalgia for the "friendship" and "cooperation" that she found in the all-female space of the cooperative, point to an evolving view of women's capabilities that increasingly take into account the conditions in which gender roles and proclivities are produced. Whereas Josefa relied on women as more or less universally "responsible" and attuned to household problems, something Eugenia repeated in her comment that "women are stronger," Lucía was more measured and more inclined to note the limits of those qualities in the context of continued expectations that women are obliged to support household endeavors even if they take on market roles. Women may be stronger, and they may be more responsible, but that strength is not limitless and those personal qualities are not guaranteed to continue. "It was good," Lucía opined as she reflected on the cooperative at the end of her interview, "but now it doesn't exist. We don't have meetings anymore, but it was good to get together, to get to know each other. It was once a week, but now I feel like people have taken sides, one on one side and one on the other. It makes me sad when I think about the group."

Other cooperative members were similarly nostalgic when thinking about gender in light of the cooperative's failure and equally nuanced in their assessment of the role of women's strengths, even in the early days of success. Cecilia Miño reflected that the group "functioned well" when I asked her if it was important that it was all female. "But now I don't know why—in the beginning everything was good. We even won a prize for being the best quesera! They've told you that, I'm sure."

JD: Yes, yes.
CM: Right. So I don't know what happened, but it fell apart. I don't know what happened, or how.

JD: But did it work better with only women, or was it not important that the group was for women?

CM: It was good, but it wasn't important. What matters is the administration. That's what was important. It was the administrator. I don't know what happened, because things worked in the beginning, but it wasn't because we were only women. . . . It would be better if they let men work.

JD: Do you think men will come into the cooperative?

CM: They haven't spoken of that, no.

A few minutes later in the interview, after commenting that life for rural women was more difficult than that of urban women, Cecilia downplayed the role of gender in daily struggles more broadly, commenting instead on the limitations placed on rural women who are unable to attain more than a basic education.

CM: A woman works as hard as a man. Or even harder sometimes. For example, in the countryside she works the same as a man. If they go pruning, they both go out into the orchard, they use the same tools, and the woman does the same work as the man. This is true in the countryside more than anywhere else. In the city, those girls are prepared, and because of this they have better work, a better post. But in the countryside—

JD: So for them life is easier?

CM: Clearly! Because they are prepared. Imagine if you only have a grade school education. I can't do anything for any kind of institution, not like that. I can't work like that. So the only thing I can do is pick up my hoe, here in the countryside.

JD: So there is inequality.

CM: Yes.

JD: But it's because of education more than gender?

CM: That's it, and because of a lack of money as well. I couldn't study because of that.

Cecilia's comments linked gender, work, and what happened in the cooperative in complex ways. For her, it wasn't so much that women are naturally more responsible, cooperative, or more attuned to fulfilling family needs but that gender is tied to economic and geographic realities such that the failure of the cooperative is the failure of a chance to participate in something other than a directly agricultural economy. Put another way, she agreed with Eugenia that women are as strong (though maybe not stronger) than men, but she resisted the notion that such strength can overcome socially structured obstacles in and of itself.

As they think about gender identities in the context of the cooperative failure, then, socias do so with a keen awareness of the settings in which such projects operate and with a critical eye toward some of the ideas about gender that continue to be propagated by project promoters and others. It is not that they believe that women are incapable of economic involvement or even success. But it is clear that their experience entering the market as women has tempered any easy belief that women are more likely to succeed simply because they are women. Indeed, cooperative members have come away from the experience less willing to rely on gendered social capital, more willing to examine the conditions that lead to uneven opportunities to participate in market economies in the first place, and more willing to consider models that would allow men to also participate in daily operations.

This heightened awareness of the social conditions that constrain women's ability to succeed economically has also reinforced nostalgia for the cooperative as an important space for mutual support, friendship, and exchange of gendered experiences. While they are skeptical of being market women, then, socias recognize and uniformly want to rekindle the cooperative as a space to be women, as an intermediate space—neither public nor private—where they can author their identities collectively and outside of usual household or agricultural roles.

ACCOUNTING FOR FAILURE

The last entry in the Libro de Actas describes a meeting that took place on February 4, 2007, in the second-story meeting room at the quesera, opened for the day by the PH promoter who had come to Chillanes to oversee the encounter. After opening with a prayer that included a petition to God to keep the group moving forward with mutual understanding between members, as well as a request that they would "act like adults," the women tackled issues of accounting, milk prices, and salaries for members working in the plant should they be able to reopen it. There was a brief and contentious discussion about the sale of the refrigerated display cases that had been used in the store, which some members felt would help finance the reopening of the plant but which others felt was shortsighted given their potential uses if operations did resume. Finally, an accountant attending the meeting at the request of PH explained to the women that they would have to use "common sense" and regularize accounting procedures, keeping a single, comprehensive ledger and using a bank account for deposits and withdrawals of all group money. This advice was followed by a last reflection that ends the written account of group activities.

> We decided to go forward with the group. It is difficult but not impossible. We can't think only of what we have lost but must put ourselves in the right frame of mind and move little by little with clearly planned events. Every meeting is the same. We know very well what we have lost, but on the other hand, we have gained much more with the construction and the equipment. (Libro de Actas 64)

The observation that the socias were well aware of what they had lost with the cessation of group activities is poignant and can be read to encompass social as well as economic capital. Where the building and the equipment are listed in the minutes as tangible reminders of what the group has gained, the unnamed losses are heavy in the room: as the women have described them throughout this chapter, these include friendships and space for reflection and support about their role in domestic spaces, as well as confidence in the institutional church and in women's ability to leverage perceived qualities of cooperation, respect, and responsibility to profitably engage emerging market structures. When the institutional church and gendered social capital failed, cooperative members remained "also outside."

The use of religious and gendered social capital in the Virgen de las Nubes Cooperative thus seemed to have offered the women resources—financial and social—on which they drew and that became foundational to group and individual identities. Especially in the early, relatively successful years of the cooperative, women perceived the institutional and sacramental church as vital to financial and social success because it provided financial and spiritual capital on which members drew and from which they formed an identity of the group as "Catholic," especially with Bible reflections in meetings and frequent contact with priests and other representatives of institutional authority. Indeed, when the group was actively engaged in cooking together, knitting, and other activities that reproduced household experiences, quotidian Catholicism in the form of daily prayers and frequent conversations about children, spouses, and household roles was integrated into regular cooperative activities, strengthening a cohesive Catholic identity. With financial failure, however, such cohesiveness was no longer present, leading to a loss of confidence in the institutional church as a vital part of local development efforts. The remaining cooperative members no longer said that the Catholic identity of the cooperative was important but rather emphasized an individualized Catholicism focused on the sacraments and home practices. There was still spiritual capital, but it was diffuse, and no longer connected to collective activities. Catholicism was privatized as a result of its interaction with capitalist markets. Just as neoliberalism moved many public services to the private sector in the name of efficiency and personal over collective profits, an emphasis on sacramental Catholicism over institutional Catholicism shifts the burden of Catholic identity from the collective to the individual who must seek out those sacraments, now understood as the primary benefit of being Catholic.

In this instance, the use of spiritual capital in economic development that fails has not resulted in a significant loss of religious identity but in a significant shift in that identity from the collective to the personal. The narratives of cooperative members reveal a church that has gone from an institution as a source of social power to a body better suited to offering spiritual goods. What appears to have been risked, and lost, is a holistic vision of the liberationist church—one capable of, and dedicated to, raising people up in social as well as spiritual spaces.

If the collision of spiritual capital and capitalist markets has resulted in the splintering of cohesive models of the church, something more like shattering may describe what happened to cooperative members' identities as women. As part of the first all-female group dedicated to cheese making, Virgen de las Nubes Cooperative members were expected to succeed because of assumptions about their abilities to cooperate, organize, and sacrifice, abilities perceived by the parent organization, and by the women themselves, as superior to those of men. As demonstrated in this chapter, such assumptions have also "gone bankrupt" in the light of financial failure. While the women still consider themselves less likely to drink or be irresponsible than their male counterparts, they no longer believe that this makes them "stronger" in ways that will make them financially successful.

For this reason, they continued to ask that men be allowed to work in the plant when they contemplated reopening. More deeply, they mourned the loss of solidarity as women that the cooperative allowed when they were not engaged in cheese production. In remembering their time together when knitting, when they would de-stress and share in reproduced household activities such as cooking, the women were remembering a use of gendered social capital that fortified visions of what they could do as women, as well as a collective sense of strength and belonging that came with those activities. In the wake of the failure, when the remaining members were deeply divided and pointing to "selfishness" and a failure to "be good," along with poor administration, as the reasons for their problems, they were highlighting the interwoven nature of social capital as a development strategy. Once married in the rhetoric and structure of a project, ideas of social and especially emotional or spiritual strengths as a foundation for financial success are difficult to tear asunder. If the project fails financially, so, too, may the assumptions on which it was built. To paraphrase Silvia Moyano, the women were indeed an example: first of what women can do and then of what they could not do.

When I completed this project in 2018, it was too early to say how permanent the changes documented in this chapter would be. Two previous presidents of the cooperative still did not speak to each other, and other friendships the cooperative originally fostered appeared to be damaged beyond repair. No other development initiative had started to replace the potential for income that the project held, and the structural challenges that contributed to the project's demise were still very much in place. There was still no reliable child care outside of family members available to women in the area, despite a local woman's effort to start a private nursery school in 2012, this in spite of the increased number of women taking jobs outside of their homes. As documented in the previous chapter, the rising middle-class economy in Ecuador has afforded more women the chance to create small businesses that were unavailable during the time of the Virgen de las Nubes project, something cooperative members may be more inclined to try, especially if they have adopted an individual as opposed to collectivist approach to poverty reduction and financial mobility.

Indeed, the real wager in the model put forth by Promoción Humana may not have been in the forms of religious or gender identities but instead in a model of cooperative development. Having pledged to work together to "provide support and motivate the advancement of peasant women out of marginalization" (Libro de Actas 1), based on a model of liberation theology that called for community organization around common causes, socias instead ended up identifying not with the collective but with the privatized model of Roman Catholicism and a view of gender focused not on the possibilities of what women can do when working together but rather on the limitations imposed by social realities. Not one of the socias I interviewed spoke about changing those realities, demonstrating a reluctance to engage in, or perhaps to consider as necessary or worthy, widespread structural change. While it is too early to proclaim the death of liberationist development models, they seem to be in dire straits, especially after failed attempts at integration into market economies. In the words of the socias, "there weren't any benefits" to such an approach.

CONCLUSION

Virgins in the Clouds

The namesake of the Virgen de las Nubes Cooperative is an apparition of the Virgin Mary that appeared in the form of clouds over Quito in 1696 as a colonial Catholic congregation processed in prayer from Guápulo church to the basilica of San Francisco, petitioning for the healing of Bishop Sancho Andrade y Figueroa. Records documenting the appearance describe the immediate healing of the bishop, as well as more than five hundred witnesses to the miraculous event. Now enshrined in Azogues, near Cuenca in the south central province of Cañar, the Virgen de la Nube, as she is called in documentary accounts, is closely associated with healing and with the reunification of migrants. Her festival is celebrated on December 30 and is specifically dedicated to families coming together after times of separation, reunions aided by the New Year's holiday the next day. The Virgen de la Nube is international and enjoys a shrine in Peru as well as her home in Azogues.

The image of the virgin in the clouds—present, witnessed, ritually effective, and then returned to vapor—is an apt metaphor for the group in Chillanes that bore its name. Images such as that of the Virgen stir the religious imagination, bring people together, support communities and households, and inspire healing of various kinds but are prone to disappear when wind and weather, literal and metaphorical, shift. They can be memorialized and reenacted but rarely captured in institutional form.

This book has traced this kind of shifting, focusing on the many ways in which the changing winds of liberation theology, neoliberal capitalism, and gendered social capital came together and then broke apart in the Virgen de las Nubes Cooperative. Imagined as currents, it is possible to conceptualize the many ways such discourses formed, informed, and eroded the institutions that merged in the creation and dissolution of the group. It is possible to understand how the women of the cooperative jumped into them, were carried by them, and at times worked to challenge and escape them in the course of authoring their identities as rural women seeking to "provide support and motivate the advancement of peasant women out of their marginalization by their own effort" (Libro de Actas 1). Such authoring included not only an assessment of their own identities as Catholics and women but also significant changes in the ways they understood and evaluated Catholicism, gender more broadly, and the ways in which women could, and could not, interact with a neoliberal market economy writ large.

The experience of the socias in becoming market women, only to find that they did not have the social or physical infrastructure adequate to support them in the endeavor, thus highlights the unevenness of access to global markets and the limits of privatized, consumer models as strategies for holistic economic and human development. In presuming a consumer ethic—that is, that the logic of individual choice and competition is the ideal way to structure everything from delivery of telecommunications to roads to healthcare—neoliberalism presumes access to and visibility in markets at the local, regional, and global levels. Certainly the women of the Virgen de las Nubes Cooperative were made more visible, and more legible, in Ecuador's increasingly neoliberal and middle-class economies with their entrance into marketized cheese production. They conceptualized themselves as "employees" in the cheese plant and during the years of their success enjoyed the accolades of Promoción Humana and other development entities, as well as the Ecuadorian government, as they were honored for their work in various settings. As the women commented, however, they were expected to "do it themselves," with no provisions to replace their domestic household and agricultural labor as they moved into full-time market production in the quesera. Unlike their imagined urban counterparts, whom cooperative members credited with more education (they are more "prepared") and thus increased access to everything from job selection to help with laundry, cooking, and childcare, the women of the cooperative expressed doubt that they could ever enter into such competitive production without expanded support, at the least in the form of men who would also work in the factory.

"Doing it themselves" proved impossible to the women asked to add paid labor to already full days and highlights the unevenness of privatized markets often described as "free." As Lind (2005) and other critics (Molyneaux 2002; Huber and Solt 2004; Bush 2010; Connell and Dados 2014) have pointed out, the transfer of state-supported infrastructure to private endeavors often requires women to replicate functions previously supported in state, or at least more collective, entities and to do so without increased assistance of men in household spaces. While the parallel is not perfect in this case — the state has never particularly supported women entering the market as entrepreneurs beyond providing the basic living subsidy ("bono") and the food provided to social groups — it is clear that without some kind of increased support — more educational opportunities, childcare, perhaps a system for the support of agricultural endeavors for women working for paid wages — entering the free market is too costly and most certainly not free for most rural women.

Indeed, the experience of cooperative members points to the unevenness of neoliberal systems in urban and rural areas. Whereas the women Lind studied in Quito found themselves replicating many of the services the state had provided in urban areas, the rural women of the cooperative found themselves confronted with a lack of access to resources that they used to define the difference between themselves and their presumably wealthier and better-educated counterparts in Ecuador's largest cities. The ethic of consumer choice that would enable a decision between wage labor and household tasks has never been available to them, a rift made even more visible by their attempts to enter the market economy. In this way, neoliberalism is indeed always local, and can make deeper the channels of inequality already in place. Forced to "do it themselves," the women of the cooperative realized they couldn't do it all, a point of contention when they asked that Promoción Humana consider allowing men to work in quesera operations.

Such experiences point to the fact that economies, and thus the development initiatives meant to bring people into intersection with them, can never be understood apart from gender and place. While neoliberalism is certainly global and asserts universal claims about efficiency, austerity, and the virtues of self-reliance, such claims can never be tested at the universal level. As development interventions seek to intersect with such claims, they will need to be attentive to the fact that development, as culture, sits in places (Basso 1996; Bebbington 2000; Escobar 2008). What is risked, and what can be gained, varies widely depending on the infrastructure on which interventions are planned and executed and how well they take into account the actual circumstances of those they aim to assist. There was certainly some of this in the wider Salinas cheese initiative, but as that initiative expanded throughout the province, the admirable goals of gender equality and opportunity, in combination with market models of success, almost guaranteed the failure of the Chillanes experiment. As cooperative members repeatedly described it, the project was "without benefits."

Development initiatives also unfold in social time, and the way cooperative members authored their identities and their experiences as group members was tempered by ongoing changes in Latin American and global Catholicism, including the rise of the charismatic movement, the global focus on missions and evangelism that unfolded in local contexts, and a renewed emphasis on the domestic church. These movements, along with local constructions and reconstructions of Santa Rita, point to new spaces in which Latin American Roman Catholic women craft religious, gender, and economic identities. Women question Santa Rita's passivity in the face of domestic violence, commenting that "she was mute," and they take to the pulpit in Holy Week missions, commenting extemporaneously on domestic issues in light of scripture. Young Catholic missionaries question Church teachings on divorce in light of domestic violence even as they prepare to reinforce Catholic teachings in Ecuador's underserved rural communities. Women increasingly serve as catechists, shoring up a renewed emphasis on sacraments that locates the liturgical church as central to Catholic identity and participation.

These things, in conjunction with a burgeoning charismatic movement that provides space for women in leadership roles as it encourages personal, and in many ways extrainstitutional, interactions with God, are changing the way Chillanense women engage the church, Ecuadorian society, and their possibility as economic actors in development settings. While traditional liberationist endeavors such as the Virgen de las Nubes Cooperative engaged in formal projects meant to intersect with or even overturn rigid economic structures, the recent Catholic emphasis on the domestic church encourages the privatization of religious life in a renewed focus on rituals and relationships in the home. The reformation of society, in this model, does not occur in outward-facing efforts meant to reform unjust social systems but in the re-creation of the home as "society's best social capital," the basis of education, healthcare, and support for the young and the elderly. This model, read in a neoliberal context, mimics neoliberalism in its preference for private solutions to widely shared problems, many of them economic in scope and origin.

In a similar manner, Juan XXIII offers the project of no project that relies on more classical ideals of charity prescribed by religious example. More akin to neoliberalism in its attention to personal relationships with the divine and private solutions (though certainly solutions encouraged in group settings as retiristas emphasized the need for continued attendance at weekly meetings and depended on one another for social and spiritual support), the arrival of Charismatic Catholicism offers new, powerful ways to imagine being female, Catholic, and economically productive. Many of these ways involve the active participation of men as partners inside and outside of domestic spaces. This double reformation of machismo, which encourages women to take on public roles even as men are more involved at home, meshes well with a growing middle-class economy in which women increasingly run businesses and work outside the household, especially as private capital is easier to come by. In this sense, charismaticism addresses some of the structural obstacles that eventually caused the cooperative to fail.

The failure of the cooperative can thus be read as a result of replicating an idealized domestic church in which pious women entered the market as Catholic women concerned with providing for their households in a uniquely gendered way. This was successful when women were indeed focused on direct benefits to their households in work that replicated traditional household tasks. But it failed when it transferred that work to market activities in market spaces without giving attention to the deficits created in domestic arenas, or to men as potential economic and social partners. In its use of gendered social capital, the cooperative reproduced only a portion of that capital, failing to fully engage the domestic church.

This may be one reason that cooperative members eventually interpreted the failure of the cheese factory as a failure of the institutional church rather than that of liturgical or quotidian Catholicism. It was not church teachings that failed but their poor implementation by administrators who seemed deaf to pleas for a more equitable vision of the domestic church. The failure of the cooperative, in other words, was interpreted and experienced socially, taking into account its positioning in time, space, and social currents. All development interventions, and their assessments, are subject to the same conditions.

A second question this work has asked and endeavored to answer revolves around the place of cooperative efforts in the individualized atmosphere of neoliberalism. What happens to collectivism in privatized economies? Here it is clear that the intersection of these currents created tensions that were difficult or impossible to navigate, though the values of collective efforts remained important to group members. One place this was particularly apparent was in the shift from knitting, which happened in a communal environment but created profits for individuals, to cheese production, which relied on collective capital of various kinds but also created salaried positions for those socias who worked in the quesera. In both instances, socias reported that "solidarity" was an important virtue, though one more easily maintained when it was not directly monetized but rather remained in the background as individual women produced knitted goods for sale. It was less effective, and would eventually become lost, when it was leveraged as a foundation for full-time market participation in the form of cheese production. Paradoxically, liberation ideals of solidarity were more effective when directly supporting individual, limited efforts than the broader and necessarily more collective marketized activity of cheese production. Indeed, solidarity was often sorely tested as women in the collective struggled over what to do with community resources, including government-supported food supplies and the refrigerated cases purchased for the failed plaza store.

In its attempt to make market women, the Virgen de las Nubes experiment demonstrates the difficulties of simultaneously engaging religious, cultural, and economic systems. As they reflected on their experiences in the group, cooperative members retained their commitment to collectivist virtues of cooperation and solidarity, even as they mourned the loss of those attributes when the cooperative collapsed. "Se fue a la quiebra"—"It went bankrupt"—eventually described not only the economic demise of the project but also the loss of camaraderie and an important space for women to share the realities and "stresses" of their daily lives. In a place and time where women have little access to public space in which they can "develop [themselves]," as Josefa Arteaga described it, the group was most effective as a human development organization when it supported women doing so primarily in domestic, rather than industrialized, contexts.

This reality points to a second major conclusion, that to use social capital as a basis for human and economic development is to risk that capital in profound ways. When the cooperative was founded in 1989,

Promoción Humana promoters told members that they had a greater chance of economic success than similar men's groups because as women they were "more responsible for [their] children, [their] husbands, for everything," and because they shared Catholic values, once again tied to gender through the widespread belief that women are "more religious" than men and thus more committed to values of solidarity, sobriety, and family. Gender and religion were thus offered as capital that the women could access as they defined themselves in community, as common experiences, values, and concerns that would motivate their actions and provide enough commonality to override potential divisions. In this sense, women's relative vulnerability was recast as a perceived strength, something that worked well when the cooperative re-created household tasks such as knitting and cooking. Culinary capital, cooking together to shore up social bonds and provide time and space for women to de-stress and share their concerns about domestic difficulties, was effective as cooperative members recalled feeling supported and strengthened in their identities as mothers, wives, and women capable of contributing to household economies. As Mercedes Huilca commented, they were capable of "buying whatever" because of the sale of knitted pieces they had produced.

The risk in wagering capital, however, became evident when its investment did not yield the expected returns. In the case of gendered social capital, cooperative members found themselves confused and to no small degree disgusted when administrators could not agree on the use of government-provided food resources, a discourse that was often punctuated by accusations of "selfishness," constructed as antithetical to women's common concerns. In a similar manner, socias cited a lack of ability to live up to their own idealized Catholic values of helping and respecting others and self-sacrifice as one reason the cooperative failed. Though they referred to common identities as Catholics and as women as a reason for their success five years after they entered cheese production, they distanced themselves almost entirely from this explanation after the cheese plant shut down.

Such tensions also point to the role that emotions play in development, especially where development efforts are tied to social capital. In the cooperative, emotions were generally classified as negative, especially as they were identified in the context of conflict. Cooperative members often described "selfishness," and "being ugly" (*se pone fea*) as problematic emotional states that interfered with a perceived natural harmony in the form of cooperation and solidarity. In contrast, charismaticism encouraged public expressions of emotions, including anger, sadness, and even fear, in meetings and other public events. Juan XXIII members uniformly described the retreats as exceptionally emotional, if difficult, as they reviewed the "movies of their lives." In this way, charismaticism did a better job than the liberationist cooperative of acknowledging the role that emotions play in building and maintaining social capital. This is not unique. Though social capital, be it religious or gendered, has clear ties to emotional experiences and expressions, emotion other than a sense of responsibility or caring does not often factor into descriptions of its strengths or even daily operations. Similar to Matthew Gutmann's (2007) critique of development constructions of masculinity that preclude men's feelings, social capital used as an intervention also sidelines emotions, positive or negative, subordinating their expression to shared identity categories. This leaves people involved in development projects using social capital in the paradoxical position of drawing on shared experience to shore up social ties even as emotional expressions of those experiences are either ignored or discouraged. In the case of the cooperative, socias described informal sharing when knitting together as positive but expressions of frustration in formal meetings as "ugly" or a sign of a personal shortcoming. This disconnect further weakened socias' ability to draw on the commonalities of religion and gender designed to hold them together in common cause.

The failure of the project, which was structured on such commonalities, left many cooperative members reevaluating their views of the Catholic Church and their abilities as women to fully participate in market economies. Forced to rethink the role of religious identity, promised as a source of strength, cohesion, and even divine support when the project began, socias after the failure cited a lack of piety and enactment of religious ideals, especially those of cooperation and caring for others, for the plant's dissolution. In addition, they divided Catholicism into constituent pieces, institutional, quotidian, and liturgical, such that a failure of the institutional church did not require distancing from its quotidian and liturgical elements, something women began speaking of as the "more important" parts of the religion. They were able to do this with the church, but it has been a harder project with gender. Whereas socias attributed the success of the project to a perceived shared sense of responsibility, participation, and solidarity when cheese production began, they no longer believed that these values, or the capital such values provided, was adequate when production ended. As the more vulnerable of the two forms of social capital on which the project was constructed, it was an identity focused on gender that was gambled and lost in the end.

To structure development projects on the foundations of social capital is to risk it, especially where that social capital is drawn from vulnerabilities such as gender, poverty, or minority status. Such risk is not currently accounted for in most development initiatives that build on social capital, an important concern as microlending and gendered interventions are increasingly popular at the beginning of the twenty-first century and as faith-based organizations such as World Vision International, Compassion International, and Islamic Relief, among others, are major contributors to international economic development efforts. As this work has shown, simply recognizing that shared vulnerabilities or values can lead to social cohesion is not a substitute for working to eliminate those vulnerabilities and their continued regeneration.

APPENDIX

1989	Virgen de las Nubes Women's Cooperative founded with twenty members. Women are trained in knitting for sale to a consortium.
1995	Community bank microlending program begins.
1997	Promoción Humana approaches group about cheese production; women vote to begin cheese production.
1998	Cheese production begins in a private home in San Juan Pamba.
1999	Promoción Humana promoter introduces the idea of a store in Chillanes's main plaza.
1999	Group purchases Quilayacu property for the quesera.
2002	Quesera opens. The cooperative has thirty-five active members.
2002	Group begins to receive Ministerio de Bienestar Social food supplies.
2004	Knitting meetings cease.
2005	Land and building deeded to cooperative by Promoción Humana
2005	Cooperative rents a storefront and sells cheese, knit goods, and sundries in Chillanes.

2005	Yogurt building funded by provincial government is opened; group begins yogurt production.
2006	Cooperative owes more than $5,000 to local milk producers and substantial amounts for water, electricity, and taxes.
2007	Padre Mateo Patenghini pays electric, water, and tax bills. The quesera is put into receivership with Promoción Humana with the agreement that it will revert to the cooperative when it resumes cheese production.
2009–2012	Promoción Humana tries repeatedly to organize and restart the cooperative with support from the remaining thirteen or so members.
2015	Cooperative ceases all operations.

NOTES

INTRODUCTION. Blessed Are the Cheese Makers?

1. Assange lived in the Ecuadorian embassy in London from June 2012 to April 2019, avoiding arrest and extradition to Sweden on sexual assault charges. The conflict at the World Health Organization summit occurred in May 2018, when Ecuador proposed an amendment that would "protect, promote, and support breast-feeding." The United States objected, stating that it was prejudicial to mothers who could not, for whatever reason, breastfeed ("Opposition to Breast-Feeding Resolution by U.S. Stuns World Health Officials" 2018).

2. See, e.g., the UN's Millennium and Sustainable Development Goals, which include "Maternal Health," "Universal Primary Education," "Reduced Inequalities," and "Responsible Production and Consumption" (United Nations 2000, 2010).

3. The naming of participants in ethnographic research remains a contested subject. Here, I follow the American Anthropological Association practices outlined in its *Ethical Guidelines*, seeking first to do no harm. It is the hope of the Virgen de las Nubes Association and of the women who chose to be named in this work that their experiences will contribute to the betterment of local development projects such as the one described in these pages wherever they are in the world. I share that hope. See also Murphy and Jerolmack 2016.

4. Eventually, Mercedes stopped charging us rent, declaring us "family." We instead contributed to family causes, building a greenhouse for Mercedes's many agricultural projects, taking over the maintenance of a guinea pig colony, and pitching in for family events with money, supplies, and help with everything from cooking to construction.

5. In 1990, the illiteracy rate in Bolívar Province was 22.1 percent; Chillanes's current illiteracy rate is 14.2 percent (INEC 2018).

6. In 1990 the canton of Chillanes had 20,477 residents, and in 2001 the number dropped to 18,685. The 2010 census counted 17,406 residents (INEC 2018).

7. Like the term "developed," "poverty" has undergone definitional changes in scholarly literature, international metrics, and lived experience. Chillanenses often talk about experiences of poverty—of perpetual lack of access to resources such as reliable water, healthcare, education, agricultural assistance, markets, or information—as "la lucha," or the struggle of daily life. See DeTemple 2012, 46–50.

ONE. Why Catholic Women Make Cheese

1. For more on the legacy of liberation theology, see Burdick 1993, 2004; Chesnut 1997, 2003a; Gill 1998.

2. In 2001, 10 percent of Ecuadorians were considered charismatic, a number that continues to grow. See Barrett and Johnson 2001.

3. The Juan XXIII he founded for clergy is not to be confused with the organization to which Elena Sánchez and other Charismatic Catholics belong.

4. The Salesian order, founded in Italy by Don Juan Bosco in 1857, has always specialized in technical and vocational training. Aside from its projects in Salinas, the order has projects in twenty-seven communities in Ecuador, as well as universities in Quito and Cuenca.

5. For a detailed account of development efforts in Salinas and their relationship to broader economic and neoliberal concerns, see North and Cameron 2003.

6. It was at this time that Ester Boserup (1970) documented the many economic roles that women do have, even in "traditional" societies. Boserup, who studied Africa, argued that women play an important role as producers and decision makers in traditional economies.

TWO. Reproducing Women

1. The GINI coefficient for Ecuador in 1987 was 50.49 (Central Intelligence Agency 2012). The coefficient measures wealth distribution within a society, with 1 equaling perfect equality and 100 equaling perfect inequality. Though imperfect due to its inability to measure local conditions, in general higher coefficient numbers mean that a society is less likely to have a functioning middle class. The GINI coefficient for Ecuador in 2016 was 45, indicating greater equality in income distribution and a growing middle class.

For comparison, in 2016 Colombia's GINI coefficient was 50.8, Peru's was 43.8, the United States's was 41.5, and Mexico's was 43.4 (World Bank 2018). For more on Ecuador's growing middle class, see chapter 4.

2. The Libro de Actas, or Book of Acts, is the official recording of all group meetings where business was transacted. The book is a requirement for registered cooperatives and foundations under Ecuadorian law.

3. Of the women who owned their own houses, four had taken advantage of a one-time grant for new construction through the Sistema de Incentivos para la Vivienda (SIV), a government program instituted in 1998 through the Ministerio de Desarrollo Urbano y Viviendas (MIDUVI; Ministry of Urban Development and Housing). The grants, worth up to $7,000, could be used to pay for construction materials on land already owned by applicants or on urban areas to put toward the acquisition of an extant structure. Applicants had to provide a minimum amount toward the house before qualifying for the grants, which then also qualified them for optimal interest rates. For the relationship of the program to neoliberalism, see Córdova 2015; Klaufus 2009; Hinojosa 2013.

4. Ecuadorian law allows for differing kinds of marriages. "Free unions" (*uniones libres*), or "uniones de hecho" in legal terms, are legal relationships recognized by the state that are less binding than formal marriages, which must be dissolved through divorce. Codified in Article 68 of the 2008 Constitution, free unions were designed to give domestic partners some protection in the event of a relationship's dissolution but do not require lengthy and expensive civil divorce proceedings. One member of the Virgen de las Nubes group solidified a longtime relationship under the union libre law. All the others were married legally, and many also had church weddings, separate from the civil ceremony.

5. Silvia was not alone in her perception that Chillanes, the most urbanized population center in the canton, was safer for women than more rural settings. Many women I interviewed and engaged with in informal conversations remarked that rural women's lives were "harder" (*más duro*) than theirs and that urban men were less likely to be physically abusive. These perceptions are validated to a certain degree by the UN Global Database on Violence against Women, which lists "rural women" as a particular point of concern in its report on Ecuador, especially as they struggle for land tenure. According to the report, 38 percent of women in Ecuador will encounter gender-based violence at least once in their lifetimes (United Nations 2015).

6. The sucre was the currency of Ecuador from 1884 until the financial crisis of 1999–2000, when Ecuadorian president Jamil Mahuad pegged the sucre to the U.S. dollar to curb runaway inflation. Ecuador adopted the U.S. dollar as its currency on March 13, 2000.

THREE. Marketing the Domestic Church

1. The law, based on the 2008 Constitution, allows both heterosexual and homosexual couples the right to civil unions, which may be dissolved at will. The unions are recognized on national identity cards, giving partners legal status. Homosexual marriages were fully legalized in June 2019, giving same-sex partners more expansive rights should they choose marriage over a civil union. (Constitución del Ecuador 2008, art. 68). Because the civil union law was relatively new in 2009, record keeping was uneven in terms of recording births, listing some women in civil unions as "married" and some as "single."

2. "Separated brothers" is a term from the Vatican II documents referring to Protestants and other non-Catholic Christians.

3. A pseudonym.

FOUR. Las Juanes

1. Andrew Chesnut (1997, 2003a) in particular argued that Pentecostals offered a rational choice for Latin Americans looking for relief from the ills of poverty, especially in the areas of healing or health. He used a rational choice model taken from economics to argue for religious choice made for similarly pragmatic reasons. Other work (Berryman 1996; Burdick 1993; Garrard-Burnett 2000; DeTemple 2005) focuses on the lived realities of poverty, such as lack of access to resources or status, that may encourage people to follow charismatic paths that may more immediately and individually address what Chesnut (1997) calls the "pathogens of poverty."

2. The literature on Pentecostal growth in Latin America is robust, from David Stoll's seminal 1990 work, *Is Latin America Turning Protestant?,* to Kevin Lewis O'Neill's 2016 examination of Pentecostal gang remediation programs in Guatemala, *Secure the Soul.* While early works focused on rising numbers of Pentecostals as part of Latin America's religious landscape, works such as O'Neill's have begun to investigate the ways in which Pentecostals both challenge and uphold political, social, and economic structures.

3. Rita Bennett has run the Christian Renewal Association, located in Edmonds, WA, since Dennis Bennett's death in 1991.

4. The text of the prayer is as follows:

Come, Holy Spirit, fill the hearts of your faithful.
And kindle in them the fire of your love.
Send forth your Spirit and they shall be created.

And you will renew the face of the earth.
Lord,
by the light of the Holy Spirit
you have taught the hearts of your faithful.
In the same Spirit
help us to relish what is right
and always rejoice in your consolation.
We ask this through Christ our Lord.
Amen.

5. "Middle class" is a notoriously difficult category to define in absolute terms. The World Bank (2012) defines being middle class as having a less than 10 percent chance of falling into poverty over a five-year period. The Pew Research Center (2015) defines the middle class using income per capita. These economic measures do not take into account access to education, banking systems, or other social structures that lead to increased levels of economic prosperity or social stability and are therefore used here not as a comprehensive indicator but as a base measure of relative economic and social circumstances within Ecuadorian realities.

6. The Instituto Nacional de Estadisticos y Censos (INEC) projects that Bolívar's rural population, counted at 137,793 in the 2010 census, will grow to only 141,644 by 2020. By contrast, the urban areas of the province, with a population of 58,838 in 2010, are projected to grow to 68,289 by 2020. This larger growth in urban areas and relative stagnation in the rural sector is projected for Ecuador as a whole. See INEC Proyección de la población ecuatoriana por los a*ños* calendarios, según regiones, provincias y sexos, www.ecuadorencifras.gob.ec/proyecciones-poblacionales/.

7. To be clear, Juan XXIII does not espouse a theology that could be easily aligned with the Prosperity Gospel. While suffering and struggle ("la lucha") were frequent topics of conversation and reflection in weekly meetings and with those I interviewed such as Rosita, no one identified rich people as especially favored by God or gave any version of a "name it and claim it" theology. There were also no references to demonic forces preventing people from flourishing of any kind.

8. See, e.g., the work of Tola Otu Pearce (2012) that examines the role of emotion in Pentecostal approaches to sexuality and marriage in southwestern Nigeria.

FIVE. "We Are Also Outside"

1. "On the last day of the feast, the great day, Jesus stood up and proclaimed, 'If anyone thirsts, let him come to me and drink.' He who believes in me as the

scripture has said, 'Out of his heart shall flow rivers of living water.' Now this he said about the Spirit, which those who believed in him were about to receive; for as yet the Spirit had not been given, because Jesus was not yet glorified" (NRSV).

2. These students, Anna Lassiter and Eve Carson, were in Chillanes with a Moorehead Scholar summer program that funds overseas internships for scholarship recipients. They went to Chillanes after Arturo Escobar, a professor at the University of North Carolina at Chapel Hill, asked me, in my last year of graduate study, to find them a placement with the women's group. They raised money from friends and family before arriving in Ecuador for six weeks with the women's group, and Anna, in consultation with me, contracted with a local lawyer in Chillanes to draft an agreement for what the money would buy and how profits were to be shared. No provision was made for division of the property in the event of the dissolution of the cooperative, something cooperative members would later characterize as "a mistake" (*un error*).

3. Choclo is traditionally eaten with queso fresco, the soft cheese that many campesinos produce at home but that is also available for purchase in Chillanes's market and small dry goods stores.

WORKS CITED

Alkire, Sabina. 2002a. "Dimensions of Human Development." *World Development* 30, no.2: 181–205.

———. 2002b. *Valuing Freedom.* New York: Oxford University Press.

Alkire, Sabina, and Ann Braham. 2005. "Supporting the MDGs: A Faith-Based Movement's Story." *Development* 48, no. 1: 122–25.

Alvarez, Sonia E. 1998. "Latin American Feminisms 'Go Global.'" In *Culture of Politics, Politics of Culture: Re-Visioning Latin American Social Movements*, ed. Sonia Alvarez et al., 293–324. Boulder, CO: Westview Press.

Andolina, Robert, Nina Laurie, and Sarah Radcliffe. 2009. *Indigenous Development in the Andes.* Durham, NC: Duke University Press.

Andrade, Susana. 1990. *Visión mundial: Entre el cielo y la tierra. Religión y desarrollo en la sierra ecuatoriana.* Quito: Abya-Yala.

Appadurai, Arjun. 1996. *Modernity at Large: Cultural Dimensions of Globalization.* Minneapolis: University of Minnesota Press.

———. 2011. "The Ghost in the Financial Machine." *Public Culture* 23, no. 3: 517–39.

Arce, Alberto, and Norman Long, eds. 2000. *Anthropology, Development, and Modernities: Exploring Discourses, Counter-Tendencies, and Violence.* New York: Routledge.

Asad, Talal. 2003. *Formations of the Secular: Christianity, Islam, Modernity.* Stanford, CA: Stanford University Press.

Baker, Joseph O. 2010. "Social Sources of the Spirit: Connecting Rational Choice and Interactive Ritual Theories in the Study of Religion." *Sociology of Religion* 71, no. 4: 432–56.

Bakhtin, Mikhail. 1981. *The Dialogic Imagination.* Austin: University of Texas Press.

Banco Central del Ecuador. 2019. "Memoria anual." https://contenido.bce.fin.ec/docs.php?path=./documentos/PublicacionesNotas/Catalogo/Memoria/.

Barbé, Lesy. 2001. "Santa Rita." Pamphlet. Barcelona: Editores Verón.

Barnett, Michael, and Janice Gross Stein, eds. 2012. *Sacred Aid: Faith and Humanitarianism.* New York: Oxford University Press.

Barrett, David, and Todd Johnson. 2001. *World Christian Encyclopedia.* 2nd ed. New York: Oxford University Press.

Barton, Carol. 2005. "Women Debate the MDGs." *Development* 48, no. 1: 101–6.

Basso, Keith. 1986. *Wisdom Sits in Places.* Albuquerque: University of New Mexico Press.

Bebbington, Anthony. 1997. "New States, New NGOs? Crisis and Transition among Rural Development NGOs in the Andean Region." *World Development* 25, no. 11: 1755–65.

———. 2000. "Reencountering Development: Livelihood Transitions and Place Transformations in the Andes." *Annals of the Association of American Geographers* 90, no. 3: 495–520.

———. 2001. "Globalized Andes? Livelihoods, Landscapes and Development." *Ecumene* 8, no. 4: 414–36.

———. 2007. "Reinventing NGOs and Rethinking Alternatives in the Andes." *Annals of the American Academy of Political and Social Science* 554: 117–35.

Bebbington, Anthony, and Thomas Perrault. 1999. "Social Capital, Development and Access to Resources in Highland Ecuador." *Economic Geography* 75, no. 4: 395–418.

Becker, Marc. 2008. *Indians and Leftists in the Making of Ecuador's Modern Indigenous Movements.* Durham, NC: Duke University Press.

———. 2011. *Pachakutik: Indigenous Movements and Electoral Politics in Ecuador.* Lanham, MD: Rowman & Littlefield.

Becker, Marc, and Kim Clark, eds. 2007. *Highland Indians and the State in Modern Ecuador.* Pittsburgh, PA: University of Pittsburgh Press.

Bedford, Kate. 2005. "Loving to Straighten out Development: Sexuality and 'Ethnodevelopment' in the World Bank's Ecuadorian Lending." *Feminist Legal Studies* 13: 295–322.

Bending, Tim, and Sergio Rosendo. 2005. "Rethinking the Mechanics of the 'Anti-Politics Machine.'" In *Development Brokers and Translators: The Ethnography of Aid and Agencies*, ed. David Lewis and David Mosse, 217–38. West Hartford, CT: Kumarian Press.

Benediktsson, Karl. 2002. *Harvesting Development: The Construction of Fresh Food Markets in Papua New Guinea.* Ann Arbor: University of Michigan Press.

Benthall, Jonathan. 2008. *Returning to Religion: Why a Secular Age Is Haunted by Faith.* London: I. B. Tauris.

———. 2016. *Islamic Charities and Islamic Humanism in Troubled Times.* New York: Oxford University Press.

Berger, Peter L. 1967. *The Sacred Canopy: Elements of a Sociological Theory of Religion.* New York: Anchor Books.

Bergeron, Suzanne. 2000. "The Post–Washington Consensus and Economic Representations of Women in Development at the World Bank." *International Feminist Journal of Politics* 5, no. 3: 397–419.

———. 2004. *Fragments of Development: Nation, Gender, and the Space of Modernity.* Ann Arbor: University of Michigan Press.

Berryman, Phillip. 1996. *Religion in the Megacity: Catholic and Protestant Portraits from Latin America.* Maryknoll, NY: Orbis.

Bhatta, Gambir. 2001. "Of Geese and Ganders: Mainstreaming Gender in the Context of Sustainable Human Development." *Journal of Gender Studies* 10, no. 1: 17–32.

Bianchi, Eugene. 1970. "John XXIII, Vatican II and American Catholicism." *Annals of the American Academy of Political and Social Science* 387: 30–40.

Boff, Clodovis. 2007. "Teologia da libertação e volta ao fundamento." *Revista Eclesiástica Brasileira* 67, no. 268: 1001–22.

Boff, Clodovis, and Leonardo Boff. 2001. *Introducing Liberation Theology.* Maryknoll, NY: Orbis Books.

Boff, Leonardo. 1985. *Church, Charism, and Power: Liberation Theology and the Institutional Church.* Eugene, OR: Wipf and Stock.

Boguslawski, Steven, and Ralph Martin, eds. 2008. *The New Evangelization: Overcoming the Obstacles.* Detroit, MI: Sacred Heart Major Seminary.

Bornstein, Erica. 2005. *The Spirit of Development: Protestant NGOs, Morality, and Economics in Zimbabwe.* Stanford, CA: Stanford University Press.

Borque, Susan C., and Kay Warren. 1981. *Women of the Andes: Patriarchy and Social Change in Two Peruvian Towns.* Ann Arbor: University of Michigan Press.

Boserup, Ester. 1970. *Women's Role in Economic Development.* New York: St. Martin's Press.

Bourdieu, Pierre. 1977. *Outline of a Theory of Practice.* Cambridge: Cambridge University Press.

———. 1980. *The Logic of Practice.* Stanford, CA: Stanford University Press.

Brouwer, Steve, Paul Gifford, and Susan D. Rose. 1996. *Exporting the American Gospel: Global Christian Fundamentalism.* New York: Routledge.

Brusco, Elizabeth. 1995. *The Reformation of Machismo: Evangelical Conversion and Gender in Colombia.* Austin: University of Texas Press.

Burdick, John. 1993. *Looking for God in Brazil: The Progressive Catholic Church in Urban Brazil's Religious Arena.* Berkeley: University of California Press.

———. 2004. *Legacies of Liberation: The Progressive Catholic Church in Brazil at the Start of a New Millennium.* Burlington, VT: Ashgate.

Bush, Evelyn. 2010. "Explaining Religious Market Failure: A Gendered Critique of the Religious Economies Model." *Sociological Theory* 28, no. 3: 304–25.

Butler, Judith. 1990. *Gender Trouble.* New York: Routledge.

Campana, Victor Alejandro. 2001. *Desarrollo, conocimiento y participación en la comunidad andina.* Riobamba: Federación de Organizaciones Indígenas de las Faldas del Chimborazo.

Cartledge, Mark J. 2006. *Encountering the Spirit: The Charismatic Tradition.* Maryknoll, NY: Orbis Books.

Casanova, José. 1994. *Public Religion in the Modern World.* Chicago: University of Chicago Press.

Castellanos Hurtado, P. Francisco. 1993. *Los Salesianos en Mexico.* Mexico City: Ediciones Don Bosco.

Castillo Lara, Lucas Guillermo. 1995. *La raigambre salesiana en Venezuela: Cien años de la primera siembra.* Caracas: Academia Nacional de la Historia.

Central Intelligence Agency. 2012. "The World Factbook: Ecuador." www.cia.gov/library/publications/the-world-factbook/geos/ec.html.

Ceria, Eugenio. 1955. *The Salesian Society: Foundation, Organization, Expansion.* Paterson, NJ: Salesian Publishers.

Certeau, Michel de. 1984. *The Practice of Everyday Life.* Berkeley: University of California Press.

Charet, Erika Silva, ed. 2008. *Genero y ambiente en el Ecuador: Aproximaciones desde lo social y lo étnico-cultural.* Quito: Abya-Yala.

Chatterjee, Nilanjana, and Nancy Riley. 2001. "Planning an Indian Modernity: The Gendered Politics of Fertility Control." *Signs* 26, no. 3: 811–45.

Chesnut, Andrew. 1997. *Born Again in Brazil: The Pentecostal Boom and the Pathogens of Poverty.* New Brunswick, NJ: Rutgers University Press.

———. 2003a. *Competitive Spirits: Latin America's New Religious Economy.* New York: Oxford University Press.

———. 2003b. "Pragmatic Consumers and Practical Products: The Success of Pneumacentric Religion among Women in Latin America's New Religious Economy." *Review of Religious Research* 45, no. 1: 20–31.

———. 2003c. "A Preferential Option for the Spirit: The Catholic Charismatic Renewal in Latin America's New Religious Economy." *Latin American Politics and Society* 45, no. 1: 55–85.

Chidester, David. 2005. *Authentic Fakes: Religion and American Popular Culture.* Berkeley: University of California Press.

———. 2014. *Empire of Religion: Imperialism and Comparative Religion.* Chicago: University of Chicago Press.

Chiriboga, Manuel, et al. 1999 *Cambiar se peude: Experiencias del FEPP en el desarrollo rural del Ecuador.* Quito: Abya-Yala.

Cisneros, Vicente. 2002. *Celebración del misterio Pascual dirigido por laicos autorizados: Domingo, Día del Señor y Semana Santa.* Quito: Diocese of Ambato.

Clarke, Matthew, ed. 2013. *Handbook of Research on Development and Religion.* Northhampton, MA: Edwin Elgar.

Cleary, Edward L. 2011. *The Rise of Charismatic Catholicism in Latin America.* Gainesville: University Press of Florida.

Clifford, James. 1988. *The Predicament of Culture: Twentieth-Century Ethnography, Literature, and Art.* Cambridge, MA: Harvard University Press.

———. 1997. *Routes: Travel and Translation in the Late Twentieth Century.* Cambridge, MA: Harvard University Press.

Colectivo de Investigación y Acción Psicosocial Ecuador. 2015. *Informe preliminar sobre las estrategias estatales de control social y represión en el Marco de Paro Nacional en Ecuador.* Quito: Investigación Acción Psicosocial.

Colloredo-Mansfeld, Rudi. 1999. *The Native Leisure Class: Consumption and Cultural Creativity in the Andes.* Chicago: University of Chicago Press.

———. 2009. *Fighting Like a Community: Andean Civil Society in an Era of Indian Uprisings.* Chicago: University of Chicago Press.

Connell, Raewyn, and Nour Dados. 2014. "Where in the World Does Neoliberalism Come From? The Market Agenda in Southern Perspective." *Theory and Society* 43, no. 2: 117–38.

Córdova, Marco Antonio. 2015. "Transformación de las políticas de vivienda social: El sistema de incentivos para la vivienda en la conformación de causimercados en Ecuador." Íconos*: Revista de Ciencias Sociales* 53: 127–49.

Cornwall, Andrea, Elizabeth Harrison, and Ann Whitehead. 2007. "Gender Myths and Feminist Fables: The Struggle for Interpretive Power in Gender and Development." *Development and Change* 38, no. 1: 1–20.

Cox, Harvey. 1995. *Fire from Heaven: The Rise of Pentecostal Spirituality and the Reshaping of Religion in the Twenty-First Century.* Reading, MA: Addison-Wesley.

Crewe, Emma, and Elizabeth Harrison. 1998. *Whose Development? An Ethnography of Aid.* London: Zed Books.

Csordas, Thomas J. "Global Religion and the Reenchantment of the World: The Case of the Catholic Charismatic Renewal." 2009. In *Transnational Transcendence: Essays on Religion and Globalization*, ed. Thomas Csordas, 73–96. Berkeley: University of California Press.

Curtis, Heather. 2018. *Holy Humanitarians: American Evangelicals and Global Aid.* Cambridge, MA: Harvard University Press.

Cush, Jonathan, ed. 1995. *The Power of Development.* New York: Routledge.

DeLanda, Manuel. 2006. *A New Philosophy of Society: Assemblage Theory and Social Complexity.* London: Continuum.

De la Torre, Carlos, and Steve Striffler, eds. 2008. *The Ecuador Reader.* Durham, NC: Duke University Press.

Deneulin, Séverine, and Masooda Bano. 2009. *Religion in Development: Rewriting the Secular Script.* London: Zed Books.

Deneulin, Séverine, and Lila Shahani. 2009. *An Introduction to the Human Development and Capability Approach: Freedom and Agency.* Sterling, VA: Earthscan.

DeTemple, Jill. 2005. "Chains of Liberation: Poverty and Social Action in the Universal Church of the Kingdom of God." In *Latino Religions and Civic Activism in the United States*, ed. Gaston Espinoza, Jesse Miranda, and Virgilio Elizondo, 219–32. New York: Oxford University Press.

———. 2012. *Cement, Earthworms, and Cheese Factories: Religion and Community Development in Rural Ecuador.* Notre Dame, IN: University of Notre Dame Press.

———. 2013. "Imagining Development: Religious Studies in the Context of International Economic Development." *Journal of the American Academy of Religion* 80, no. 1: 107–29.

———. 2015. "Inca Roads, Protestant Hospitals, Catholic Cheese, and the Fluctuating State: Religion and Development in Ecuador." In *The Routledge Handbook of Religions and Global Development*, ed. Emma Tomalin, 156–66. Oxford: Routledge.

DeTemple, Jill, Erin Eidenshink, and Katrina Josephson. 2009. "How Is Your Life Since Then? Gender Doctrine and Development in Bolivia." In *Bridging the Gaps: Faith-Based Organizations, Neoliberalism and Development in Latin America and the Caribbean*, ed. Julie Adkins, Tara Hefferan, and Laurie Occhipinti, 119–32. Lanham, MD: Lexington Books.

Dijkstra, A. Geske, and Lucia C. Hanmer. 2000. "Measuring Socio-Economic Gender Inequality: Toward an Alternative to the UNDP Gender-Related Development Index." *Feminist Economics* 6, no. 2: 41–75.

Drogus, Carol Ann. 1997. *Women, Religion, and Social Change in Brazil's Popular Church.* South Bend, IN: University of Notre Dame Press.

Dubach, José. 1998. *Diez años del Proyecto queserias rurales del Ecuador.* Quito: Fondo Ecuatoriano Popularum Progressio.

Dupré, Louis. 1993. *Passage to Modernity: An Essay in the Hermeneutics of Nature and Culture.* New Haven, CT: Yale University Press.

———. 2008. *Religion and the Rise of Modern Culture.* Notre Dame, IN: University of Notre Dame Press.

Ecklund, Elaine Howard. 2003. "Catholic Women Negotiate Feminism: A Research Note." *Sociology of Religion* 64, no. 4: 515–24.

Edbaugh, Helen Rose, Janet Saltzman Chafetz, and Paula Pipes. 2005. "Faith-Based Social Service Organizations and Government Funding: Data from a National Survey." *Social Science Quarterly* 86, no. 2: 273–92.

Engelke, Matthew, and Matt Tomlinson. 2006. *The Limits of Meaning: Case Studies in the Anthropology of Christianity.* New York: Berghahn Books.

Escobar, Arturo. 1995. *Encountering Development: The Making and Unmaking of the Third World.* Princeton, NJ: Princeton University Press.

———. 2000. "Culture Sits in Places: Reflections on Globalism and Subaltern Strategies of Localization." *Political Geography* 19: 139–74.

———. 2008. *Territories of Difference: Place, Movement, Life,* Redes. Durham, NC: Duke University Press.

Ferguson, James. 1984. *The Anti-Politics Machine: "Development," Depoliticization, and Bureaucratic Power in Lesotho.* Minneapolis: University of Minnesota Press.

Ferreira, Francisco H. G., Julian Messina, Jamele Riolini, Luis-Felipe López-Calca, Maria Ana Lugo, and Renos Vakis. 2012. *Economic Mobility and the Rise of the Middle Class.* Washington, DC: World Bank.

Ferris, Elizabeth. 2005. "Faith-Based and Secular Human Organizations." *International Review of the Red Cross* 87, no. 1: 311–25.

Figueroa, Adolfo. 1990. "La agricultura campesina en Ámerica Latina: Desafios para los 90." *Estudios Rurales Latinoamericanos* 13, no. 1–2: 85–113.

Fine, Ben. 1999. "The Development State Is Dead—Long Live Social Capital?" *Development and Change* 30: 1–19.

———. 2001. *Social Capital versus Social Theory: Political Economy and Social Science at the Turn of the Millennium.* London: Routledge.

———. 2010. *Theories of Social Capital: Researchers Behaving Badly.* New York: Palgrave Macmillan.

Fraser, Arvonne, and Irene Tinker. 2004. *Developing Power: How Women Transformed International Development.* New York: Feminist Press at the City University of New York.

Freire, Paulo. 2006. *Pedagogy of the Oppressed.* New York: Continuum.

Friedmann, John, Rebecca Abers, and Lilian Autler, eds. 1996. *Emergences: Women's Struggles for Livelihood in Latin America.* Los Angeles: UCLA Latin American Center Publications.

García Martín, Julio. 1998. *La actividad misionera según la doctrina y la legislación de la Iglesia.* Buenos Aires: Editorial Claretiana.

Gardner, Kay, and David Lewis. 1996. *Anthropology, Development and the Post-Modern Challenge.* London: Pluto Press.

Garrard-Burnett, Virginia, ed. 2000. *On Earth as It Is in Heaven: Religion in Modern Latin America.* Wilmington, DE: Scholarly Resources.

Gavilanes del Castillo, Luis María. 1992. *Monseñor Leonidas Proaño y su misión profético: Liberadora en la Iglesia de America Latina.* Quito: Fondo Ecuatoriano Populorum Progressio.

Gibson-Graham, J. K. 2006. *Postcapitalist Politics*. Minneapolis: University of Minnesota Press.

Gill, Antony. 1998. *Rendering unto Caesar: The Catholic Church and the State in Latin America.* Chicago: University of Chicago Press.

Gobierno del Canton Chillanes. 2009. *Catastro de las patentes comerciantes de Chillanes*. Chillanes.

Goody, Jack. 2003. "Religion and Development: Some Comparative Considerations." *Development* 46, no. 4: 64–67.

Grameen Bank. 2012. "What Is Microcredit?" www.grameeninfo.org/index.php?option=com_content&task=view&id=28&Itemid=108.

Gudeman, Stephen. 1976. *Relationships, Residence and the Individual.* London: Routledge & Kegan Paul.

———. 1986. *Economics as Culture: Models and Metaphors of Livlihood.* London: Routledge & Kegan Paul.

Guerrero Cazar, Fernando, and Pablo Ospina Peralta. 2003. *El poder de la comunidad: Ajuste estructural y movimiento indígena en los Andes ecuatorianos.* Buenos Aires: Consejo Latinoamericano de Ciencias Sociales (CLACSO).

Gupta, Akhil. 1998. *Postcolonial Developments.* Durham, NC: Duke University Press.

Gutiérrez, Gustavo. 1971. *Teología de la liberación: Perspectivas.* Lima: CEP.

———. 1999. "The Task and Content of Liberation Theology." In *The Cambridge Companion to Liberation Theology*, ed. Christopher Rowland, 19–38. Cambridge: Cambridge University Press.

Gutmann, Matthew. 1996. *The Meanings of Macho: Being a Man in Mexico City.* Berkeley: University of California Press.

———. 2007. *Fixing Men: Sex, Birth Control, and AIDS in Mexico.* Berkeley: University of California Press.

Guyer, Jane. 1988. "Dynamic Approaches to Domestic Budgeting: Cases and Methods from Africa." In *A Home Divided: Women and Income in the Third World,* ed. Daisy Dwyer and Judith Bruce, 155–72. Stanford, CA: Stanford University Press.

Haidari, Shokrullah Hamd, and Susan Wright. 2001. "Participation and Participatory Development among the Kahlor Nomads of Iran." *Community Development Journal* 36, no. 1: 53–62.

Hardt, Michael, and Antonio Negri. 2000. *Empire.* Cambridge, MA: Harvard University Press.

Harris, Richard, and Jorge Nef, eds. 2008. *Capital, Power and Inequality in Latin America and the Carribean*. New York: Rowman & Littlefield.

Haynes, Jeffrey. 2007. *Religion and Development: Conflict or Cooperation?* New York: Palgrave.

Hefferan, Tara. 2007. *Twinning Faith and Development: Catholic Parish Partnering in the U.S. and Haiti*. West Hartford, CT: Kumarian Press.

Hefferan, Tara, Julie Adkins, and Laurie Occhipinti, eds. 2009. *Bridging the Gaps: Faith-Based Organizations, Neoliberalism, and Development in Latin America and the Caribbean*. Lanham, MD: Lexington Books.

Hennelly, Alfred T. 1990. *Liberation Theology: A Documentary History*. Maryknoll, NY: Orbis Books.

Hinojosa Lara, Héctor David. 2013. "El bono de la vivienda en el Ecuador: Su alcance y perspectiva, periodo 2007–2011." PhD dissertation, Universidad Católica del Ecuador.

Hippert, Christine. 2011. "The Politics and Practices of Constructing Development Identities in Rural Bolivia." *Journal of Latin American and Caribbean Anthropology* 16, no. 1: 90–111.

Hirschman, Albert O. 1967. *Development Projects Observed*. Washington, DC: Brookings Institution.

———. 1984. *Getting Ahead Collectively: Grassroots Experiences in Latin America*. New York: Pergamon Press.

———. 1985. *A Bias for Hope: Essays on Development in Latin America*. Boulder, CO: Westview Press.

———. 1986. *Rival Views of Market Society*. New York: Viking Books.

"Historia de las queseras rurales del Ecuador." 2008. www.salinerito.com/downloads/historia.queseras.doc.

Hoadley, J. Stephen. 1981. "The Rise and Fall of the Basic Needs Approach." *Cooperation and Conflict* 16, no. 3: 149–64.

Hogan, John P. 2003. *Credible Signs of Christ Alive: Case Studies from the Catholic Campaign for Human Development*. Lanham, MD: Rowman & Littlefield.

Hoksbergen, Roland. 1986. "Approaches to Evaluation of Development Interventions: The Importance of World and Life Views." *World Development* 14, no. 2: 283–300.

Holland, Dorothy, William Lachiotte Jr., Debra Skinner, and Carole Cain. 1998. *Identity and Agency in Cultural Worlds*. Cambridge, MA: Harvard University Press.

"Homalía del Papa sobre la familia en el Parque Samanes en Guayaquil." 2015. ACI Prensa. www.aciprensa.com/noticias/texto-completo-homilia-del-papa-sobre-la-familia-en-el-parque-samanes-en-guayaquil-54183.

hooks, bell. 1990. *Yearning: Race, Gender, and Cultural Politics.* Toronto: Between the Lines.

Huber, Evelyne, and Fred Solt. 2004. "Successes and Failures of Neoliberalism." *Latin American Research Review* 30, no. 3: 150–64.

Hula, Richard, Cynthia Jackson-Elmore, and Laura Reese. 2007. "Mixing God's Work and the Public Business: A Framework for the Analysis of Faith-Based Service Delivery." *Review of Policy Research* 24, no. 1: 67–89.

Hurtado, Oswaldo. 1969. *Dos mundos superpuestos: Ensayo de diagnóstico de la realidad ecuatoriana.* Quito: Instituto de Planificación para el Desarrollo Social.

———. 2010. *Portrait of a Nation: Culture and Progress in Ecuador.* Trans. Barbara Sipe. Lanham, MD: Madison Books.

Illich, Ivan. 1977. *Toward a History of Needs.* New York: Pantheon.

———. 1981. *Shadow Work.* Boston: Marion Boyars.

Instituto Nacional de Estadísticos y Censos, Ecuador (INEC). 2018. www.ecuadorencifras.gob.ec/institucional/home/.

Jaquette, Jane S., and Gale Summerfield, eds. 2007. *Women and Gender Equity in Development Theory and Practice: Institutions, Resources, and Mobilization.* Durham, NC: Duke University Press.

Kabeer, Naila. 2005. "Gender Equality and Women's Empowerment: A Critical Analysis of the Third Millennium Development Goal." *Gender and Development* 13, no. 1: 13–24.

Kelkar, Govind, and Dev Nathan. 2002. "Gender Relations and Technological Change in Asia." *Current Sociology* 50, no. 3: 427–41.

Khabeer, Su'ad Abdul. 2016. *Muslim Cool: Race, Religion, and Hip Hop in the United States.* New York: New York University Press.

Klaufus, Christien. 2010. "The Two ABCs of Aided Self-Help Housing in Ecuador." *Habitat International* 34: 351–58.

Klenk, Rebecca M. 2004. "'Who Is the Developed Woman?': Women as a Category of Development Discourse, Kumaon, India." *Development and Change* 35, no. 1: 57–78.

Kochhar, Rakesh. 2015. "A Global Middle Class Is More Promise than Reality: From 2001 to 2011, Nearly 700 Million Step out of Poverty, but Most Only Barely." Pew Research Center, Washington, DC.

Libro de Actas. 2009. "Virgen de las Nubes Women's Cooperative." Unpublished document. Chillanes, Ecuador.

Lin, Nan. 2001. *Social Capital: A Theory of Social Structure and Action.* New York: Cambridge University Press.

Lind, Amy. 1997. "Gender, Development and Urban Social Change: Women's Community Action in Global Cities." *World Development* 28, no. 9: 1205–23.

———. 2002. "Making Feminist Sense of Neoliberalism: The Institutionalization of Women's Struggles for Survival in Ecuador and Bolivia." *Journal of Developing Societies* 18, no. 2–3: 228–58.

———. 2003a. "Feminist Post-Development Thought: 'Women and Development' and the Gendered Paradoxes of Survival in Bolivia." *Women's Studies Quarterly* 31, no. 3–4: 227–46.

———. 2003b. "Gender and Neoliberal States: Feminists Remake the Nation in Ecuador." *Latin American Perspectives* 30, no. 1: 182–207.

———. 2005. *Gendered Paradoxes: Women's Movements, State Restructuring, and Global Development in Ecuador.* University Park: Pennsylvania State University Press.

Lofton, Kathryn. 2011. *Oprah: The Gospel of an Icon.* Berkeley: University of California Press.

Lomnitz, Larissa Adler. 1978. "Mecanismos de articulación entre el sector informal y el sector formal urbano." *Revista Mexicana de Sociología* 40, no. 1: 131–53.

———. 1988. "Informal Exchange Networks in Formal Systems: A Theoretical Model." *American Anthropologist*, n.s., 90, no. 1: 42–55.

Long, Charles. 1986. *Significations: Signs, Symbols, and Images in the Interpretation of Religion.* Minneapolis, MN: Fortress Press.

Lyons, Barry. 2006. *Remembering the Hacienda: Religion, Authority, and Social Change in Highland Ecuador.* Austin: University of Texas Press.

Lyons, Barry, with Angel Aranda and Dina Guevera. 2008. "Simple People." In *The Ecuador Reader*, ed. Carlos de la Torre and Steve Striffler, 403–14. Durham, NC: Duke University Press.

Malinowski, Bronislaw. 1961. *Argonauts of the Western Pacific.* New York: Dutton.

Malloch, Theodore Roosevelt. 2003. "Social, Human and Spiritual Capital in Human Development." Templeton Foundation, Working Group of the Spiritual Capital Project: Harvard University. www.spiritualcapitalresearch program.com/pdf/malloch.pdf.

Marshall, Katherine 2004. "Faith Perspectives for Development Institutions: New Faces of Compassion and Social Justice." *International Journal* 59, no. 4: 893–901.

Martin, David. 1990. *Tongues of Fire: The Explosion of Protestantism in Latin America.* Oxford: Basil Blackwell.

Martinez-Hernandez, Raul, Gareth Thomas, Luís Kluwe Aguiar, and Francisco Gonzalez-Diaz. 2007. "The Salinas Cheese Factories: Factors Affecting the Competitive Strategy in Ecuador." Paper presented at the 17th Annual Forum and Symposium IAMA Conference, Parma, Italy.

Masuzawa, Tomoko. 2005. *The Invention of World Religions, Or, How Universalism was Preserved in the Language of Pluralism.* Chicago: University of Chicago Press.

Mayer, Enrique. 2002. *The Articulated Peasant: Household Economics in the Andes.* Boulder, CO: Westview Press.

McAlister, Elizabeth. 2013. "Humanitarian Advocacy, Transnational New Apostolic Missions, and Evangelical Anti-Dependency in a Haitian Refugee Camp." *Nova Religio: Journal of Alternative and Emergent Religions* 16, no. 4: 11–34.

McCutcheon, Russell T. 1997. *Manufacturing Religion: The Discourse on Sui Generis Religion and the Politics of Nostalgia.* New York: Oxford University Press.

Meisch, Lynn. 2002. *Andean Entrepreneurs: Otavalo Merchants and Musicians in the Global Arena.* Austin: University of Texas Press.

Migration Policy Institute. 2007. "Ecuador: Diversity in Migration." www.migrationinformation.org/USfocus/display.cfm?ID=575.

Mitlin, Diana, Sam Hickey, and Anthony Bebbington. 2007. "Reclaiming Development? NGOs and the Challenge of Alternatives." *World Development* 35, no. 10: 1699–1720.

Molyneaux, Maxine. 2002. "Gender and the Silences of Social Capital." *Development and Change* 3, no. 2: 167–88.

Mörner, Magnus. 1985. *The Andean Past: Land, Societies, and Conflicts.* New York: Columbia University Press.

Moser, Carolyn. 1993. *Gender Planning and Development: Theory, Practice and Training.* London: Routledge.

Mosse, David. 2004. "Is Good Policy Unimplementable? Reflections on the Ethnography of Aid Policy and Practice." *Development and Change* 35, no. 4: 639–71.

Muehlebach, Andrea. 2013. "The Catholicization of Neoliberalism: On Love and Welfare in Lombardy, Italy." *American Anthropologist* 115, no. 3: 452–65.

Munck, Thomas, and Denis O'Hearn. 1999. *Critical Development Theory: Contributions to a New Paradigm.* London: Zed Books.

Murphy, Alexandra, and Colin Jerolmack. 2016. "Ethnographic Masking in an Era of Data Transparency." https://contexts.org/blog/ethnographic-masking-in-an-era-of-data-transparency-2/.

Nagle, Robin. 1997. *Claiming the Virgin: The Broken Promises of Liberation Theology*. New York: Routledge.

Napolitano, Valentina. 1998. "Between 'Traditional' and 'New' Catholic Church Religious Discourses in Urban, Western Mexico." *Bulletin of Latin American Research* 17, no. 3: 323–39.

"New Evangelization Inseparable from Family." 2011. *Osservatore Romano*, December 2. www.osservatoreromano.va/en/news/new-evangelization-inseparable-from-family.

North, Liisa, and John Cameron, eds. 2003. *Rural Progress, Rural Decay: Neoliberal Adjustment Policies and Local Initiatives.* Bloomfield, CT: Kumarian Press.

North, Liisa, with Wade Kipp and Rob Koep. 2003. "Rural Land Conflicts and Human Rights Violations in Ecuador." Cerelac Working Paper Series, Toronto.

Nussbaum, Martha. 2000. *Women and Human Development: The Capabilities Approach.* Cambridge: Cambridge University Press.

Occhipinti, Laurie. 2005. *Acting on Faith: Religious Development Organizations in Northwestern Argentina.* Lanham, MD: Lexington Books.

Ochoa Chucuyán, Andrea Cristina. 2015. "Incremento en las recaudaciones en el impuesto a la renta y su impacto en el crecimiento económico del Ecuador, período 2006–2012." PhD dissertation, Universidad Católica de Santiago de Guayaquil.

Olivier de Sardan, Jean-Pierre. 2005. *Anthropology and Development: Understanding Contemporary Social Change.* London: Zed Books.

O'Neill, Kevin Lewis. 2015. *Secure the Soul: Christian Piety and Gang Prevention in Guatemala.* Berkeley: University of California Press.

"Opposition to Breast-Feeding Resolution Stuns World Health Officials." 2018. *New York Times*, July 8. www.nytimes.com/2018/07/08/health/world-health-breastfeeding-ecuador-trump.html.

Orsi, Robert. 1997. "Everyday Miracles: The Study of Lived Religion." In *Lived Religion in America: Toward a History of Practice*, ed. David D. Hall, 3–21. Princeton, NJ: Princeton University Press.

Pallares, Amalia. 2002. *From Peasant Struggle to Indian Resistance: The Ecuadorian Andes in the Late Twentieth Century.* Norman: University of Oklahoma Press.

Parpart, Jane L., Shirin M. Rai, and Kathleen Staudt. 2002. *Rethinking Empowerment: Gender and Development in a Global/Local World.* London: Routledge.

Pastoral Challenges in the Context of Evangelization. 2014. Rome: Vatican.

Paul VI. 1964. *Encyclical Letter: Lumen Gentium.* Washington, DC: United States Catholic Conference.

———. 1967. *Encyclical Letter: Populorum Progressio.* Washington, DC: United States Catholic Conference.

Pearce, Tola Otu. 2012. "Reconstructing Sexuality in the Shadow of Neoliberal Globalization: Investigating the Approach of Charismatic Churches in Southwestern Nigeria." *Journal of Religion in Africa* 42, no. 4: 345–68.

Pearson, Ruth. 2000. "Moving the Goalposts: Gender and Globalisation in the Twenty-First Century." *Gender and Development* 8, no. 1: 10–19.

Peattie, Lisa. 1981. *Thinking about Development.* New York: Plenum Press.

Pew Research Center. 2014. "Religion in Latin America: Widespread Change in a Historically Catholic Region." www.pewforum.org/2014/11/13/religion-in-latin-america/.

Phillips, Lynne, ed. 1998. *The Third Wave of Modernization in Latin America: Cultural Perspectives on Neoliberalism.* Wilmington, DE: Scholarly Resources.

Pigg, Stacy Leigh. 1992. "Inventing Social Categories through Place: Social Representations and Development in Nepal." *Comparative Studies in Society and History* 34, no. 3: 491–513.

Poewe, Karla, ed. 1994. *Charismatic Christianity as Global Culture.* Columbia: University of South Carolina Press.

Polo F., Padre Antonio. 1993. *Un nuevo paradigma para el desarrollo: La empresa comunitaria andina. Entrevista con el padre Antonio Polo sobre la experiencia autogestionaria de Salinas.* Quito: Comunidec.

———. 2002. *La puerta abierta: 30* años de *aventura misionera y social en Salinas de Bolívar, Ecuador.* Quito: Abya Yala.

Pottier, Johan, Alan Bicker, and Paul Sillitoe. 2003. *Negotiating Local Knowledge: Power and Identity in Development.* London: Pluto Press.

Pribilsky, Jason. 2007. *La Chulla Vida: Gender, Migration, and the Family in Andean Ecuador and New York City.* Syracuse, NY: Syracuse University Press.

Pritchard, Elizabeth. 2000. "The Way Out West: Development and the Rhetoric of Mobility in Postmodern Feminist Theory." *Hypatia* 15, no. 3: 45–72.

Putnam, Robert. 2000. *Bowling Alone: The Collapse and Revival of American Community.* New York: Simon & Schuster.

Radcliffe, Sarah A., Nina Laurie, and Robert Andolina. 2003. "The Transnationalization of Gender and Reimagining Andean Indigenous Development." *Signs: Journal of Women in Culture and Society* 29, no. 2: 387–415.

Radio Amigo Chillanes. 2009. "Tema Santa Rita." Radio broadcast, May 14.

Rahnema, Majid, and Victor Bawtree, eds. 1997. *The Post-Development Reader.* London: Zed Books.

Ratzinger, Joseph Cardinal. 1985. "Notification to Father Leonardo Boff." www.vatican.va/roman_curia/congregations/cfaith/documents/rc_con_cfaith_doc_19850311_notif-boff_en.html.

Ratzinger, Joseph Cardinal, and Vittorio Messori. 1985. *The Ratzinger Report: An Exclusive Interview on the State of the Church.* San Francisco: Ignatius Press.

República del Ecuador. 2008. Constitución de 2008. http://pdba.georgetown.edu/Constitutions/.

Rhoades, Robert E., ed. 2006. *Development with Identity: Community, Culture, and Sustainability in the Andes.* Cambridge, MA: CABI Publishing.

Rist, Gilbert. 1997. *The History of Development: From Western Origins to Global Faith*. London: Zed Books.

Rittich, Kerry. 2003. "Engendering Development/Marketing Equality." *Albany Law Review* 67: 575–93.

Robalino Gonzaga, César Raúl. 1969. *El desarrollo económico del Ecuador*. Quito: Junta Nacional de Planificación y Coordinación.

Rowland, Christopher, ed. 1999. *The Cambridge Companion to Liberation Theology.* Cambridge: Cambridge University Press.

Roy, Ananya. 2010. *Poverty Capital: Microfinance and the Making of Development.* New York: Routledge.

Rueschemeyer, Dietrich, et al. 1992. *Capitalist Development and Democracy.* Chicago: University of Chicago Press.

Sachs, Jeffrey D. 2005. *The End of Poverty: Economic Possibilities for Our Time.* New York: Penguin Books.

Schech, Susanne, and Jane Haggis. 2000. *Culture and Development: A Critical Introduction.* Oxford: Blackwell.

Schech, Susanne, and Sanjugta Vas Dev. 2007. "Gender Justice: The World Bank's New Approach to the Poor?" *Development in Practice* 17, no. 1: 14–26.

Segarra, Monique. 1996. "Redefining the Public/Private Mix: NGOs and the Emergency Social Investment Fund in Ecuador." In *The New Politics of Inequality in Latin America: Rethinking Participation and Representation*, ed. Douglas A. Chalmers, Carlos M. Vilas, Katherine Hite, Scott P. Martin, Kerri Pster, and Monique Segarra, 489–515. New York: Oxford University Press.

Scheper Hughes, Jennifer. 2009. *Biography of a Mexican Crucifix: Lived Religion and Local Faith from the Conquest to the Present.* New York: Oxford University Press.

Scott, James. 1998. *Seeing Like a State: How Certain Schemes to Improve the Human Condition Have Failed.* New Haven, CT: Yale University Press.

Seales, Chad E. 2013. *The Secular Spectacle: Performing Religion in a Southern Town.* New York: Oxford University Press.

Seligson, Mitchell, and John T. Passé-Smith. 1998. *Development and Underdevelopment: The Political Economy of Global Inequality.* Boulder, CO: Lynne Rienner.

Sen, Amartya. *Development as Freedom*. 1999. New York: Alfred A. Knopf.

Sharma, Renuka, and Purushottama Bilimoria. 1999. *The Other Revolution: NGO and Feminist Perspectives from South Asia.* New Delhi: Sage.

Shaull, Richard, and Waldo Cesar. 2000. *Pentecostalism and the Future of the Christian Churches: Promises, Limitations, Challenges.* Grand Rapids, MI: Eerdmans.

"Sismo afecto 240 viviendas en Chillanes provincia de Bolívar." 2018. *TeleAmazonas*, September 8. Guayaquil, Ecuador.

Smith, James Howard. 2008. *Bewitching Development: Witchcraft and the Reinvention of Development in Neoliberal Kenya.* Chicago: University of Chicago Press.

Smith, Jonathan Z. 1982. *Imagining Religion: From Babylon to Jonestown*. Chicago: University of Chicago Press.

Smith, Steven Rathgeb, and Michael R Sosin. 2001. "The Varieties of Faith-Related Agencies." *Public Administration Review* 61, no. 6: 651–70.

Sobrino, John, and Ignacio Ellcuría. 1993. *Systematic Theology: Perspectives from Liberation Theology*. Maryknoll, NY: Orbis Books.

Spickard, James. 1998. "Rethinking Religious Social Action: What Is 'Rational' about Rational Choice Theory?" *Sociology of Religion* 59, no. 2: 99–115.

Stern, Nicholas. 2002. *A Strategy for Development.* Washington, DC: World Bank.

Stoll, David. 1990. *Is Latin America Turning Protestant?* Berkeley: University of California Press.

Taussig, Michael T. 1980. *The Devil and Commodity Fetishism in South America.* Chapel Hill: University of North Carolina Press.

Tinker, Irene, ed. 1990. *Persistent Inequalities: Women and World Development.* New York: Oxford University Press.

Tomalin, Emma. 2009. "Buddhist Feminist Transnational Networks: Female Ordination and Women's Empowerment." *Oxford Development Studies* 37, no. 22: 81–100.

______. 2013a. "Gender, Buddhism and the Bhikkhuni Ordination: Transnational Strategies for the Feminist Transformation of Religion in the 21st Century." In *Religion, Gender and the Public Sphere*, ed. Niamh Reilly and Stacey Scriver, 108–19. New York: Routledge.

———. 2013b. "Gender, Religion and Development." In *Handbook of Research on Development and Religion,* ed. Matthew Clarke, 183–200. Northhamton, MA: Edwin Elgar.

———. 2013c. *Religions and Development.* New York: Routledge.

———. 2015. *The Routledge Handbook of Religions and Global Development.* New York: Routledge.

Tomalin, Emma, and C. Starkey. 2013. "Buddhism and Development." In *Handbook of Research on Development and Religion*, ed. Matthew Clarke, 31–50. Northhampton, MA: Edwin Elgar.

Tsing, Anna Lowenhaupt. 1993. *In the Realm of the Diamond Queen.* Princeton, NJ: Princeton University Press.

———. 2000. "The Global Situation." *Cultural Anthropology* 15, no. 3: 327–60.

Tweed, Thomas A. 2006. *Crossing and Dwelling: A Theory of Religion.* Cambridge, MA: Harvard University Press.

Tyndale, Wendy. 2000. "Faith and Economics in 'Development': A Bridge across the Chasm?" *Development in Practice* 10, no. 1: 9–18.

———. 2006. *Visions of Development: Faith Based Initiatives.* Burlington, VT: Ashgate, 2006.

"Unitatis Redintegratio." Document of the Second Vatican Council. Rome, Italy. www.vatican.va/archive/hist_councils/ii_vatican_council/documents/vat-ii_decree_19641121_unitatis-redintegratio_en.html.

United Nations. 2000. *Millennium Development Goals.* www.un.org/millenniumgoals/.

———. 2010. *Sustainable Development Goals.* https://sustainabledevelopment.un.org/.

———. 2015. "Concluding Observations on the Combined Eighth and Ninth Periodic Reports of Ecuador." United Nations Convention on Eliminating All Forms of Discrimination against Women. http://evawglobaldatabase.unwomen.org//media/files/un%20women/vaw/country%20report/america/ecuador/ecuador%20cedaw%20co.pdf?vs=552.

United States Peace Corps. 2006. *Participatory Analysis for Community Action Training Manual.* Washington, DC.

Van Fleet, Krista. 2011. "On Devils and the Dissolution of Sociality: Andean Catholics Voicing Ambivalence in Neoliberal Bolivia." *Anthropological Quarterly* 84, no. 4: 835–64.

Vásquez, Manuel A. 2011. *More than Belief: A Materialist Theory of Religion.* New York: Oxford University Press.

Vásquez, Manuel A., and Phillip J Williams. 2005. "Introduction: The Power of Religious Identities in the Americas." *Latin American Perspectives* 32, no. 1: 15–26.

Verter, Bradford. 2003. "Spiritual Capital: Theorizing with Bourdieu against Bourdieu." *Sociological Theory* 21, no. 2: 150–74.

Vicuña Izquierdo, Leonardo. 2000. *Política económica del Ecuador: Dos décadas pérdidas, los años 80–90.* Quito: ESPOL.

de Vries, Pieter. 2007. "Don't Compromise Your Desire for Development! A Lacanian/Deleuzian Rethinking of the Anti-Politics Machine." *Third World Quarterly* 28, no. 1: 25–43.

Weber, Max. 1985. *The Protestant Ethic and the Spirit of Capitalism.* Trans. Talcott Parsons. London: Unwin.

Weisbrot, Mark, Jake Johnston, and Stephan Lefebvre. 2013. "Ecuador's New Deal: Reforming and Regulating the Financial Sector." Center for Economic and Policy Research, Washington, DC.

Weismantel, Mary. 1988. *Food, Gender, and Poverty in the Ecuadorian Andes.* Philadelphia: University of Pennsylvania Press.

Whitaker, Morris D., and Dale Colyer. 1990. *Agriculture and Economic Survival: The Role of Agriculture in Ecuador's Development.* Boulder, CO: Westview Press.

Whitten, Norman, ed. 1981. *Cultural Transformations and Ethnicity in Modern Ecuador.* Urbana: University of Illinois Press.

———. 2003. *Millennial Ecuador.* Iowa City: University of Iowa Press.

———. 2004. "Ecuador in the New Millennium: 25 Years of Democracy." *Journal of Latin American Anthropology* 9, no. 2: 439–50.

Wilk, R. R., ed. 1989. *The Household Economy: Reconsidering Domestic Modes of Production.* Boulder, CO: Westview Press.

Wong, Sam. 2007. *Exploring "Unseen" Social Capital in Community Participation: Everyday Lives of Poor Mainland Chinese Migrants in Hong Kong.* Amsterdam: Amsterdam University Press.

World Bank. 2018. "GINI Index." http://data.worldbank.org/indicators/SI.POV.GINI.

Wright, Wendy M. 2004. *Heart Speaks to Heart: The Salesian Tradition.* Maryknoll, NY: Orbis Books.

Young, Robert J. C. 1995. *Colonial Desire: Hybridity in Theory, Culture and Race.* London: Routledge.

Yúdice, George. 2003. *The Expediency of Culture: Uses of Culture in the Global Era.* Durham, NC: Duke University Press.

INDEX

JILL DeTEMPLE

is associate professor of religious studies at Southern Methodist University. She is the author of *Cement, Earthworms, and Cheese Factories: Religion and Community Development in Rural Ecuador* (University of Notre Dame Press, 2012).

www.ingramcontent.com/pod-product-compliance
Ingram Content Group UK Ltd.
Pitfield, Milton Keynes, MK11 3LW, UK
UKHW020841290926
15470UKWH00004B/1480

9 780268 107451